AF838986

Progressive Laws in Patriarchal Societies

Progressive Laws in Patriarchal Societies

Lessons from Pakistan

By Sara Malkani

BLOOMSBURY ACADEMIC
NEW YORK • LONDON • OXFORD • NEW DELHI • SYDNEY

BLOOMSBURY ACADEMIC
Bloomsbury Publishing Inc, 1385 Broadway, New York, NY 10018, USA
Bloomsbury Publishing Plc, 50 Bedford Square, London, WC1B 3DP, UK
Bloomsbury Publishing Ireland, 29 Earlsfort Terrace, Dublin 2, D02 AY28, Ireland

BLOOMSBURY, BLOOMSBURY ACADEMIC and the Diana logo are trademarks of Bloomsbury Publishing Plc

First published in the United States of America 2025

Copyright © Bloomsbury Publishing Inc, 2025

Cover images:
© hadynyah/E+/Getty Images

All rights reserved. No part of this publication may be: i) reproduced or transmitted in any form, electronic or mechanical, including photocopying, recording or by means of any information storage or retrieval system without prior permission in writing from the publishers; or ii) used or reproduced in any way for the training, development or operation of artificial intelligence (AI) technologies, including generative AI technologies. The rights holders expressly reserve this publication from the text and data mining exception as per Article 4(3) of the Digital Single Market Directive (EU) 2019/790.

Bloomsbury Publishing Inc does not have any control over, or responsibility for, any third-party websites referred to or in this book. All internet addresses given in this book were correct at the time of going to press. The author and publisher regret any inconvenience caused if addresses have changed or sites have ceased to exist, but can accept no responsibility for any such changes.

ISBN: HB: 978-1-6669-1714-7
ePDF: 979-8-7651-9294-8
ePUB: 979-8-7651-9295-5
eBook: 978-1-6669-1715-4

Typeset by Deanta Global Publishing Services, Chennai, India

For product safety related questions contact productsafety@bloomsbury.com.

To find out more about our authors and books visit www.bloomsbury.com
and sign up for our newsletters.

Contents

Acknowledgments

I am indebted to many friends and colleagues who have helped shape the ideas I've tried to communicate in this book. I am deeply grateful to Farieha Aziz for her invaluable support as well as her sharp insights and observations on the topics covered in this book. Scholar Ayesha Khan has deeply influenced my views and understanding of gender politics in Pakistan and the role of law in struggles for gender justice. Conversations with friend and activist Moneeza Ahmed have also shaped my understanding of ongoing challenges to gender equality in Pakistan. Thought-provoking conversations with lawyer Asad Jamal have helped me to understand and articulate realities of the criminal justice system. I am very thankful to scholar Yasser Kureshi for reviewing early drafts of some chapters and providing such thoughtful comments and suggestions. Maria Khan, Zahra Batool, Kashif Ali, and Sadam Bhutto provided valuable research support.

I interviewed many experts while writing this book, and I am extremely grateful to them for their time and insights. These experts include Maliha Zia Lari, Nida Ali, Amar Sindhu, Bushra Gohar, Majida Rizvi, Anis Haroon, Khawar Mumtaz, Shehnaz Wazir Ali, Saba Shaikh, Sabahat Riaz, Uzma Noorani and her helpful colleagues at Panah Shelter Home.

Much of this book was written while I was at the University of Oxford as a Rangoonwala Fellow at the Contemporary South Asian Studies Programme (CSASP). I am very grateful to staff and faculty at CSASP as well as to the Rangoonwala Foundation for an excellent opportunity.

My husband, Umair Vadria, reviewed drafts of the book and helped in other countless ways. Zahra and Anum Malkani give me much to think about in my work and have always been there to hear my ideas and frustrations. My father, GM Malkani, has always encouraged me to read, write, and think for myself. My late mother, Rubina Malkani, has always been my driving inspiration to live and work for justice and love.

Chapter 1

Women Shape Laws

Over the last two decades, Pakistan has seen major legislative changes in the areas of gender-based violence and harassment. This book explores their impact. The legislative changes are remarkable in the context of the deep patriarchy and parochialism that permeates Pakistan's society and culture. The legal developments are the product of a combination of factors, not least of which is a strong women's rights movement that has consistently demanded that the state act to protect and promote the rights of women.

This book considers the impact of a wave of progressive legislative changes from 2006 to the present in the areas of rape and sexual violence, domestic violence, child marriages, and honor killings. A frequent refrain in political and social commentary in Pakistan is that these laws, while transformative on paper, have not translated to actual change in the lives of women and girls because of poor implementation. Widespread incidents of violence against women in the home, in the workplace, and in public places persist. Women and girls who approach state institutions, such as police and courts, in the hope of some accountability for violence confront patriarchal attitudes and corruption and inefficiency of state actors, leading to deep frustration and retraumatisation. Online spaces, where misogynist targeting of women and girls is rampant, amplify their insecurities.

Historically, feminism in Pakistan has relied heavily on the power of the law to promote gender justice. For much of Pakistan's history, feminists formed alliances with state actors and institutions to achieve their goals. This was in part due to the state's receptivity to demands for progressive laws and policies to promote the status of women. General Zia ul Haq's decade of rule over Pakistan from 1977 to 1988 was an aberration with long-standing impact. Zia initiated sweeping changes to laws as part of his "Islamisation" campaign that led to the detention of women on accusations of adultery and fornication, promoted impunity for sexual violence, and threatened to demote women to the status of second-class citizens. A women's-rights movement grew in response to Zia's policies and devoted many years fighting against his regressive changes.

The passage of gender progressive laws in recent years marks a dramatic shift in the state's attitude toward women's rights, compared to the state's attitude during Zia's rule. Years after the passage of some of the gender progressive laws, however, their effective implementation remains a distant goal. Legislatures and some mainstream political parties may have affirmed their faith in gender equality but pushing state machinery to meaningfully activate legislation is proving to be an immensely difficult task. Given the disjuncture between gender progressive laws on the one hand and the lived experiences of women and girls in Pakistan on the other, the following question should be investigated closely: *what are the barriers to enforcement of gender progressive laws, and what can be done to eliminate or at least reduce the barriers?*

This is a crucial question for the women's-rights movement in Pakistan, which has adopted reform of legal frameworks as one of its central aims. While the women's-rights movement that grew from the activism against Zia's rule has premised its work on the assumption that a liberal democratic state will help advance the goal of gender equality, the current scenario casts doubt on the effectiveness of state power, even with gender progressive laws in place, to meet feminist goals. Assessing the obstacles to implementation is important for women's-rights activists to understand not only how law reform can be made more meaningful but also to determine the extent to which they should prioritize law-reform advocacy in their work.

As a practicing lawyer in Pakistan for over a decade, I have worked closely with state institutions, state and nonstate actors, and survivors of gender-based violence to operationalize gender progressive laws. Through my work, I have directly encountered barriers to implementation. Over the years, I have observed laws on gender-based violence passed to much fanfare and self-congratulation by political parties, NGOs, and donors. The celebration is in stark contrast to my frustrations as a lawyer trying to convince police, judges, and bureaucrats to fulfil their obligations by enforcing these landmark laws. These personal experiences drove me to closely assess the impact of law-reform advocacy and document barriers to implementation. My assessment of the implementation of laws in this book is based on my experiences in courts and police stations, in interactions with survivors, and in encounters with legislators and government officials. I also rely on interviews with legislators and activists and records of cases before courts and tribunals. I also compare findings in Pakistan to research in other countries in South Asia with similar legal systems and cultural norms, as these comparisons illuminate some entrenched features of progressive law reform on gender in patriarchal societies.

Table 1.1 Gender Progressive Laws from 2010 Onward

Year	Federal Legislation
2010	Protection Against Harassment of Women in the Workplace Act
2011	Acid Control and Acid Crime Prevention Act
2011	Prevention of Anti-Women Practices Act
2016	Criminal Law (Offences Relating to Rape) Amendment Act
2016	Criminal Law (Offences in the Name or Pretext of Honour) Amendment Act
2016	Prevention of Electronic Crimes Act
2021	Anti Rape (Investigation and Trial) Act
2021	Criminal Law (Amendment) Act
Year	**Provincial Legislation**
2013	Sindh Child Marriage Restraint Act
2013	Sindh Domestic Violence (Prevention and Protection) Act
2014	Balochistan Domestic Violence (Prevention and Protection) Act
2016	Punjab Protection of Women Against Violence Act
2021	Khyber Pakhtunkhwa Domestic Violence Against Women (Prevention and Protection) Act

Before I analyse recent law reform and its impact, I will introduce the main actors that enabled these legal changes. Their roles, the challenges they faced, and their strategies provide the context in which these laws were passed.

MAIN ACTORS

A key force behind the passage of laws was a women's-rights movement that gained strength over the decades, particularly during the 1980s and beyond. Women legislators in elected parliaments gained strength in numbers after reserved seats were reinstated in 2002 and supported the demands of women's-rights activists. Pronouncements by the judiciary on the state's responsibility to prevent and punish gender-based violence gave impetus to advocacy for legislative change. These factors led to fertile ground for the enactment of gender progressive legislation.

Activists and NGOs

Initiatives for law reform in Pakistan have been led by women's-rights activists through collectives and civil-society organisations. Women's-rights activism in Pakistan has deep roots going back to the creation of the state in 1947. The only two women in Pakistan's first constituent assembly formed the United Front for Women's Rights (UFWR) and successfully lobbied for a law permitting women to inherit agricultural property in 1951.[1]

A left-wing women's organization called Anjuman Jamhooriat Pasand Khawateen (Democratic Women's Association) was formed in 1948 and advocated for working-class women.[2]

The All Pakistan Women's Association (APWA) was formed in 1948 to uplift women through economic welfare and empowerment initiatives. Ra'ana Liaquat, the wife of Pakistan's first prime minister who later became governor of the province of Sindh, was one of the founders of APWA. In 1955 when Prime Minister Muhammad Ali Bogra married his second wife, APWA protested against the religion-based personal law that permitted a Muslim man to marry up to four wives without seeking permission from his existing wives. Their protest pushed the government to reevaluate Muslim family laws, which until then were not codified and were applied by the state based on vague interpretation of Shariah by religious scholars.[3] The government formed the Rashid Commission, comprising leading legal experts, to make recommendations for the reform of Muslim family laws, leading to a codified family law—the Muslim Family Law Ordinance of 1961.

Until the 1980s, women's-rights activism in Pakistan was met with a degree of benign accommodation by the state. Following the imposition of discriminatory laws by General Zia-ul-Haq, women's-rights activists adopted a confrontational stance toward the state and challenged its promotion of patriarchy and its Islamization agenda. Zia ul Haq notoriously imposed "Islamisation" on laws and policies, and a crucial pillar of his project was to undermine women's freedom and autonomy. He openly stated that women should be confined in the home or "*chadar chaar divari*."[4] He made extensive changes to criminal laws through the Hudood Ordinances. One piece of legislation, the Offence of Zina (Enforcement of Hudood) Ordinance 1979 took rape provisions outside the Penal Code and placed them in purportedly Shariah-based laws that conflated rape with adultery, with the result that many women, including those who had in fact been raped, faced adultery trials that could lead to the death penalty.[5] His government's reforms to the Evidence Act 1872 to supposedly bring it in compliance with Shariah stipulated that, in financial matters, a woman's testimony is worth half that of a man. This change was perceived as state-sponsored discrimination against women and the imposition of second-class status on women. It was met with strong resistance from women activists who, in February 1983, demonstrated outside the Lahore High Court and were confronted with police brutality, leading to the imprisonment of several women, some of whom went on to become leaders of the women's movement that played a significant role in the resistance against Zia's dictatorship.[6]

Activists formed the Women's Action Forum, a collective that advocated for the reversal of General Zia's regressive legal measures. It comprised women lawyers, journalists, and academics and established chapters in cities across the country. During the 1980s, activists in the Women's Action Forum (WAF) simultaneously established and strengthened NGOs that lent institutional support to their advocacy agenda. Shirkat Gah, an NGO formed in 1975–1976, became a prominent voice in the struggle against the Zia regime and included activists such as Khawar Mumtaz and Farida Shaheed.[7] The Aurat Foundation was formed in 1986 by Shahla Zia and Nigar Ahmed as a research and advocacy organization focusing on the rights of women.[8] Over the years it developed legislative expertise and regularly issued analyses of laws, legal proposals, and recommendations for legislative change. The Aurat Foundation released a newsletter called *Legislative Watch* that monitored legislative advocacy and made recommendations for law reform. The Human Rights Commission of Pakistan was founded in 1986 by leading lawyers and activists, including Asma Jahangir and Hina Jilani, and became a major force for advocacy for rights of women and research and documentation of human-rights abuses.

With the end of Zia's regime and the return of elected governments in 1988, the women's movement pushed for state recognition of women's equal status and a legal regime that guaranteed the equality of women. The 1990s saw the expansion of a nationally prominent women's movement, and women led civil society organisations that directly interacted with and confronted state power to demand repeal of Zia's laws and the implementation of laws that protect women from patriarchal violence.

Western donors and the UN provided funding to these organizations, allowing some of them to expand rapidly to major cities across Pakistan.[9] These organizations developed ties to a global human-rights community and in particular the global women's-rights movement that achieved crucial gains in the international human-rights system through the decades of the '80s and '90s. Benazir Bhutto attended the 1994 International Conference on Population and Development in Cairo and the 1995 World Conference on Women in Beijing. NGOs such as Shirkat Gah and Aurat Foundation participated in the conferences and also worked with the government to prepare conference reports.[10] The Pakistan government signed and ratified the Convention on the Elimination of Discrimination Against Women in 1996 in response to demands from WAF and other NGOs. Leading activists took roles in the UN human-rights system, which enabled them to strengthen human-rights norms globally and also enhanced the credibility of their domestic advocacy. Asma Jahangir was appointed as a UN special rapparteur on extra-judicial killings and then on freedom of religion. Hina Jilani was appointed as a special representative to the Secretary General on Human Rights Defenders. NGOs also developed ties to feminists in South Asia becoming founding members of South Asians for Human Rights (SAHR). Shirkat Gah joined a network of Muslim feminists known as Women Living Under Muslim Laws to share experiences of women living in Muslim countries and to advocate for law reform.

Women's rights activists and NGOs used their resources to raise awareness around pervasive violence against women during the decade of the 1990s. They led vigorous agitation against honour killings of women, which were reported in the media and highlighted by activists. The case of Samia Sarwar, who was killed by her mother in the office of lawyer Hina Jilani after she left her husband and sought a divorce, received widespread media and international attention.[11] It stoked the flames of outrage against increasing reports of women being murdered with impunity. "Honour" killings were exonerated because of amendments to the Penal Code provisions on murder and assault brought about as a result of Zia ul Haq's push to "Islamize" criminal laws. Known as the "Qisas and Diyat" amendments, which were first introduced through ordinance and then enacted by parliament in 1997, these legal changes made murder a "compoundable" offence —one for which punishment in the form of imprisonment could be avoided if the heirs of the victim agree to be compensated by the murderer.[12] Activists highlighted incidents of sexual violence and condemned the failure of the state to hold perpetrators accountable for these incidents. The NGO War Against Rape, founded in 1989, publicized incidents of sexual violence and provided aid and legal representation to survivors.[13] Activism through the 1990s led to increased public awareness and societal condemnation of gender-based violence, paving the ground for legislative changes that were to come years later.

Activism in Pakistan was fueled by the international women's-rights movement of the 1990s, which made violence against women one of its central advocacy goals. *Violence against women* (VAW) became an established phrase, assuming an important role in the international human-rights system. The concept incorporated the recognition that violence in both public and private spheres falls within the human-rights obligations of governments. The 1993 Vienna World Conference on Human Rights was a watershed moment for the recognition of women's rights as human rights. The Vienna Declaration and Programme of Action that emerged from the conference reflected the recognition that women have the right to be protected from violence in the private sphere.[14] States acknowledged their responsibility to prevent and punish harms caused to women within the family and to address the harmful effects of traditional and customary practices. The UN General Assembly passed a declaration in 1993, soon after the Vienna Convention, that recognized that violence against women "is a manifestation of historically unequal power relations between men and women, which have led to domination over and discrimination against women."[15] The declaration explicitly covered violence occurring in private as well as public life. In 1994 a UN special rapparteur on violence against women who submitted annual reports to the UN General Assembly was appointed. These accomplishments of the international women's-rights movement reinforced the women's movement in Pakistan against patriarchal violence, which gained strength through the 1990s and the first decade of the twentieth century.

Activist fervor and donor-funded NGO agendas combined to lay the groundwork for criminal legislation on violence against women. The resistance of activists to gender-based violence and their inclination to hold the government accountable for its inaction met with the rights-based, law-reform–oriented priorities of NGOs, whose agendas were influenced by UN human-rights norms and foreign donor priorities. Resistance to the state, a hallmark of the 1980s activism, was tempered over a period of time to accommodate reformist agendas that found openings within Pakistan's constitutional and legal framework to address patriarchal violence. Over time, activists and NGOs found allies in political parties and legislatures.

Political Parties, Legislators, and a National Women's Commission

The return of civilian governance in the 1990s did not lead to a reversal of Zia's regressive laws. Although much hope was placed in the first government of Prime Minister Benazir Bhutto, it did not repeal the Zina Ordinance or discriminatory provisions in Zia's law of evidence. According to a former member of the Pakistan People's Party (PPP) and the National Assembly, Dr. Shahnaz Wazir Ali, the PPP governments of the 1990s were continuously besieged by the military establishment and aggressive opposition within the parliament. In this environment, Benazir Bhutto and the PPP focused on political survival and could not afford to take on the religious right by repealing laws that were ascribed a religious justification.[16]

The two tenures of Benazir Bhutto's government (1988–1990 and 1993–1996) did, however, create space for women activists and NGOs to advocate with legislators and government departments. Bhutto's participation in the 1994 International Conference on Population and Development and the 1995 Beijing Conference signaled an openness to demands for gender equality and a willingness to engage with activists and NGOs. In her second government, Prime Minister Benazir Bhutto formed a Commission on the Inquiry of the Status of Women, which included lawyers and activists Asma Jahangir and Shahla Zia and was chaired by a Supreme Court judge. In 1997, the commission released its report, which gave comprehensive recommendations for political and legal reform in the areas, among others, of criminal laws, violence against women, family laws, and political participation.[17] The recommendations in the area of criminal legislation included the repeal of Zia's Hudood Ordinances. The commission's report contained a chapter on the theme of *Violence Against Women*, which included a recommendation that "[s]pecific legislation on domestic violence by husbands or in-laws should be enacted" and that there "should be no mitigation of any sentence in any case of honour killing."[18] It also called for a law "making it mandatory for all employers to respond to and monitor incidents of violence and harassment in the workplace."[19] The report also contained a chapter on *Institutionalisation*, which included recommendations on protection measures for persons vulnerable to violence. It called for shelters throughout the country that are "only protective and not custodial or reformatory."[20] The commission's inquiry report included a set of recommendations on political participation. It recommended that 33 percent of seats in both houses of parliament—the Senate and the National Assembly—be reserved for women and that women in the reserved seats be elected directly.

In 1999, Pakistan's short-lived experience with elected governments was cut short as another military leader, General Pervez Musharraf, came into power in a coup. General Musharraf led the country until 2007. Unlike Pakistan's previous military dictator, Musharraf made some attempts to portray a progressive outlook, including on issues of gender. As scholar Ayesha Khan has noted, "in attempting to demonstrate to the educated elite within the country and the outside world that his government was not anti-women and was indeed progressive in matters of religion and social policy," he made institutional reforms that enabled significant gender progressive legislation.[21]

The most significant institutional reform during Musharraf's years was the restoration of reserved seats for women in elected bodies. The 1973 Constitution provided that 5 percent of seats were reserved for women in the National Assembly and provincial assemblies, but this provision lapsed in 1980. General Zia-ul-Haq held elections in 1985 on a nonparty basis with a 20 percent reservation for women. Provision for reserved seats lapsed again in 1990, and for twelve years there were no reserved seats for women. In the three general elections that took place between 1990 and 1997, the number of women in parliament declined significantly: there were only two women in the 1990–1993 National Assembly and four in the 1993–1996 National Assembly. Musharraf's Legal Framework Order of 2001 granted women a reservation of 33 percent of seats at all three tiers of local government and a reservation of 17.5 percent of seats in national and provincial legislative bodies. This dramatically increased the representation of women in subsequently elected assemblies. Following the 2002 general elections more than seventy women became members of the National Assembly.[22] The National Assembly formed after the 2008 general elections had seventy-six women representatives (sixty on reserved and sixteen on general seats).[23]

Women on reserved seats were elected indirectly by directly elected representatives from their political parties on a proportionate basis, in contrast to the recommendation of the Commission on Inquiry of Status of Women in its 1997 report, which called for direct elections of women on reserved seats. The indirect elections meant that women representatives retained a status that was secondary to that of the mostly male members of their political party who voted them into the seats. They were nonetheless instrumental in the passage of gender progressive legislation in national and provincial assemblies over the years.[24] The legal changes initiated by General Musharraf were a response to the consistent demands made by women activists for reserved seats. They were able to take advantage of General Musharraf's desire to appear progressive—primarily to appeal to a Western audience during the War on Terror—and succeeded in the partial implementation of their demands.

Another significant institutional measure from General Musharraf was the National Commission on the Status of Women. The 1997 Commission on the Inquiry of the Status of Women, recommended the establishment of a permanent commission to oversee and monitor the enforcement of women's rights as an independent, autonomous body. In 2000, General Musharraf set up the National Commission on the Status of Women (NCSW) by presidential ordinance. Justice Majida Rizvi, a recently retired judge of the Sindh High Court, was appointed to chair the NCSW in 2002. She spearheaded initiatives to repeal the Hudood Ordinances, setting up a committee of legal experts to devise proposals. The law committee included women's-rights lawyers Shahla Zia and Hina Jilani and met regularly over several months to discuss legal and ethical arguments against the Hudood Ordinances, culminating in a report published in 2003. The NCSW took steps to widely disseminate the report. Justice Rizvi travelled across the country over several months, speaking to community members and leaders about the exploitative impacts of the law to build support for legal reform.[25] These efforts were instrumental in the passage of the Protection of Women (Criminal Laws Amendment) Act of 2006, which amended key provisions of the Offence of Zina (Enforcement of Hudood) Ordinance 1979 (Zina Ordinance). The 2006 law did not repeal the Hudood Ordinances in their entirety but made it procedurally very difficult to initiate cases alleging adultery.[26]

National elections held in 2008 marked a return to civilian government with the PPP emerging victorious after the assassination of its leader, Benazir Bhutto. The PPP came to power with the most progressive agenda among mainstream parties on the issue of gender. Its origins in populist democracy in the 1970s as well as its leadership by Benazir Bhutto, the first Muslim woman to lead a Muslim country, are among the factors that contributed to its progressive outlook and rhetoric on gender. The party also formed a government in the province of Sindh. The provincial assemblies acquired greater legislative power following the eighteenth constitutional amendment in 2010, which devolved more areas of governance from the federal government to the provinces.

With a critical mass of women legislators in assemblies, the momentum for women's rights and progressive legislation accelerated in the 2008–2013 period. This period also saw the first woman speaker of the National Assembly, Fahmida Mirza, who supported the women legislators in their efforts to bring progressive legislation to the floor. Women legislators formed cross-party alliances to pass these laws, using the Women's Parliamentary Caucus as an important forum for discussion and debate on legislation.[27] Civil-society organisations also engaged with the caucus, providing crucial resources and support while lobbying for legislative measures. National and provincial legislatures during this time passed a number of gender progressive laws, including the Protection against Harassment of Women in the Workplace Act 2010, the Acid Control and Acid Crime Prevention Act 2011, the Sindh Child Marriage Restraint Act 2013, and the Sindh Domestic Violence (Prevention and Protection) Act 2013. This legislation was perceived to be groundbreaking as it provided legal guarantees to women and girls of state protection against harassment, violence, and traditional patriarchal norms in the private sphere of the home and in the workplace.

Women legislators had to work hard to gain support for progressive legislation. It is a testament to their determination that they met with some success, even though the enacted laws often did not take the most desirable shape due to protracted negotiations with ambivalent or hostile legislators. Senator Sherry Rehman of the PPP points to the many hurdles women legislators faced to push through progressive legislation, including from bodies such as the Council of Islamic Ideology. Progressive bills are often referred to the Council for Islamic Ideology for approval, which effectively relegates them to "legislative graveyards."[28] Women legislators are often unable to oppose conservative right-wing opposition to progressive laws.

During this period, the National Commission on the Status of Women (NCSW) was also led by a seasoned women's-rights activist, Anis Haroon, one of the founders and leading members of the WAF. Women members of the PPP—specifically Sherry Rehman and Shahnaz Wazir Ali—encouraged Anis Haroon to apply for the position of chairperson, indicating that the party was keen to have the NCSW chaired by an effective leader who would push for legal and policy improvements.[29] During 2008–2013, the NCSW played a crucial role as a bridge between civil-society organisations and legislators, providing a forum for advocacy for gender progressive laws. The NCSW held focus-group discussions and seminars, bringing together activists, legislators, and government officials to discuss legislative and policy measures to address sexual harassment, domestic violence, and child marriages. This in spite of the fact that the NCSW had to struggle to maintain its status as an independent entity, as the government wished to preserve the financial dependence of the body on government ministries and their bureaucracies. During the tenure of Anis Haroon, the NCSW was formally recognized as an autonomous body.[30]

The elected National Assembly completed its tenure, and elections held in 2013 marked a shift in power to the Pakistan Muslim League (PML-N), led by Nawaz Sharif. During its two tenures in the 1990s the PML-N under Nawaz Sharif was no friend of the women's movement or its causes. On the contrary, WAF campaigned energetically against attempts by Nawaz Sharif to Islamise the legal system during both of his tenures in the 1990s. In his first tenure (1990–1993), Sharif bulldozed through the parliament the Shariat Act, a vaguely worded law that declared that Shariah is the supreme law of the land and that, in the interpretation of any statue, the meaning most consistent with Shariah will prevail.[31] In his second stint in office (1997–1999), Nawaz Sharif proposed a constitutional amendment that would give the federal government the power to enforce Shariah, a measure that was also strongly opposed by the WAF, which saw it as an attempt to extend Zia ul Haq's Islamisation agenda and to pave the way for more regressive legislation concerning women.[32] Nawaz Sharif's party's attitude toward women's rights shifted somewhat when he took office in 2013. In 2016, the National Assembly made amendments to the Pakistan Penal Code and Criminal Procedure Code that strengthened criminal penalties against rape and amended procedures for evidence collection in sexual assault cases. The year 2016 also saw amendments to the Pakistan Penal Code that attempted to restrict the application of Qisas and Diyat provisions in the case of honour killings against women—but unfortunately the amendments were not effective. The amendments to the anti–honour-killing law were set in motion after the murder of social media celebrity Qandeel Baloch, whose murder by her brother[33] became national and international news. In 2016, the PML-N–dominated National Assembly passed the Prevention of Electronic Crimes Act, which contained criminal penalties for offending the "modesty of a natural person."[34] Free-speech activists and journalists protested against the law that imposed draconian restrictions on online speech, but it was nonetheless enacted while being portrayed as a law that would protect women in online spaces.

Over the last two decades, women politicians combined forces with women's-rights activists and NGOs to achieve the legislative reform discussed in this book by building support within their parties and overcoming opposition from conservative forces within assemblies. The judiciary has supported their goals at times through progressive jurisprudence and directives holding government actors accountable for their legal and constitutional obligations.

Judiciary

Women's-rights activists have pursued cases of gender-based violence in trial courts for decades to attain convictions for specific incidents and also to influence the mindsets of judges and law-enforcement officers through public advocacy around these cases. During the 1980s, women's-rights lawyers and activists represented people detained under the Zina Ordinance. Their representation led to the documentation of gross due-process violations and raised public consciousness against the law. The judiciary was an important forum in which to raise public consciousness about the draconian impact of the law, particularly in the absence of a democratically elected parliament in the 1980s that would be receptive to demands of women activists. During the 1990s and onwards, WAF and NGOs such as War Against Rape brought cases of gender-based violence to criminal courts, seeking convictions of perpetrators.

The "superior" judiciary in Pakistan comprises the Supreme Court and high courts (one in each province and the Islamabad capital territory) with appellate jurisdiction, while trial courts (sometimes referred to as "lower" judiciary) try criminal cases and resolve civil disputes at the local level. Special courts that focus on specific areas, such as family law, operate at the district level. The superior judiciary has appellate jurisdiction as well as limited original jurisdiction to hear matters specified in the Constitution. Pakistan's Constitution gives high courts the jurisdiction to hear matters involving the enforcement of fundamental rights guaranteed in the Constitution. The Supreme Court also has the original jurisdiction to hear matters of public importance that involve the enforcement of fundamental rights. This is sometimes referred to as public-interest litigation, which may be initiated by those directly aggrieved by the fundamental rights violation as well as concerned "public-spirited" citizens or organisations. The public-interest jurisdiction of high courts and the Supreme Court has created space over the years for women's-rights activists to advance some of their goals through courts. Judgments from superior courts has supported legislative advocacy on violence against women. For example, in 2012 the Supreme Court ordered that collection of DNA evidence be mandatory in rape cases, following the filing of a petition by concerned citizens, seeking directions to law-enforcement authorities to improve investigation processes in rape cases.[35] The pronouncements of the Supreme Court influenced amendments made to the Criminal Procedure Code in 2016. In 2021, the Lahore High Court banned the invasive and demeaning "two finger test" or virginity test that was performed by medico-legal officers on rape survivors on a public-interest petition filed on behalf of activists.[36] Subsequently, a law passed in 2021 to improve investigation and trial procedures in rape cases prohibited the use of the "two finger test."

As I discuss in subsequent chapters of the book, the judiciary has a crucial role to play in the enforcement of recently enacted legislation on gender-based violence. Unfortunately, trial courts have not enabled the implementation of these laws, and, even after the passage of progressive legislation, the burden has largely remained on survivors, victims' families, and activists to enforce these laws in courts. Delays in proceedings impose severe psychological and financial costs on survivors and their families. Poor awareness about gender progressive laws, lack of competence, and patriarchal attitudes prevent prosecution and conviction and deter survivors from pursuing cases in courts. While some pronouncements by the high courts and the Supreme Court, calling for improvements in prosecution of violence cases, have influenced the attitudes of trial court judges to some extent, the overall culture of courts is unwelcoming to survivors.

In recent years, the representation of women in the judiciary has increased. In 2022, Justice Ayesha Malik became the first woman judge appointed to the Supreme Court in the history of Pakistan. In 2023, another woman, Justice Mussarat Hilali, was sworn as a judge of the Supreme Court. These significant milestones aside, the overall representation of women in the judiciary leaves much to be desired. For example, in the district level judiciary in Sindh, only 13 percent of all judges are women, while, in Punjab, women judges comprise 17 percent of the district judiciary.[37] In Sindh High Court, women judges comprise 9 percent of the total number, while, in Lahore High Court, 5 percent of judges are women.[38]

FEMINISTS IN THE HALLS OF POWER

Women in Pakistan have made inroads into key governance institutions to make their voices heard. Women activists effectively raised their voices in centres of power—parliaments, political parties, judiciary, government bureaucracies, and international governance bodies in the UN and INGOs. They are no longer marginalized to the peripheries of political decision-making or media and public discourse. The extent to which this translates to gains for gender equality is to be investigated and analyzed, and this book attempts to do so with respect to violence against women.

The space that women have made for themselves in centres of power is remarkable, given the overall state of gender inequality in Pakistan. If we consider some indicators that convey the extent of patriarchy embedded in the society (46 percent of girls of primary-school age are out of school[39]; the maternal mortality rate in Pakistan is 186 deaths per 100,000 live births[40]; and female labour-force participation is 25 percent[41]), it is particularly impressive that women activists, women-led NGOs, and women legislators are able to work effectively with state institutions to influence legal norms and bring about substantial legislative changes.

In her book, *Governance Feminism*, legal scholar Janet Halley raises the following questions for feminists in light of the fact that we now "walk the halls of power":

> Exactly what forms of "feminism" make sense to power elites as they gradually let women in? What happens when feminists and feminist ideas find their way into legal institutions and change legal thought and operations? Whose nongovernmental organisations get funding from international aid and development agencies and from ideologically driven private donors? Once feminists gain a foothold in governance, what do they do there, and what particular legal forms are they most invested in? What are the distributive consequences of the partial inclusion of some feminist projects? Who benefits and who loses? Can feminism foster a critique of its own successes?[42]

These are important questions to answer to assess the impact of the violence-against-women agenda for feminists in Pakistan. Halley and her coauthors use the term governance feminism to "mean every form in which feminists and feminist ideas exert a governing will within human affairs."[43] Governance feminism indicates the "state, state-like and state-affiliated" power that feminists come to adopt. The strands of the women's movement in Pakistan that I have discussed in this chapter share many features with governance feminism. The movement has taken the state to be the central repository of its rights claims and at various stages has confronted, collaborated with, and taken on the mantle of state authority to achieve its goals for gender equality and freedom. As women's-rights activists pursued their demands from the state through collectives and NGOs, they began to move from outsider status closer to the centres of power. These gains were hard won, a result of feminists devoting their lives to their causes, often at grave personal risk. They were also the product of rigorous intellectual activity to understand institutions and their complex rules and procedures, to build an extensive body of research to identify and support advocacy-based causes, and to develop sophisticated public messaging and consciousness-raising strategies. The successes of governance feminism in Pakistan are evident.

These successes nonetheless demand critical analysis and thorough assessment. This book attempts to critically assess the success attained by governance feminism in Pakistan in the legal recognition of many forms of violence against women and legislative enactments to introduce new criminal offences, enhance criminal penalties, and establish protection mechanisms. By tracing the background momentum that led to these changes, it considers why this particular solution—criminal regulation and accountability—gained more recognition than other potential approaches to tackle violence against women. The book looks at how the successes impacted the intended beneficiaries of these gains: women and girls who face patriarchal violence and attempt to utilize these legislative gains. It also sheds light on the costs of these gains, costs that may be incurred through both the failures of implementation as well as the successful utilization of criminal law and processes. Finally, it asks women's-rights activists in Pakistan who continue to raise concerns about gender-based violence to assess options for future advocacy. While working out how criminal-justice–based approaches may be made more effective they should also consider how approaches outside the criminal-justice system may be explored and leveraged. I suggest that these questions be answered not from a standpoint that idealizes state power or an opposite perspective that rejects any emancipatory potential of state institutions. In fact, the evidence about the impact of gender progressive laws illustrates that a superior framework rejects a state/nonstate binary. Instead, it identifies elements of state power that can be harnessed to pursue feminist goals while incorporating emancipatory activism that de-centres the punitive state.

Here I introduce three broad concerns raised by feminist scholars and practitioners about strides made by governance feminism in different parts of the world. These concerns are relevant to the assessment of gains by governance feminism in Pakistan in criminal laws to address violence against women. As I analyze legal frameworks and their impact in subsequent chapters of the book, these concerns become relevant to varying degrees. One concern is based on a critique often leveled against the international women's-rights movement on violence against women: it exaggerates the role of culture in the perpetuation of patriarchal violence, thereby encouraging stereotypes of communities, especially from the Global South, while underplaying the role of contemporary forces, including that of the modern state, in promoting violence against women. The second concern is critical of feminist approaches that rely on the punitive powers of the state. It is argued that these approaches, sometimes labelled "carceral" feminism, support and even legitimize the arbitrary excesses of the police state and ignore the impact of punitive state power on marginalized individuals and communities. A third concern is that the violence-against-women agenda centres patriarchy as the cause of violence while obscuring structural economic hierarchies that promote violence against women and entail that its impact is experienced differently by women based on their class background.

I consider all three concerns here briefly as they inform much of the analysis of gender progressive laws in the remainder of the book, while also emphasizing that these concerns apply to Pakistan's context in very specific ways.

The International Women's Rights Movement and Violence against Women

The focus on violence against women by the women's movement in Pakistan in the 1990s intensified as the international feminist activism on this issue made significant strides. The global campaign against violence against women was very successful in establishing the responsibility of states and the international human-rights system to address all forms of violence faced by women, particularly in the private sphere, and to challenge traditions and cultural practices that condone and promote patriarchal violence. Globally, these measures led to the recognition that women and girls are not simply the subjects of families and communities but, rather, bearers of fundamental human rights that states and the international human-rights order must protect and promote.

The extent and nature of the focus of the international women's-rights movement on violence against women has faced some criticisms from within the feminist movement. One criticism is that it promotes an essentialist view about women as victims that obscures the complexities and diversities of women's experiences, based on class, race, nationality, religion, and other crucial identity-defining factors.[44] Such essentialist viewpoints privilege the position of a certain kind of woman—upper class, heterosexual, white, and from the Global North—women who are most likely to experience gender as the biggest and primary obstacle to equality, in comparison to women from other backgrounds who face intersecting harms based on characteristics other than gender.[45] Women in the Global South are particularly vulnerable to simplistic essentialization within the international women's-rights movement because they tend to be portrayed as perpetual victims of regressive cultures, and these cultures are themselves subject to racist stereotyping. Feminists caution that this has serious implications for strategies adopted by the women's movement and has encouraged conservative and protectionist responses from states. The emphasis on the woman as a "victim subject" in the discourse on violence against women has lent support to punitive criminal laws that impose state restrictions on the very women and girls that they claim to protect.[46] It is argued that VAW discourse has encouraged a feminist discourse that is "protectionist" and "conservative."[47]

While there is some degree of truth to such criticism, it must be applied with a great deal of nuance to feminist discourse and activism on violence against women in Pakistan. Concerns about patriarchal violence against women in Pakistan is rooted in issues arising in domestic contexts and have not been transplanted into local movements from foreign sources. Concerned individuals and groups based in Pakistan have built movements around violence against women motivated primarily by domestic social conditions—the widespread incidence of domestic violence, honour killings, and sexual violence—rather than foreign agendas. The women's movement in Pakistan galvanized in the 1980s around domestic political conditions, especially regressive laws introduced by General Zia ul Haq that promoted impunity for sexual violence as well as the detention of women on accusations of adultery. The movement was crucial in bringing the issue of sexual violence against women into the public discourse and to raising consciousness. The women's movement that grew in opposition to regressive legal measures began to develop agendas, advocacy projects, and a body of research to address gender inequality more broadly. As the media became more sensitized, reporting of incidents of gender-based violence increased. While the international women's movement enabled the domestic advocacy to gain global prominence, which in turn gave it more credibility within the Pakistani state and society, the domestic advocacy was nonetheless rooted in concerns and priorities arising from social, cultural, and political contexts in Pakistan. It would therefore be incorrect to say that the movement around violence against women in Pakistan is driven by the normative assumptions of a transnational feminist movement that privileges the viewpoint of the white woman from the Global North.

It is important, however, to consider the extent to which the movement against violence against women in Pakistan and globally has motivated a legislative agenda that is "protectionist and conservative." Subsequent chapters of the book will show that some criminal legislation passed in Pakistan in recent years has relied on increased criminalization and an enhanced role for the police and prisons to prevent and punish gender-based violence. Legislative changes to the Pakistan Penal Code provision on rape, for example, enhanced criminal penalties in 2016 and 2021. The Sindh Child Marriage Restraint Act 2013 also increased criminal penalties for parents and adult males as well as persons who solemnize child marriages. These punitive approaches have been emphasized over welfare-based approaches, such as improved protection mechanisms in the form of well-resourced shelters and counseling services as well as availability of education and employment opportunities for women and girls vulnerable to violence.

Another criticism of the international anti–violence-against-women agenda is that it "reifies" cultural norms and practices and obscures the modern political and social forces—including those unleashed by the modern state—that perpetuate violence against women. Kapur states that some "cultural practices have come to occupy our imaginations in ways that are totalizing of a culture and its treatment of women, and are nearly always overly simplistic or a misrepresentation of the practice."[48] Kapur gives the example of the movement around dowry deaths in India that became the cause of vigorous local and global advocacy and was represented as an "ancient Hindu practice" that has existed "since time immemorial."[49] Such depictions ignore the fact that dowry murders are a "thoroughly modern and contemporary phenomenon"[50] rooted in desires and aspirations of a consumerist market-driven economy that has encouraged a practice of "bargaining" between the families of grooms and brides and expectations that the bride's family will provide certain goods to the husband's family. Given the modern nature of dowry murders, Kapur argues that analyzing the practice through the lens of culture and tradition does not advance a useful understanding of the phenomenon.

The discourse about violence against women in Pakistan has succumbed at times to this cultural reification, and this is reflected in law-reform advocacy. Some forms of violence against women in Pakistan, such as child marriage and honor killing, are depicted as cultural practices rooted in centuries-old traditions and tribal norms, ignoring or downplaying the modern social and political forces that shape the contemporary nature of these practices. Honour killing is believed to be a practice rooted in tribal values that equate a family's or community's honour with women's sexuality. Child marriage is also deemed to be rooted in centuries-old cultural norms about girls' sexuality and beliefs about their essential roles as wives and mothers. The fact that opposition to efforts to curb these practices invokes tradition and religion further solidifies narratives about their historical cultural origins. One consequence of such assumptions about these practices is that they create space for the state to intervene as the institution through which discriminatory practices promoted by nonstate actors—communities, tribes, families with their cultural norms and values—are regulated.

The cultural reification of such practices supports advocacy for state intervention premised on a dichotomy of *state vs. communities* and *law vs. culture*. These dichotomies perpetuate false assumptions by obscuring the way in which modern forces, including the modern state, shape these occurrences as they take place today. With respect to honour killings, for example, research on the phenomenon in Sindh shows how the formal legal system enables nonstate actors, including community elders and tribal leaders, to promote impunity for murders. Nafisa Shah's study reveals how many murders portrayed as "honour killings" are in fact motivated by other grievances, such as property or financial disputes, but are ascribed this label to use as a bargaining chip for a settlement between parties in lieu of criminal penalties—settlements in which state actors, such as the police and the judiciary, play active roles. She describes honour killings in Sindh as a "contemporary cultural product that often articulates social hierarchies and contests over marriages and resources."[51] The reality of honor killings as a contemporary practice therefore not only contradicts their portrayal as timeless cultural practices but also shows how formal and informal actors come together to promote some forms of gender-based violence.

The contemporary nature of child marriage in Pakistan also reflects the limitation of culture-based accounts of the phenomenon, since many such marriages are self-arranged by adolescents. A large number of child marriage cases coming before the police and courts do not involve marriages forced on girls by parents and communities—the paradigmatic instances of child marriage. Rather, they are marriages entered into voluntarily by girls, often to escape a forced marriage imposed by parents or as a consequence of a discovery of a consensual romantic relationship.[52] The cases discussed in the book show how the role of the state here is not to advance the agency and freedom of the girl but, rather, to reinforce control by families and communities. Again, the reality of child marriage disrupts the assumption that it is essentially a cultural practice and one that the state is in a best position to regulate through the enforcement of criminal legislation.

This book discusses how the law-reform advocacy achieved through activism in Pakistan on violence against women has adopted some unhelpful essentialisations of forms of gender-based violence. The advocacy has assumed a distinction between state and nonstate actors that has led to law reforms that are inconsistent with the reality of these challenges. To this extent, the criticism of the international movement on violence against women applies to advocacy for law reform in Pakistan.

Carceral Feminism

Debates among feminists globally on carceral approaches to gender-based violence provide some useful context to recent law reform in Pakistan. The term carceral feminism is used to denote the reliance of feminist activists on state intervention and a "law and order" approach to attain gender-related justice. Coined by Elizabeth Bernstein primarily to describe alliances between feminist activists and Christian evangelical groups in the United States against sex trafficking, carceral feminism describes an approach that emphasizes the role of the punitive state—through police and prisons—and a "drift from the welfare state" to address gender-based violence.[53] Such "approaches seek to maximise punishments against perpetrators of GBSV [gender-based sexual violence], push for reforms to anti-violence laws, and often work collaboratively with agents of the carceral system to imagine women's safety as something that accompanies the surveillance, prosecution, and incarceration of perpetrators."[54]

Among the criticisms of carceral feminism is that it legitimizes punitive state power that is prone to arbitrary and exploitative excesses. To that extent, it helps to "whitewash" institutions, such as the police and courts, that often engage in or condone human-rights violations. Feminists have pointed out that this is particularly detrimental for marginalized communities and racial and ethnic groups that are vulnerable to excessive policing and incarceration.[55] Support among women's-rights activists for enactment or implementation of criminal laws creates risks for women belonging to marginalized communities. Approaches relying on criminal law also intensify focus on individual perpetrators and specific instances of violence while obscuring the structural causes of patriarchal violence.[56] Carceral feminists who are satisfied with the conviction and imprisonment of individual perpetrators let all other structural forces, including the state and economic and racial hierarchies, off the hook for their role in promoting and enabling violence against women.

The legal changes discussed in this book rely on criminalization to address sexual violence, domestic violence, and child marriage. Much of the advocacy by the women's-rights movements in cases of gender-based violence has demanded that perpetrators be arrested and imprisoned. Activists and NGOs also from time to time join forces with punitive state institutions, such as the police, to arrest and imprison perpetrators. Acquittals in sexual-violence cases are deemed failures of the criminal-justice system, while long prison sentences are assumed to indicate that the system is or at least can "work" for women.

While the term carceral feminism is often used pejoratively, I argue that punitive approaches should not always be dismissed as regressive and counterproductive, given the seriousness and complexity of patriarchal violence and limitations of approaches to address the problem. I agree with those feminists who call for an imagining of justice beyond the carceral/anticarceral binary, based on the recognition of the urgency of dealing with patriarchal violence that threatens many women and girls on a daily basis while at the same time acknowledging the need to think through and implement a vision of accountability and prevention that relies less on punitive powers of the state and more on the transformative and healing potentials of communities, movements, and public institutions.

My own experience as a lawyer who has worked with dozens of survivors of gender-based violence over the years shows that many do seek criminal punishment of perpetrators because they believe that it is the most serious sanction available. Opinions about criminal sanctions vary—some people are satisfied with arrest and detention of a few days, while others choose to pursue more protracted sentences. The motivation for seeking imprisonment is protection, as detention of the perpetrator is the only way some survivors can feel safe. Other times the motivation is retribution for the harm they have faced. There are many others who prefer mediation or simply want support (legal, financial, or otherwise) as they try to move away from abusive partners or family members. For feminist activists who work with survivors on a daily basis, it becomes difficult to reject carceral approaches outright when these seem to be what survivors want and sometimes need.

It should be acknowledged that the demands of women activists for state intervention was and is a response to grave threats faced by women and girls from nonstate actors in the form of violence and cultural practices, often engaged in by family members, that are condoned by communities. The alliance between women's-rights activists and the state in Pakistan was therefore necessary to afford protection to women premised on claims of equality and fundamental rights against the state. It would be misguided and counterproductive to dismiss the strides made by women's-rights activists by taking advantage of openings, where available, in legislatures, bureaucracies, and the judiciary to advance their cause against gender-based violence. At the same time, however, the significant and serious obstacles between the passage of the gender progressive laws on the one hand and prevention and accountability for gender-based violence on the other call for a critical analysis of the strides achieved so far. The subsequent chapters of the book attempt to do just that—they consider the costs of criminalization that are borne not only by perpetrators but also by survivors, and the consequences of prioritizing punitive over welfare measures.

Marginalizing Economic Inequalities

One longstanding criticism of the women's-rights movement in Pakistan is that it has not prioritized demands for equitable and fair distribution of economic resources.[57] Women'srights activists have largely emphasized political and legal equality but have obscured the economic hierarchies that prevent women from reaping the benefits of greater political recognition and progressive legal frameworks. It is argued that the movement has also ignored the disparate experiences of women, experiences that vary based on their class background. The fact that many of the leaders of the women's movement come from upper-class and upper-middle-class backgrounds has entrenched the perception that the women's movement in Pakistan is class-blind.

It is true that the women's movement in Pakistan that emerged from the 1980s has, to a very large extent, focused on political and legal discrimination. This was largely motivated by Zia ul Haq's policies that sought to relegate women to second-class status. From the 1980s onwards, the goal of the movement was to reverse his regressive laws. During the 1990s, influential NGOs promoting women's rights, such as the Aurat Foundation, focused on increased political representation for women through reservations in legislatures and local government bodies. A significant emphasis was placed on the state's responsibility to protect women from patriarchal violence by nonstate actors. In making these demands, the women's-rights movement perceived its target, gender hierarchy, as the central and defining power relation. The main thrust of feminist politics during this time was what renowned feminist scholar Nancy Fraser has called the "politics of recognition"—the dominant feminist politics from the 1980s onward that foregrounds identity and difference rather than economic structures.

Fraser contrasts the "politics of recognition" with the ideological underpinnings of the 1960s wave of global feminism that challenged capitalist economies for their gender exclusions. This feminism adopted many claims of the socialist left's challenge to capitalism but added to it a radical critique of patriarchy: "[p]oliticizing the 'personal', they expanded the boundaries of contestation beyond socioeconomic distribution—to include housework, sexuality and reproduction."[58] By the 1980s, the socialist project was undermined severely across the world with the fall of the "Eastern bloc," emergence of a unipolar world, and the dominance of free-market ideologies. Feminism adapted to the ideological shifts by adjusting its claims: equality through transformation of economic relations was no longer the aspiration; rather, equality through recognition of women's cultural identity animated feminist ideology. Fraser writes, "The result was a major shift in the feminist imaginary: whereas the previous generation has sought to remake political economy, this one focused more on transforming culture."[59]

The global anti–violence-against-women agenda of the 1990s rose to prominence when free-market ideology was at its peak, which coincided with the period when the "politics of recognition" became the centerpiece of feminist struggle. The agenda foregrounded women's gender identity and cultural values subordinating their gender as a crucial, if not the most crucial, impediment to gender equality. The women's movement in Pakistan, which has always been in conversation with global feminist struggles, was affected by this trajectory. While recent years have seen some mobilisations led by women for economic rights (for example, the Lady Health Workers movement for secure employment and higher wages), the mainstream women's movement is preoccupied with questions of political and cultural status rather than economic redistribution.

The legislative enactments on violence against women discussed in this book are a product of the politics of recognition, which has been very successful in Pakistan and globally over the last three to four decades in defining states' responsibility to punish acts of patriarchal violence enabled by patriarchal cultures. Recent criminal-law reforms that emphasize accountability and punishment tend to assume, however, that all women, irrespective of their class background, have the resources to approach police, courts, and lawyers to secure protection and accountability. In their resort to the punitive rather than to welfare mechanisms of the state, these legal enactments obscure economic conditions that limit access to legal institutions. As lawyer and leading human-rights activist Hina Jilani writes in an assessment of the women's movement in Pakistan,

> So do the women of today have a better deal? In a narrow, legal sense the answer is yes. And in the cities at least, there is a lot more confidence to be seen . . . Even so, a lot needs to be resolved. The movement needs grassroots outreach, though this seems unachievable in the near future, considering the status of women in rural communities. But as Bangladesh has demonstrated, there is no substitute for economic empowerment in raising the status of women.[60]

In the absence of economic empowerment of women, patriarchy will persist. Therefore, those concerned with violence against women will have to address economic deprivation of women and how this is entrenched in Pakistan's highly unequal, class-stratified economy. It is possible to recognize women's subordinate cultural status and simultaneously to challenge economic structures that prevent the vast majority of women, particularly those of poor and working class backgrounds, from accessing justice. The subsequent chapters of the book discuss how barriers to accessing justice prevent women from taking advantage of legal reforms. It is hoped that the analysis sheds some light on how questions about economic empowerment and entitlements are inextricably linked to concerns about violence.

ASSESSING LAW REFORM

This book considers the impact of recent law reform in the following areas: domestic violence, rape, child marriage, and honor killings. In each of these areas, I discuss the impetus behind the legal change and then the obstacles to its implementation. Legal scholar Upendra Baxi posits that law-reform efforts may be characterized as "(1) regulatory law reform, namely, changes to statute law or other legal doctrine; (2) governance reform or changes in institutional practices; and (3) social reform or changes in social attitudes."[61] This typology is helpful toward understanding the limits of law reform in Pakistan. Women's-rights advocacy in Pakistan has attained the most significant gains in regulatory-law reform through the passage of gender progressive laws. Advocates have not, however, been able to make significant inroads in governance reform due to weak and corrupt state institutions. Social reform also remains a distant goal, as the cultural constraints on women continue to hamper their ability to take advantage of gender progressive laws and access state institutions for justice. By tracing the way in which the state, civil society, feminists, and women responded to these laws, this book aims to shed light on why regulatory reform does not lead to desired governance or social reform.

In the chapter on rape, I show how law reform on sexual violence was motivated by activism against the Zina Ordinance of 1979 that conflated rape with adultery, leading to the criminalization, under the adultery prohibition, of women who approached the police with complaints of rape and sexual violence. Women's-rights activists also galvanized around certain publicized and politicized cases of rape, including those of Mukhtaran Mai and Shazia Khalid in the 2000s. The activism around rape led to reforms in the Pakistan Penal Code and the Criminal Procedure Code, most notably in 2016 and 2021, to strengthen the capacity of the criminal-justice system to prosecute rape. The reforms, among others, entailed liberalization of the definition of rape, enhancement of punishments, and the introduction of procedural changes through collection of DNA evidence and legal-aid support for survivors. This book presents evidence to show that the implementation of these reforms is slow and inconsistent, with long delays between the passage of the law and the enforcement of measures by courts, police, and other bureaucracies. There are also major inconsistencies in implementation across geographies, so that the experiences of rape survivors and their families with the criminal-justice system remain deeply painful. The impact of law reform on rape affirms the gap between regulatory reform and governance reform, as it shows how the statutory changes to the meaning of rape as well as the introduction of legal requirements regarding procedures and processes do not directly lead to changes in institutional behavior. The absence of meaningful governance reform diminishes the possibility of social reform being achieved through the legislative change.

In Chapter Two, I discuss how activism to amend the 1929 child marriage law has focused on raising the minimum age of marriage and strengthening criminal penalties. This advocacy has been successful in one province, Sindh, which passed child-marriage legislation in 2013 that raised the minimum age of marriage to eighteen for both boys and girls and increased the criminal penalties imposed on parents who arrange child marriages, adult males who enter into marriage with minors, and persons who solemnize a child marriage. Attempts to make similar amendments at a federal level have failed due to resistance from religious parties and the Council of Islamic Ideology. The 2013 enactment in Sindh was met with strong approval from the human-rights community in Pakistan, but it has had unintended consequences that are counterproductive for the cause of gender justice. As I show in the chapter, the child-marriage legislation has been used, along with other Penal Code provisions on rape and kidnapping, by parents against adolescents entering into self-arranged marriages. Review of prominent court cases as well as interviews with women and girls who entered into self-arranged child marriages and who were, with their partners, then apprehended by the police show how the criminal law, intended to curtail a human-rights violation, can be wielded by patriarchal forces to impose controls on young persons. Research on child marriage shows how social realities undermine the positive impact of laws intended to curtail discriminatory practices due to the inability of vulnerable persons—in this case, girls—to use the laws against patriarchal forces and the ability of stronger parties to use these laws against young people. Again, to use Baxi's typology, regulatory reform in the area of child marriages did not lead to desired governance or social reform, as it failed to promote effective institutional practices or cultural attitudes that recognize the capacities and freedoms of minors, especially girls.

The chapter on domestic-violence legislation focuses on laws passed in Sindh and Punjab and shows how resistance to implementation of these laws by law enforcement, courts, and bureaucracies hampers their effectiveness. In both provinces, the laws remained more or less dormant for many years. It took years before women started approaching courts to avail themselves of remedies offered in the law. In Sindh, the first case was admitted in court almost four years after the law was passed. In Punjab, the law on domestic violence that was passed in 2016 was not immediately effective throughout the province. The law itself specified that it would only become effective in an "area" upon notification by the provincial government, and, in its initial years, the law was effective in only one area, Multan. The validity of the law was also challenged before the Federal Shariat Court, which rejected the challenges in 2022. In both provinces, there are signs of incremental implementation, with an increasing number of cases filed in courts and the activation of some protection mechanisms, but the progress is very slow. The experience with domestic violence—to use Baxi's typology—shows that, when successful regulatory reform does not lead to governance reform, its capacity to bring about social reform is diminished.

Chapter Five considers the advocacy against legal changes to the Pakistan Penal Code in the decade of the 1990s, known as the Qisas and Diyat amendments, which permit defendants in murder cases to escape criminal penalities by entering into compromises with the heirs of victims. The Qisas and Diyat amendments are perceived by women's-rights activists to be a significant obstacle in the way of accountability for these crimes. The chapter considers changes to the penal code, particularly those enacted in 2016, in response to advocacy against the Qisas and Diyat amendments, and shows how these changes were cosmetic and did not repeal the provision for compromise. Shedding a critical light on advocacy against honour killings in Pakistan, I suggest that the focus on the perniciousness of the Qisas and Diyat amendments should be diffused onto other, structural failures in the criminal-justice system that impede accountability for honour crimes.

These structural features are more difficult to address than statutory law, as they require not only legislative enactments but also accountability and training within complex and often corrupt and inefficient bureaucracies. Endemic structural weaknesses prevent the formal justice system from bringing about accountability for honour killings and also help entrench the legitimacy of informal justice processes in Pakistan (known as jirgas, panchayats, or *faislo*) that often mediate compromises between murderers and victims' families in honor-killing cases. Advocacy against honour killings and informal justice processes illustrates how the regulatory reform advocated for by women's-rights activists assumes the efficacy of the formal adjudicative and carceral processes to uphold gender justice. The advocates' assumption, however, is not borne out by the evidence, as formal processes have consistently failed to bring about gender justice and have in fact worked with informal processes to promote impunity for gender-based crimes.

The final chapter assesses the overall impact of women's-rights advocacy for criminal-law reform and considers the paths and strategies available for current and future activism. It looks at contemporary feminist movements in Pakistan, particularly the Aurat March collectives that developed after widely attended public protests in 2018 and 2019. The contemporary movements, primarily comprising women's-rights activists that came of age at least one generation after the WAF-led movement of the 1980s, are skeptical of the role of law and legal institutions to tackle patriarchy. Hence their attitudes toward criminal law and enforcement are ambivalent, even though they advocate very vocally against gender-based violence. The final chapter considers some of the shifts in approaches toward criminal-law reform and suggests how current and future generations of activists may adopt diverse models of accountability for gender-based violence.

Law-reform advocacy in multiple areas that we discuss in the book—child marriage, rape, domestic violence, and honour killings—shares some common features. The majority of law reform relating to gender-based violence in recent years relies on the criminal-justice system for accountability and prevention. In the case of rape, child marriage, and honour killings, significant emphasis is placed on increasing criminal penalties and expanding the range of criminalizable behaviour. Relatedly, the legal changes rely on an adversarial judicial mechanism that assesses evidence to make determinations of guilt or liability for gender-based violence and harassment. The burden is largely on the survivors' or victims' families, either themselves or through the state, to convince a neutral forum that a criminal violation has occurred. The primary responsibility for implementing these laws lies with the judiciary and the police. With respect to some laws, such as legislation relating to domestic violence and child marriage, there is also a reliance on bureaucracies, such as the women's development and social welfare departments, to provide protection services, such as shelters and counselling. As I show in subsequent chapters of the book, the many barriers to the implementation of these laws share common features: there is resistance on the part of police and courts to enforce the laws, governments do not devote financial or human resources to sustain protection and welfare mechanisms required by the laws, and there is an overwhelming burden on survivors and their families to utilize the law and interact with reluctant and often hostile actors working in government institutions.

NOTES

1. Farida Shaheed and Sohail Akbar Warraich, "The Context of Women's Activism," in *Shaping Women's Lives: Laws, Practices and Strategies in Pakistan*, eds. Farida Shaheed and others (Shirkat Gah, 1998), 273–74.
2. Ibid., 273.
3. Ibid., 274.
4. Xari Jalil, "Women Recount 1983 Protest against Discriminatory Laws," *Dawn*, Lahore, February 13, 2020, <https://www.dawn.com/news/1534095>, accessed August 16, 2024.
5. Martin Lau, "Twenty-Five Years of the Hudood Ordinance—A Review," *Washington and Lee Law Review* 64, no. 4 (2007): 1291, 1295.
6. Shahla Zia, "Some Experiences of the Women's Movement: Strategies for Success," in *Shaping Women's Lives: Laws, Practices and Strategies in Pakistan,* eds. Farida Shaheed and others (Shirkat Gah, 1998), 377.
7. Farida Shaheed and Sohail Akbar Warraich, "The Context of Women's Activism," in *Shaping Women's Lives: Laws, Practices and Strategies in Pakistan*, eds. Farida Shaheed and others (Shirkat Gah, 1998), 278.
8. See the Aurat Foundation website: https://www.af.org.pk/.
9. Ayesha Khan, *The Women's Movement in Pakistan: Activism, Islam and Democracy* (I. B. Tauris, 2018), 148.
10. Ibid., 147.
11. The Guardian, "A Question of Honour," *The Guardian* (May 27, 1999), <https://www.theguardian.com/world/1999/may/27/gender.uk1>, accessed date.
12. Pakistan Criminal Law (Amendment) Act 1997.
13. Khan, n 9, 145.
14. Vienna Declaration and Programme of Action adopted by the World Conference on Human Rights (June 25, 1993).
15. Declaration on the Elimination of Violence Against Women, UNGA Res 48/104 (December 20, 1993).
16. Dr. Shahnaz Wazir Ali, interview by Sara Malkani and Farieha Aziz, Karachi, April 15, 2022.
17. *Report of the Commission of Inquiry for Women, Pakistan* (1997).
18. Ibid.
19. Ibid.

20. Ibid.

21. Khan, n 9, 245.

22. Zaffar Abbas, "Pakistan's New-Look Parliament," *BBC News* (November 21, 2002), <http://news.bbc.co.uk/1/hi/world/south_asia/2498425.stm>, accessed August 16, 2024.

23. Khan, n 9, 249.

24. According to Senator Sherry Rehman, "The debate about the merits of the 17 percent quota system aside, which was introduced in 2002, having more women in parliament has undoubtedly altered the fabric of Pakistani law and government . . . Where men previously dominated, women parliamentarians have brought a qualitative change in the nature of parliamentary business and discourse. As the Human Rights Commission found, apart from women's bills, a majority of the human rights legislation in Pakistan was moved by women, which in a cascade of political debates successfully changed the discourse, tone and, to some extent, the voting dynamics of parliament." Sherry Rehman, "The Parliament Percentage," in *Womansplaining: Navigating Activism, Politics and Modernity in Pakistan*, ed. Sherry Rehman (Folio Books, 2021).

25. J. Majida Rizvi, interview by Sara Malkani and Farieha Aziz, April 12, 2022.

26. Protection of Women (Criminal Laws Amendment) Act 2006.

27. Shahnaz Wazir Ali, interview by Sara Malkani and Farieha Aziz, Karachi, April 15, 2022.

28. Sherry Rehman, "The Parliament Percentage," in *Womansplaining: Navigating Activism, Politics and Modernity in Pakistan*, ed. Sherry Rehman (Folio Books, 2021), 101.

29. Anis Haroon, interview by Sara Malkani and Farieha Aziz, March 31, 2022.

30. Ibid.

31. Khan, n 9, 156.

32. Ibid., 158.

33. Mariyam Suleman Anees, "'Honor Killings' Continue Unabated in Pakistan," *The Diplomat* (July 28, 2022), <https://thediplomat.com/2022/07/honor-killings-continue-unabated-in-pakistan/>, accessed August 16, 2024.

34. Prevention of Electronic Crimes Against Women 2016, s. 19.

35. *Salman Akram Raja v. Government of Punjab* (2013) SCMR 203.

36. *Sadaf Aziz & Others v. Federation of Pakistan & Others* (2021) PCrLJ 205 (Lahore High Court).

37. Nida Usman Chaudhry, "The State of Women's Representation in the Judiciary 2023: Supplementary Report" (Women in Law Initiative, Pakistan, 2024).

38. Ibid., 21.

39. Juan D. Baron, Lauren Dahliln, and Jessica D. Lee, "Five Major Challenges to Girls' Education in Pakistan" (The World Bank, June 2024), <https://datatopics.worldbank.org/dataviz/girls-education-pakistan/>, accessed August 15, 2024.

40. National Institute of Population Studies and ICF, "2019 Pakistan Maternal Mortality Survey Summary Report" (Islamabad, Pakistan, and Maryland, US, 2020),<https://dhsprogram.com/pubs/pdf/SR267/SR267.pdf>, accessed August 15, 2024.

41. The World Bank, "Female Labor Force Participation in Pakistan: What Do We Know?" (World Bank Group, February 2018), <https://documents1.worldbank.org/curated/en/444061529681884900/pdf/Female-labor-force-participation-in-Pakistan-what-do-we-know.pdf>, accessed date.

42. Janet Halley, "Preface: Introducing Governance Feminism," in *Governance Feminism: An Introduction*, eds. Janet Halley and others (University of Minnesota Press, 2018), ix.

43. Ibid.

44. Ratna Kapur, "The Tragedy of Victimization Rhetoric: Resurrecting the Native Subject in International/Postcolonial Feminism Legal Politics," *Harvard Human Rights Law Journal* 15 (2002):1, 10.

45. Ibid., 6.

46. Ibid., 6.

47. Ibid., 7.

48. Ibid., 12.

49. Ibid., 13.

50. Ibid., 13.

51. Nafisa Shah, *Honour Unmasked: Gender Violence, Law and Power in Pakistan (2016)* (Oxford University Press, 2016), 3.

52. See Chapter 3 in this book.

53. Elizabeth Bernstein, "The Sexual Politics of the 'New Abolitionism,'" *Differences-A Journal of Feminist Cultural Studies* 18, no. 3 (2007): 143.

54. Maddie Brockbank and Saara Greene, "Beyond the Carceral/Anti-Carceral Binary: Considerations for Addressing Gender-Based and Sexual Violence," *The British Journal of Social Work* 52, no. 8 (2022): 5027.

55. Ibid.

56. Ibid.

57. Afiya Shehrbano Zia, "Contesting the Class Question: Moving Beyond Piety and Patriarchy," in *Womansplaining*, ed. Sherry Rehman (Folio Books, 2021).

58. Nancy Fraser, *Fortunes of Feminism: From State Managed Capitalism to Neo-Liberal Crisis* (Verso, 2013), 3.

59. Ibid., 4.

60. Hina Jilani, "In Her Own Voice," in *Womansplaining*, ed. Sherry Rehman (Folio Books, 2021).

61. Prabha Kotiswaran, "Governance Feminism in the Postcolony: Reforming India's Rape Laws," in *Governance Feminism—An Introduction*, eds. Janet Halley and others (University of Minnesota Press, 2018), 81 (citing a conversation with Upendra Baxi).

Chapter 2

Prosecuting Rape

In September 2020, the rape of a woman on a motorway outside the city of Lahore sparked several protests and media outrage across the country.[1] The woman was stranded in the motorway in the early hours of the morning when her car broke down. She called the motorway police on their helpline for assistance, but while she was waiting two armed men approached her, forced her out of her car, and raped her.

In the years preceding the incident, feminist collectives known as Aurat March had formed in some cities across the country, and they played a key role in mobilizing protests against the rape in public spaces as well as through media, particularly social media. Activists and media commentariat blamed the state for its failure to prevent sexual assault against women and demanded accountability. At a press conference, Lahore's chief of police told the press that the rape survivor should have checked her gas tank before making the drive.[2] This comment triggered waves of condemnation among women's-rights activists who said that this thoughtless remark amounts to victim blaming.

Accountability for this incident was swift. The accused men were arrested and brought to trial in antiterrorism court. Within a few months, the men were convicted and sentenced to death. Their appeals are pending before the Lahore High Court. Imran Khan's Pakistan Tehreek Insaaf (PTI)–led government of the time was also quick to propose law reform in wake of the incidents and protests around it. In December 2020, the president of Pakistan promulgated two Ordinance that made significant changes to the Pakistan Penal Code provisions on rape and sexual assault and also introduced a range of procedures and mechanisms for investigation and prosecution of sexual violence cases. The legal changes were pushed through without any meaningful consultation with women's-rights groups and civil-society organisations working with sexual-assault survivors. Nor did the PTI government introduce its law reform as a bill to be considered by parliament. Instead, it introduced these changes in the form of a presidential ordinance that was valid for up to 120 days, after which it would lapse unless it was passed by a legislature. The haste with which PTI introduced these reforms (which will be discussed in more detail later in this chapter) was a response to widespread protests around the case and the realization that a swift response would be to the government's credit.

Moving forward more than two years, another rape incident shook the country, and this time with a very different outcome. On February 2, 2023, a woman reported to the police that she had been raped in a park in the capital city of Islamabad.[3] She reported that she had gone to the park at night with a friend. Two men approached them and held them at gunpoint. Both men raped the woman. The incident sparked protests and outrage on electronic and social media.

Around two weeks after the crime, the police announced that they had killed the rapists in an "encounter" while attempting their arrest.[4] This claim was false; shortly before this announcement, the police had informed the rape survivor that they had arrested the suspects and had asked her to come to the police station to identify the rapists, which she did.[5] A high-profile rape case therefore closed without investigation or a trial. The rape survivor's lawyer and other activists held a press conference, declaring that no justice had in fact been done, as the police employed illegal force to kill the perpetrators. The rape in an Islamabad park in February 2023 served as another stark reminder that, even after the convictions in the Lahore motorway rape case and law reform by the government, sexual crimes against women remain endemic in Pakistan and that the state apparatus is ineffective in its response.

In response to consistent activism by women's-rights groups, Pakistan's state has come a long way in the last three decades or so in its acknowledgement that sexual violence exists and that it has a responsibility to prevent and punish this human-rights violation. Women's-rights activists, however, are dissatisfied with the extent to which this acknowledgment translates into effective and meaningful change in the way the state addresses sexual violence.

This chapter traces the history of women's-rights activism in Pakistan around rape and sexual violence. In its initial years, advocacy around sexual violence confronted regressive laws enacted during Zia ul Haq's regime. One of the demands during this period was to restore rape provisions in the Pakistan Penal Code. In the 1990s, advocacy expanded to include demands for state accountability for rape and sexual abuse. Activists focused on some high-profile incidents of rape, including those of Mukhtaran Mai and Shazia Khalid, which I discuss later in this chapter. The state's response in the 1990s and 2000s was denial and hostility. It took sustained advocacy around the issue, driven by NGOs such as War Against Rape, the Aurat Foundation, and the Human Rights Commission of Pakistan (HRCP), to instill acknowledgment of this human-rights violation among some political actors. Over time, the state's oppositional stance diminished and shifted toward alliance building with NGOs. In 2006, the Protection of Women (Criminal Amendment) Act was passed to bring rape back into the Pakistan Penal Code and make prosecution for adultery and fornication very difficult. In 2016, amendments were made to the Pakistan Penal Code and the Pakistan Code of Criminal Procedure to expand the range of criminal sexual offences and to improve investigation and prosecution procedures. Further amendments were made in 2021 with similar intent.

Discussion of rape-law reform in this chapter underscores the gap between formal changes in the law and their implementation. Legal amendments in 2016 and 2021 have not so far led to significant improvement in conviction rates for rape. Outcomes of recent cases show that the conflation of rape and adultery along with the high evidentiary requirements imposed by the Zina Ordinance for proving rape influence courts in spite of the law reform of 2006. Regressive laws seem to have long-lasting impact on the mindsets of state actors even after progressive law reform. Poor resource allocation for investigation and prosecution mechanisms and lack of accountability for officials in the criminal-justice system mean that severe obstacles for survivors and their families persist.

In her analysis of rape-law reform in India, scholar Prabha Kotiswaran refers to legal theorist Duncan Kennedy's caution that "criminal laws against the sexual abuse of women will never operate 24/7 and that the legal system will always tolerate a certain level of sexual abuse, namely, the tolerated residuum of abuse, which in turn depends on social decisions about what abuse is and how important it is to prevent it."[6] Kotiswaran notes that this idea of the "tolerated residuum of abuse" questions "the very assumption that the law can eliminate sexual abuse" and "tempers unrealistic expectations of regulatory reform."[7] The analysis of rape trials in this chapter and evidence of nonimplementation of legal reforms in Pakistan is indicative of the "tolerated residuum of abuse" that persists in spite of legislative changes and progressive jurisprudence. For feminists in Pakistan this means that even as they emphasize the significance of law reform, they must adjust their expectations of its impact.

Table 2.1 Timeline of Milestones

2006	Protection of Women (Criminal Laws Amendment) Act is passed
2011	Supreme Court acquits Mukhtaran Mai's rapists
2013	Supreme Court rules that DNA testing is admissible in rape cases; samples must be collected from accused persons and from the rape survivor with the survivor's consent
2016	2016 Criminal Law (Second Amendment) Act and 2016 Criminal Law (Amendment)(Offences Relating to Rape) Act 2016 make a series of changes to the Pakistan Penal Code and Code of Criminal Procedure provisions on rape and sexual violence
September 2020	Woman is raped by two men outside Lahore while her car is stranded on a motorway, triggering protests across the country
December 2020	President of Pakistan promulgates two Ordinance that amend definition of rape and punishments for sexual offences and that introduce new procedures for investigation and prosecution of sexual-violence cases
2021	Supreme Court of Pakistan and Lahore High Court rule that "two finger" and hymen testing results in rape cases for the purposes of "ascertaining the virginity" of rape survivor are inadmissible as evidence and these tests violate rights of survivors
December 2021	2021 Criminal Laws (Amendment) Act and 2021 Anti Rape (Investigation and Trial) Act is passed in parliament

REVERSING "ISLAMISATION" OF CRIMINAL LAWS

Changes to criminal laws initiated by General Zia-ul-Huq from 1979 onward were a huge setback for accountability for sexual violence. In 1979, the Pakistan Penal Code provision on rape was repealed with the promulgation of the Offence of Zina (Enforcement of Hudood) Ordinance, which made all sexual intercourse outside marriage a criminal offense. The Zina Ordinance introduced the offences of adultery and fornication in addition to prescribing penalties for rape.[8] The maximum punishment for rape and adultery was stoning to death for adult married Muslims and one hundred lashes for adult non-Muslims and adult single women.[9] The maximum punishment could be decreed only when the crime was witnessed by four male witnesses of good character or with confession by the accused.[10] Where the burden of proof for the maximum punishment (*hadd*) was not met, the crime may still be punishable by a lesser sentence, known as *tazir*.[11]

Because the Zina Ordinance lumped the crimes of adultery and rape together, women who approached the police with the complaint of rape would find themselves in a legal trap. If a woman's accusation of rape was not proven, she had admitted to sexual intercourse that was possibly consensual. This opened her up to the charge of adultery.

In their book, *The Hudood Ordinance: A Divine Sanction?*, lawyers Asma Jahangir and Hina Jilani describe many cases of such entrapment. After fifteen-year-old Jehan Mina's father died, her mother remarried, and Jehan Mina was left with her maternal grandfather. She was sent to the home of her ailing aunt to take care of household chores. When she returned, it was discovered that she was pregnant. She told her uncle that she was raped by her aunt's husband and son, and her maternal uncle filed a complaint of rape with the police on her behalf. At trial, the accused were acquitted as Jehan Mina's version was disbelieved. However, her state of pregnancy and the absence of a finding of guilt of the accused men was deemed a confession of adultery, and she was sentenced to the maximum punishment (*hadd*) of one hundred lashes. On appeal, the Federal Shariat Court upheld the conviction but reduced the sentence to a lesser punishment or *tazir*.[12]

While the Zina Ordinance remained in effect, trial courts imposed the maximum penalty of *hadd* for adultery (stoning to death or one hundred lashes), but the vast majority of convictions were overruled by appellate courts. No one was executed by stoning under the law; however, as noted by Asma Jahangir and Hina Jilani in their book, there were numerous convictions for adultery under *tazir*, the lesser punishment of incarceration. Another case described in their book is of a woman who was accused of adultery by her former husband. Shahida Parween married Muhammad Sarwar after she was divorced. Her former husband denied divorcing her. Even though she placed a divorce deed on record, it was not registered by the Union Council as required under the law. On this basis, the trial court found the marriage between Shahida Parween and her current husband illegal, and they were sentenced to stoning to death for engaging in illicit sex. Their convictions were appealed before the Federal Shariat Court, which ordered a retrial during which both were acquitted.[13]

Repeal of the Zina Ordinance became a rallying cry for activists and galvanized the women's-rights movement. During the 1980s women activists were up against strong resistance from Zia ul Haq's regime, but, even after elected civilian governments came to power in 1989, repeal of the laws was an uphill struggle. Successive elected leaderships throughout the 1990s wanted to avoid any backlash that would come with efforts to repeal the laws that had a stamp of religious sanction. As noted by scholar Martin Lau, a powerful reason behind the resilience of the Zina Ordinance is "rooted in the nature and legitimacy of the state of Pakistan itself."[14] The construction of a Pakistani national identity around Islam meant that even nonreligious political parties and their leadership did not want to be *accused* of secularizing laws and policies or reversing purportedly Islam-based legal reforms.

The laws therefore remained on the books until 2006, when a major victory for the women's movement was achieved with the Protection of Women

(Criminal Laws Amendment) Act 2006. The 2006 Act did not fully repeal the Zina Ordinance but significantly diluted its most reprehensible and dangerous aspects. The rape provision was returned to the Pakistan Penal Code and disentangled from its equation with adultery under the Zina Ordinance. Rape is therefore no longer governed by the Zina Ordinance. The offence of adultery remains in the Zina Ordinance, with the addition of a new definition of "confession."[15] A "confession" must now be an explicit oral statement admitting the commission of the offence. This provision prevents a court from inferring a confession or admission of offence of adultery from the inability of a person to prove an accusation of rape.

The 2006 Act also removes any reference to the lesser punishment of *tazir* for adultery. This means that the only punishment for adultery is the maximum—death by stoning—and it can only be decreed if there are four pious male Muslim witnesses to the act of adultery. The 2006 Act also made substantial procedural changes that make the very prosecution of adultery unlikely. A court cannot even charge a person with adultery unless four adult male eyewitnesses to the sexual act make a statement before a court under oath and satisfy the court that they are "truthful" persons.[16]

Women's-rights activists had long demanded that the Zina Ordinance be repealed in its entirety. While the 2006 Act did not meet this demand, it did away with the most pernicious aspects of the Zina Ordinance, making the detention and conviction of people for adultery and fornication extremely difficult.

The 2006 law reform succeeded because it was portrayed to be consistent with an Islamic legal framework. The lengthy Statement of Objects and Reasons for the 2006 Act notes that it aims to bring the Zina Ordinance in line with Islam and that, in their current form, they are inconsistent with Islamic law. The Statement also notes that the Zina Ordinance "facilitated abuse" because they led to the prosecution of women victims of rape for adultery.[17] Notably but unsurprisingly, the Statement avoids expressing any intent to secularize criminal laws and instead affirms the commitment to keep the legal framework consistent with Islam. Neither does the Statement convey any intent to decriminalize or destigmatize adultery or fornication. Instead, the Statement highlights the danger of wrongful imprisonment and conviction of *innocent* women (i.e., women who are not adulteresses or fornicators) due to the Zina Ordinance. Couched in religious terminology and protectionist language, the 2006 Act was portrayed as a paternalistic concession in recognition of the abuses triggered by the Zina Ordinance, and lawmakers tried as much as possible to avoid affirming sexual and bodily autonomy of women.

Some high-profile rape cases that were covered extensively by global and local media in the early 2000s also contributed to increasing pressure on the government to make further changes to the legal framework on sexual violence. I discuss two of these cases below, those of Mukhtaran Mai and Shazia Khalid, cases that galvanised public discourse around sexual violence in Pakistan and exposed the state's resistance to accountability for reducing such crime.

RAPE CASES GO PUBLIC

Mukhtaran Mai's rape in 2002 was a watershed case for women and human-rights activists in Pakistan. A local village council (panchayat) ordered that Mukhtaran Mai be raped to punish her for the alleged sighting of her younger brother with a woman of a higher caste.[18] Eight days after the incident, Mukhtaran Mai filed a complaint with the police. She was supported by a local sympathetic maulvi. Local press reported on the incident, and it came to the knowledge of an NGO, Pattan, and an activist, Farzana Bari. Pattan organized a rally that drew a large crowd and triggered more public protest. The Supreme Court took notice of the case and ordered the Inspector General of the Punjab Police to provide information about the investigation.[19]

Fourteen men were charged with the crime, and their case was tried in an antiterrorism court. Four were accused of committing the rape, while the remainder were accused of aiding and abetting the crime through their involvement in the panchayat that ordered Mukhtaran Mai's rape. The court sentenced six of the accused men to death while acquitting the remaining eight accused men. The decision was appealed to the Lahore High Court by the prosecution and the defendants. In 2005, the Lahore High Court overturned the verdict—only one man was declared guilty and awarded a life sentence, while all other accused persons were acquitted. The verdict was appealed to the Supreme Court.

The Supreme Court finally reached a decision in 2011, when a majority of the three-member bench upheld the decision of the Lahore High Court,[20] to the shock and outrage of Mukhtaran Mai and the many activists and NGOs who supported her through the years. An analysis of the eighty-four-page decision of a three-member bench of the Supreme Court shows the pitfalls at every stage of the criminal-justice process that make the successful prosecution of rape cases so difficult.

The Supreme Court concluded that eight of the accused persons were rightly acquitted as their names were not mentioned in the FIR (first information report) and no clear role was attributed to them. The dissenting judge agreed with the majority view to this extent. With respect to the remaining six accused, two were convicted by the trial court for aiding and abetting rape, given their role in the panchayat, while the other four were convicted for committing gang rape. The Lahore High Court upheld the conviction of only one person, acquitting the rest on the grounds that the prosecution failed to establish its case beyond a reasonable doubt. The Supreme Court agreed with the Lahore High Court that the conviction of only one person—Abdul Khaliq—could be upheld since he admitted to sexual intercourse with Mukhtaran Mai.

In its explanation of its reason for acquitting all but one accused person, the Supreme Court pointed to the delay in registration of the first information report, which cast doubt on the credibility of the complainant.[21] It also pointed to the absence of medical evidence to corroborate the accusation of gang rape: no physical sample was dispatched for DNA testing. The Supreme Court noted established precedent that in rape cases the solitary statement of the rape victim may be sufficient to support a conviction. However, it stated that the solitary statement must be viewed in light of other facts that diminish the credibility of Mukhtaran Mai's statement.[22] The Supreme Court noted with incredulity that Mukhtaran Mai was taken by the rapists to the home of one of the accused persons in the presence of her father and maternal uncle. According to the Supreme Court, it seemed unlikely that they would be unable to stop the incident.

The Supreme Court believed that an alternative version of events may be possible. It said that there was some credence to the defense claim that the panchayat had in fact decided that Mukhtaran Mai would be married to one of the accused, Abdul Khaliq, while her brother would marry his sister, Salma, with whom he was accused of engaging in illicit relations. After this "watta satta" or bride swap was finalized, Mukhtaran Mai and Abdul Khaliq had sexual intercourse. However, six days later, Khaliq's sister, Salma, was married off to another person and not to Mukhtaran Mai's brother, as arranged. This may have led Mukhtaran Mai to take revenge for her betrayal, and in this she was supported by the local maulvi, who encouraged her to make the complaint. According to the Supreme Court, the maulvi was the "mastermind" of the episode, and he "orchestrated" the case.[23] However, the motive of the maulvi to orchestrate this case was not established in the Supreme Court judgment. The maulvi was in litigation over some dispute with the father-in-law of one of the accused, but there was no evidence of any possible ill will or enmity toward any of the other accused. Also, if the Supreme Court was of the view that the alternative explanation is plausible, i.e., that intercourse between Mukhtaran Mai and Abdul Khaliq took place after they were married in accordance with the decision of the panchayat, it's unclear how Abdul Khaliq's rape conviction could be sustained.

The single dissenting judge upheld the conviction of Abdul Khaliq and his sentence of life imprisonment for rape and also found that four other accused persons should be found guilty for aiding and abetting the rape. The dissenting opinion took the view that Mukhtaran Mai's testimony about the incident should be deemed credible and that the medical evidence showing "healed bruises" on her body established that she was assaulted.[24] The dissent emphasized that the delay in reporting the rape case is understandable in light of the power difference between the tribe of the accused rapist and the tribe to which Mukhtaran Mai belonged. The accused rapists were from the more powerful tribe of Mastois, while Mukhtaran Mai and her family belonged to the more humble Gujjar caste. The power difference, which was not considered by the Supreme Court in its majority opinion, explains why Mukhtaran Mai and her family would be reluctant to go to the police immediately after the incident.[25] The strength of the Mastoi tribe also explains why the father and maternal uncle of Mukhtaran Mai were helpless as she was dragged away by the rapists.

The dissent also points out that many of the contradictions in the statements of witnesses, as emphasized by the Lahore High Court and the Supreme Court, are based on comparisons between witness testimony at trial and the statements supposedly made to the police during a fact-finding inquiry into the case ordered by the police chief of the district in which the incident took place.[26] The witness testimony before the court should not have been compared against the statements to the police during the fact-finding inquiry, which was not a part of the main investigation, and the inspector recording the statements was not even produced before the court as a witness. The fact-finding inquiry was conducted by the police in response to complaints regarding the investigation, but ironically it was the fact-finding report that was used to assail the credibility of the witnesses in support of the prosecution case. This is one indication of how the overzealousness of the government and the pressure it put on the police ended up harming the chances of conviction. This may be why leading human-rights lawyer Hina Jilani concluded that the government's attempt to take control of the case led to its ruin.[27]

This case was a stark reminder of the persistent failures of the criminal-justice system and the rigid barriers in the way of accountability for sexual

Table 2.2 Outcomes of Mukhtaran Mai's Rape Case

Courts in Mukhtaran Mai's Rape Case	Convicted of Rape (number)	Convicted of Aiding and Abetting Rape (Number)	Acquitted (Number)
Trial Court	6	0	8
Lahore High Court	1	0	13
Supreme Court	1	0	13
Supreme Court (dissent)	1	3	10

violence. There was little physical evidence, partly because of the failure of the investigation authorities to conduct a thorough investigation and partly due to the lapse of time between the incident and the reporting of the crime, a lapse that is common in rape cases. Because rape trials rely so much on the oral testimony of the complainant, there is a huge burden on her to convince the court of her credibility. The Supreme Court in Mukhtaran Mai's case set an extremely high standard of credibility for Mukhtaran Mai, and this is typical of the burden placed on survivors. If Mukhtaran Mai, with her bravery and support from so many activists and NGOs locally and internationally, could not get justice, what hope was there for other victims of sexual violence?

The judicial outcome of the Mukhtaran Mai case raises some questions that continue to come up in sexual violence cases and remain unanswered:

- To what extent do sexual-violence cases require deviation from the principle that in criminal cases the prosecution must build a case that proves guilt beyond a reasonable doubt? The burden of proof in criminal cases is high in order to minimize any chance of an erroneous conviction. Generally, testimonies of victims require corroborating evidence to support criminal convictions, but the Supreme Court and high courts in Pakistan sometimes make exceptions for rape cases, given the nature of the crime, the likelihood that it will not happen before witnesses, and the difficulties of obtaining physical evidence. The Supreme Court and high courts in Pakistan have held that a solitary statement of the survivor in sexual-violence cases that is trustworthy and reliable may sustain a conviction in the absence of corroborating evidence.[28] The Supreme Court in Mukhtaran Mai's case, however, did not accept the survivor's testimony in light of other perceived gaps and weaknesses. In advocating for a loosening of prosecution standards in rape and sexual-violence cases, are feminists standing in opposition to other human-rights principles?
- When does the push for harsh penalties for crimes of sexual violence reduce the chances of a conviction? The Supreme Court opinion reflects a reluctance to sustain a finding of gang rape. The only sentence for gang rape under the applicable provision at the time of the offence against Mukhtaran Mai (Section 10(4) of Offence of Zina (Enforcement of Hudood) Ordinance, 1979) was death. Given the mandatory death penalty, it is understandable why judges may be reluctant to convict the accused of gang rape even where there is only a shadow of a doubt. In fact, the dissenting judge stated that this is why he was reluctant to make a finding of gang rape and explains why he found only one person guilty of rape itself,[29] while four other accused persons were found by him to be guilty of aiding and abetting rape.

- Does high-level government pressure promote or deter proper investigation? One dilemma faced by feminists and human-rights activists is that, in their normal course, investigations of crimes in general, including rape, are ridden with flaws that make a conviction very difficult. In the absence of intervention from senior police officers or government officials, investigative officers are likely to be negligent in their duties. Unfortunately, added government pressure in specific cases can jeopardize the investigation even further as it may lead to overzealous and hasty investigation that skips crucial steps. In Mukhtaran Mai's case, in its eagerness to show seriousness the police named eight persons on its charge sheet against whom no specific allegations or evidence were put forward, and this impacted the credibility of the police investigation. The Supreme Court majority also pointed to the fact-finding inquiry conducted by the police in response to complaints of negligence to cast doubt on the credibility of the witnesses, and therefore the fact-finding exercise weakened rather than strengthened the prosecution's case.

Mukhtaran Mai was an exceptional rape survivor. She became a leader and role model for her community and galvanised activism against sexual violence in Pakistan. Global human-rights organisations, such as Amnesty International and Human Rights Watch, consistently called for accountability, while journalist Nicholas Kristoff regularly wrote about the case for the *New York Times*. Her case had far-reaching implications for the government of General Pervez Musharraf, who responded quite vengefully to the global outrage that the case had generated. In 2005 a United States–based women's-rights group invited Mukhtaran Mai to speak in the United States, and Musharraf's government placed her name on the Exit Control List and canceled her passport.[30] This triggered a wave of international condemnation, causing Musharraf's government to retract the cancellation and permit Mukhtaran Mai to travel. During the War on Terror following the 9/11 attacks in New York City, Musharraf was trying hard to promote himself as an "enlightened moderate" to court the West, and his attempt to stop Mukhtaran Mai from "maligning" Pakistan abroad backfired.

This was not the only high-profile rape case that shook Musharraf's government.

Dr. Shazia Khalid and Politicisation of Rape

In 2005, a medical doctor named Shazia Khalid was raped allegedly by an army officer inside the heavily guarded Sui Southern gas facility in Balochistan. In her case, there was no investigation or trial. Her rape and the

Musharraf government's response to her accusation sparked an insurgency among Balouch nationalists that continues to this day.

Dr. Shazia Khalid was employed by an oil company, Pakistan Petroleum Limited (PPL), and lived on her own in a housing complex inside the Sui Southern gas facility. In January 2005, she was attacked in her apartment while she was sleeping. The assailant blindfolded her, tied up her hands, and threatened to kill her with a pistol if she screamed. He assaulted her all night and left the room at sunrise. Dr. Khalid managed to untie herself and went to the hospital at the PPL facility. There, company officials told her to keep quiet about the case and did not provide medical treatment. Dr. Khalid contacted her husband, who worked in Libya, and he travelled to Balochistan to be with her.[31]

The Sui Southern gas facility was guarded by a branch of the Pakistan military, the Defense Security Guards. They took over the crime scene and did not allow the police to investigate. Other staff members informed local politicians that the rapist was an army officer and identified him as Captain Hammad. After word spread that the rapist was allegedly an army officer, President General Musharraf announced publicly that the suspect was completely innocent, even though an investigation had not taken place.[32] One of Pakistan's leading lawyers and human-rights activists, Asma Jahangir, is reported to have said at the time, "If the President of the country comes on television without the investigation being carried out and says that the accused he can assure people is innocent, I believe as a citizen he has no right to say it and if he does he is part of the cover up."[33]

Dr. Khalid was sent to Karachi against her will by the government, where she was kept under effective house arrest. She was not allowed to speak to media or lawyers. Meanwhile stories began to appear in newspapers to damage the credibility and reputation of Dr. Khalid, some even suggesting that she was a prostitute. Asma Jahangir said that President Musharraf himself told one of the editors of the newspaper that, "if he were to speak of Dr. Shazia, he didn't want to but he could say a few things too." Asma Jahangir added, "I mean what kind of an insinuation is that?"[34]

The incident heightened the tensions with nationalists in Balouchistan who had long-standing grievances against the federal government and the army's usurpation of natural-gas resources in the province. One of the leaders of the insurgents, Nawab Akbar Khan Bugti, declared that his tribe would avenge the rape and fired rockets at the Sui Southern gas facility. Musharraf's response to the outrage of human-rights activists and the insurgents was politically disastrous. Shortly after the incident, Musharraf visited the United States, and in an interview with *The Washington Post*, he was quoted as saying, in response to a question about Dr. Khalid's rape, "This has become a money making concern. A lot of people say if you want to go abroad and get a visa for Canada or citizenship and be a millionaire, get yourself raped."[35] This statement sparked renewed protests in Pakistan.

Shazia Khalid was told by the government to leave Pakistan and was sent off to London with her husband and adopted child. She wanted to go on to Canada as she had relatives residing there, but the government did not give her any support when she arrived in London. The insurgency in Balouchistan continued, and the army refused to concede on the issue of investigation of rape or the distribution of the province's natural resources among locals. In 2006, Musharraf ordered the assassination of Nawab Akbar Khan Bugti, which was not only a crime but also a huge political blunder as it only gave more fuel to the insurgency, which continues to this day.

Even though neither Mukhtaran Mai nor Shazia Khalid attained justice, they exposed what Pratiksha Baxi calls the "public secret" of rape—a feature of society that is generally known but not talked about.[36] They brought the crime of sexual violence to the centre of public discourse and made it increasingly difficult for the state to deny that it is systemic and goes unpunished. In their advocacy around these cases, women's-rights activists built constituencies in the public and among political actors who supported the reforms to rape laws that came years later. The law reform itself, widely celebrated, is an exposure of the public secret; but when we consider the actual experiences of rape survivors in the criminal-justice system, even after law reforms, we see how institutions work to perpetuate secrecy around rape by silencing survivors or punishing them for speaking out.

RAPE LAWS REFORMED

The momentum for accountability for sexual violence led to criminal-law amendments in 2016. The first act was passed in March 2016, and it introduced a new range of sexual offences, including "child pornography" and sexual abuse of a minor.[37] Another set of amendments, Criminal Law (Amendment)(Offences Related to Rape) Act 2016, increased the criminal penalties for rape. The act inserted a provision stating that whoever commits the offense of rape on a minor or a person with disabilities shall be punished with death or imprisonment for life. A "public servant" found guilty of committing rape while taking advantage of his official position was make liable to punishment with death or imprisonment for life. Whoever commits the offence of rape while also committing the offense of grievous "hurt" shall be punished with death or imprisonment for life. Disclosing the identity of the rape victim was declared illegal. The act also repealed a provision in the law of evidence—known as Qanun-e-Shahadat Act of 1984—that permitted a rape victim's testimony to be impeached by introducing evidence of her "immoral character."[38]

To improve the investigation of cases, a provision was introduced that criminalized the failure of a public servant to carry out the investigation of a case "properly or diligently." Failure to do so was punishable by imprisonment of up to three years. The law also made it mandatory to conduct a medical examination of a rape victim "where practicable." It specifically provided that DNA samples must be collected from a rape victim with her consent or that of her parents. This codified a Supreme Court ruling from 2013 that DNA testing should be mandatory in rape cases.[39] This overruled an opinion of the Council of Islamic Ideology—a body that advises the parliament on the consistency of laws with Islamic injunctions—that DNA evidence cannot be relied on as primary evidence in rape trials as it runs contrary to evidentiary procedures prescribed in Islam.[40] The act also introduced a requirement in the Code of Criminal Procedure that rape trials must be concluded in three months.

2016 Criminal Law Amendments and Implementation Challenges

The amendments to the Pakistan Penal Code and the Code of Criminal Procedure by and large did not make a significant dent on conviction rates for rape. Data collected in the province of Punjab in 2022, six years after these amendments, revealed that only 3 to 4 percent of registered rape cases resulted in convictions.[41] One major reason for nonimplementation is the poor resource allocation put toward investigation and prosecution mechanisms. For example, the requirement that DNA samples be collected and analyzed in all rape cases required the existence of laboratories where such investigation could be conducted and technicians that understand how to analyze DNA evidence. In the largest city in Pakistan, Karachi, the first DNA analysis laboratory was established as late as 2019.[42]

Police stations and courts remained hostile spaces for survivors of sexual assault in spite of the legal changes. Although amendments to the law required that rape cases be decided within three months, rape trials stretch for much longer. In spite of the amendment to the law on evidence that prohibited questions about "immoral character," trial judges continue to make references to women's sexual history.[43]

A study of rape cases in the Lodhran district in Punjab, conducted in 2016–2017 after the 2016 laws were passed, found that the law reforms had virtually no impact on the prosecution of rape cases.[44] The study found that the average duration of a rape case from the registration of the first information report to the decision is 560 days,[45] considerably more than the three months mandated under the law after the 2016 amendments. The study also found that the registration of first information reports or FIRs continues to be delayed: the average duration between the incident and the registration of an FIR is twenty-five days. The report also notes that persistent delays in the medical examination of victims often rendered the medical examinations useless. In a majority of cases, the medical examination of the accused was not conducted, which made the use of DNA evidence impossible even if samples were collected from the survivor.

The study also found that a majority of rape trials are terminated due to out-of-court settlements: 84 percent of the rape cases studied in 2016–2017 resulted in acquittals due to resiling of witnesses.[46] In most of these cases, the resiling takes place after parties have reached an out-of-court compromise. Rape (unlike some other criminal offences in the Pakistan Penal Code, including murder) is not a compoundable offence, which means that it cannot be excused or mitigated by the victim of the crime or the victim's family. In spite of that, however, parties in rape cases reach out-of-court settlements, after which the survivors resile their testimony against the perpetrator, and courts close the case. Without the testimony of the victim, there is usually little to no physical evidence available to sustain a conviction. Although the study does not have specific findings on reasons why survivors or their families reach out-of-court compromises, some aspects of the criminal-justice system suggest why such compromises may be desirable. Due to the long duration of rape trials and the uncertainty of outcomes, many people would rather terminate the trial than spend more time in and money on the proceedings. Threats from perpetrators or their families and the absence of a functioning witness-protection program could also lead to out-of-court settlements.

The 2016 legal changes attempted to improve accountability for sexual violence through the criminal-justice system, which works very poorly for crimes in general, and the overall conviction rates in Pakistan are therefore very low.[47] This has many causes, including poorly trained and corrupt police, underqualified and overburdened prosecution and judicial officers, very poor knowledge of investigation techniques, and lack of accountability of law enforcement. Due to these underlying systemic problems, legal reform is not downstreamed to police stations, medico-legal hospitals and courts, where the encounter of the rape victim with the criminal-justice system takes place and where the foundation for any accountability must be established.

2020 Ordinance

Even though the 2016 changes to the Pakistan Penal Code and the Code of Criminal Procedure were not implemented, the federal government pushed to add another layer of reforms in response to widespread protests after the Lahore motorway rape in September 2020. In December 2020, the president of Pakistan promulgated a presidential ordinance that amended rape provisions in the Pakistan Penal Code. Rape was now defined as a crime that can be committed by a person of any gender on a person of any gender.[48] Prior to these amendments, rape was defined in the Pakistan Penal Code as a crime that could be committed only by a man upon a woman. The ordinance also specifically included forced oral sex and penetration using any body part or object other than the penis in the definition of rape. A definition of "consent" was also added to the Pakistan Penal Code, which stated that consent must be based on an "agreement" and the absence of physical resistance should not be equated with consent for sex:

> *Consent means an unequivocal voluntary agreement when B by words, gestures or any form of verbal or non-verbal communication, communicates willingness to participate in the specific sexual act;*
>
> *Provided that if B who does not physically resist to the act of penetration, it shall not by the reason only of that fact, be regarded as consenting to sexual activity.*[49]

The ordinance added an additional penalty for rape: imprisonment for the remainder of the perpetrator's natural life.[50] It also introduced the punishment of "chemical castration" for "exceptional first offenders" or "repeat offenders."

A second presidential ordinance promulgated at the same time specified a slew of procedures for law enforcement and courts with respect to rape cases.[51] The ordinance called for the establishment of "special courts" to deal with cases of gender-based violence, the creation of "anti-rape" cells in each administrative district, which would bring together the range of services required by a rape survivor for the initiation of a criminal case of rape, special sexual-offences investigation units in the police, independent support advisers, and establishment of a register for sex offenders. The ordinance explicitly stated that the "two finger virginity testing for the purposes of medico-legal examination of a victim shall be strictly prohibited."[52]

The government led by Imran Khan's Pakistan Tehrik-e-Insaaf (PTI) initially chose to impose these laws as presidential Ordinance rather than put them through parliamentary vote. In December 2021, both Ordinance were enacted by the parliament with very few substantive changes. One notable change in the finally enacted version of the laws is that the penalty of "chemical castration" was removed due to opposition from the Council of Islamic Ideology, which claimed that such a penalty was against the injunctions of Islam.[53]

There was no broad-based consultation with women's-rights groups or sexual-violence experts on the contents of the laws that were drafted with considerable haste. Some women's-rights activists and experts working in areas of sexual violence raised serious skepticism about the breadth of procedural changes and mechanisms introduced in the Ordinance and wondered how these would be implemented when the earlier procedural requirements introduced by law were not even close to being implemented.[54]

The absence of broad-based consultation prior to making these significant legal changes is in contrast to the momentum leading to rape-law amendments in India in 2013. India's Criminal Law Amendment Act of 2013 was passed shortly after a rape and murder in Delhi—known as the Nirbhaya case—that sent shockwaves across the country. Soon after the incident, the Indian government formed the Verma Committee to consider law reform. The committee interacted with ninety-two feminist organisations and individuals before releasing its recommendations.[55]

Pakistan's 2020 ordinance and 2021 Act have borrowed considerably from India's 2013 law. India's 2013 Criminal Law Amendment Act amended the definition of rape to cover penile and nonpenile penetration, a change that Pakistan enacted in 2021. The law in India, however, retains the gender specificity of rape, in contrast to Pakistan's amendment. The "Explanation" of consent in India's 2013 law is also almost identical to the one adopted by Pakistan in 2021.

Whereas these amendments in India's law were the product of deliberation that included inputs from many feminist organisations, the significant changes in Pakistan's law were initiated by PTI legislators without feedback from the public or a broad base of feminists and human-rights activists. The changes to the definition of rape and the meaning of consent mark a significant shift and are by no means a reflection of a common or even predominant understanding within Pakistan of the meanings of these terms. The introduction of a gender-neutral definition of rape, for example, was not the result of long-standing advocacy by LGBT groups in Pakistan; nor was there any discussion among women's-rights groups in Pakistan on the implications of a gender-neutral definition. Again, this is in contrast to India where feminists and LGBT activists clashed over the introduction of a gender-neutral definition, with many feminists insisting that the gender specificity be retained to emphasize the vulnerability of cis-gender women to rape. When it was decided that the 2013 Criminal Laws Amendment Act would retain the gender-specific meaning of rape, LGBT advocates expressed their dismay that the experiences of transgender persons were marginalized.[56]

In 2020–2021, Pakistan's legislators sidestepped the possibility of any fraught debate and passed a gender-neutral definition without opposition. While many feminists in Pakistan (including myself) believe that the definition is a significant improvement, it is not obvious that it reflects a broad-based acceptance of an expansive definition. Whether or not the definition is controversial, the legislative enactment seems to have settled any disagreement, perhaps prematurely. It is important to consider whether the lack of discourse and absence of measures to raise awareness about the significant legal changes have implications for the implementation of law reforms.

The meaning of consent was also inserted without any deliberation on the implications of this definition for prosecutions or acknowledgement of the difficulties of conveying this meaning of consent to law-enforcement officials and judges, many of whom believe that the absence of physical resistance implies consent to a sexual act. The plain language of the amended statute requires that consent be an "unequivocal" agreement, expressed verbally or nonverbally, which entails that consent must be affirmative; otherwise, sex is rape.[57]

The affirmative consent requirement is a significant departure from how courts in Pakistan assessed consent prior to these amendments. Affirmative consent requirements have been debated vigorously in some contexts. In the United States, for example, there has been considerable resistance to this requirement, even among feminists.[58] In Pakistan, however, this explanation of consent was adopted without meaningful debate among legislators, legal experts, or women's-rights activists. The application of this meaning of consent will be difficult, partly because it is ambiguous. In particular, it does not clarify on whom the burden of proof falls to establish the absence of consent, and recent Supreme Court jurisprudence, discussed later in this chapter, shows how some key questions about factual determinations on consent in rape cases remain unresolved.

Some provisions in the new laws set forth procedures that had already been mandated under existing laws or rules. For example, special courts to try cases of gender-based violence existed in some districts in the country. Laws already existed for the provision of legal aid to victims of crimes. The 2016 amendments to the Code of Criminal Procedure already provided for the in camera trial of rape victims. Activists and lawyers with experience in working with survivors of gender-based violence cases argued that prior to the reintroduction of these procedures in a new law there should have been some assessment of why the previous interventions had not worked.[59] Without such assessment, it is likely that the new laws would be similarly ineffective.

Other procedural innovations introduced seemed highly ambitious. For example, the provision of "independent support advisers" would require recruitment of a whole cadre of trained personnel to perform the important and sensitive task of providing support to sexual-violence victims. This would need sufficient budget allocation and training. Similarly, the establishment of a special investigation unit within the police requires extensive training and monitoring of personnel to perform these investigations as desired. It is doubtful whether the police force has the capacity for such training and monitoring.

Since the laws were enacted, implementation has been very gradual. The first Anti-Rape Crisis Center required under the Anti Rape Act 2021 was inaugurated in Karachi in August 2023, almost two years after the law was passed by parliament and almost three years after the presidential Ordinance.[60] Most districts still do not have a crisis centre. Past experience has shown that governments do not devote the financial and human resources required to implement reforms to improve investigation and prosecution of cases of sexual violence. It is difficult to see how these procedures will effectively address sexual violence when they were overlaid on already existing institutions, police, and courts that are riddled with systemic flaws.

Some evidence suggests that conviction rates for sexual offences are higher in special courts that hear cases involving gender-based violence. A study conducted in 2017–2019 of such a special court in Lahore, Punjab found that the conviction rate for rape and sexual cases tried was 16 percent, significantly higher than the conviction rate for rape in other criminal courts.[61] The Legal Aid Society reports that the conviction rate for rape in Sindh, where courts specialising in cases involving gender-based violence exist in each district, was 11 percent by the end of 2022, significantly higher than the national rates.[62] More studies of such special courts are needed to understand why they are convicting at a significantly higher rate. A court hearing cases involving gender-based violence in Karachi, where I have appeared frequently, does not appear to work differently from any other criminal court; the judge and the prosecutor assigned here seem to approach cases with the same level of bias and lack of competence observed in other cases. A case of sexual abuse of a minor tried before a court that specialises in cases of gender-based violence in 2022–2023 in Karachi is discussed in some detail later in this chapter as an example.

Lawyer and human-rights activist Maliha Zia Lari, who has worked extensively with the government and UN agencies on legislative reform, says that the laws enacted to promote women's rights and to prevent and punish sexual violence are often removed from the reality of how law-enforcement institutions and courts actually function. She says that there is a gap between desired outcomes and practical outcomes, which explains why law reforms on rape are not adequately implemented. She also points out that drafting of laws and legal amendments of rape laws is often driven by civil-society groups and international donors with little buy-in from the government actors in fact responsible for implementing the legal changes.[63]

The set of reforms made in 2020–2021, like the ones introduced in 2016, are premised on the assumption that specific gender-focused interventions can be effective toward addressing gender-based violence. Institutions are unable to address gender-based violence, however, in large part because of systemic flaws that make them incompetent to address crimes in general. For gender-based crimes, the institutional failures are magnified because they are compounded by the prejudices of law-enforcement officials as well as the larger systemic barriers faced by women in accessing justice in the face of patriarchal societal norms. Interventions to address the latter, when implemented, will only be so effective so long as the underlying structural flaws remain unaddressed. When poorly implemented, these interventions are not likely to succeed.

In light of these realities, recent law reforms seemed geared to whitewashing state failures rather than making practical improvements. The fact that a punishment such as chemical castration was prescribed temporarily is indicative of how governments want the laws to symbolize their outrage about rape and that practical considerations about implementation are secondary. The introduction of harsh and extraordinary punishments does not address the problem of low conviction rates—punishments can only be meted out after there is a conviction. While conviction rates remain low, any deterrence effect of harsh punishments will remain negligible.

High Court and Supreme Court Jurisprudence

Over the years, the Supreme Court and the high courts in Pakistan have developed precedent to make rape convictions easier. For decades, superior courts have held that the solitary statement of a complainant that is trustworthy and reliable is sufficient to sustain a rape conviction. These judgments recognize that rapes typically are not witnessed and that it is very difficult to convict if a survivor's statement is required to be corroborated. The application of this precedent, however, is inconsistent. In Mukhtaran Mai's case, for example, the Supreme Court noted that, while a solitary statement of a complainant may be sufficient to support a conviction, the statement must be considered in light of other facts that could damage the credibility of the complainant. The Supreme Court then pointed to a number of aspects of the prosecution's case that it found to be implausible or inconsistent and that therefore cast doubt on the credibility of the Mukhtaran Mai's statement. In this case, the Supreme Court set a very high standard for the credibility and trustworthiness of a survivor's statement to support a conviction.[64]

Significant progress in sexual-violence jurisprudence was made in 2021, when the Lahore High Court and the Supreme Court passed judgments outlawing the archaic and invasive practice of the "two finger test" by medico-legal doctors during rape investigations. The practice involves the insertion of two fingers in a woman's vagina to assess elasticity. The elasticity is used to determine whether a woman claiming to be raped was a virgin and also whether she was "habituated" to sexual activity. Previously, medico-legal reports about rape survivors noted whether a woman was a virgin, with the determination made based on the so-called "two finger test." A woman deemed habituated to sexual activity was less likely to be believed in rape cases—an assessment concluding that a woman's vagina was loose meant that she had an "easy virtue," and courts consistently assumed that her claim lacked credibility.[65]

In a petition by activists, the Lahore High Court ruled that the practice violates a woman's constitutional right to dignity. It further concluded that the test's results have no evidentiary value. The Supreme Court, while deciding a criminal appeal, also considered whether the "two finger test" should be deemed admissible evidence in rape cases. The Supreme Court determined that the test has "no basis in medical science."[66] It further noted that a "woman, whatever her sexual character or reputation may be, is entitled to equal protection of the law" and that whether or not a woman is "accustomed" to sexual intercourse has no bearing on her credibility in rape cases.[67]

Implementation of superior court rulings, like that of legal reform initiated by legislatures, is fraught. An investigation conducted by Vice World News showed that the "two finger test" practice used on rape survivors persisted after the Supreme Court and high court judgments.[68] An examination of medical reports and interviews with rape survivors showed that the practice continued with impunity up to the time that the Vice report was published in September 2021. As recently as October 2023, the Lahore High Court noted with concern, while hearing a bail application on behalf of a man accused of rape, that the medical report about the rape survivors indicated that the two finger test was performed.[69] The Lahore High Court ordered disciplinary action against doctors who were continuing the outlawed practice.

Superior Court judgments on the two finger test were an important milestone in jurisprudence on rape cases in Pakistan not only because they outlawed a regressive, invasive, and forensically useless practice but also because they affirmed the irrelevance of a woman's sexual history in assessing the credibility of her accusation. The judgments rejected patriarchal assumptions about the "good rape victim" who is virginal and pure, in contrast to the woman of "loose character" who does not deserve justice. Poor implementation of the judgments, however, shows how patriarchal and sexist notions persist in spite of progressive pronouncements at the highest level of the judiciary.

While women's-rights activists consider progressive superior-court judgments to represent victories for their cause, these decisions often fail to impact trial-court adjudication. Even though these judgments constitute binding precedent, trial-court judgments generally make little to no reference to them and often display poor understanding of their content. A review of trial-court judgments in the Lodhran district in Punjab found that 90 percent of trial-court judgments in rape cases in 2016–2017 did not mention legal precedent.[70]

Confusions about Consent

Within the superior judiciary, confusion about rape adjudication persists. A Supreme Court judgment announced on June 26, 2024, overturning a rape conviction, shows how the highest court of the country continues to impose a very high burden to prove nonconsensual sex. The fact that the Supreme Court in this case convicted the accused person of fornication under the Pakistan Penal Code after concluding that the sex between the parties was consensual shows how the dangerous legacy of Zia's laws continues. The dissenting opinion, authored by Justice Ayesha Malik (Pakistan's first woman on the Supreme Court), underscores the complicated and contradictory Supreme Court jurisprudence regarding the burden of proof in rape cases. These contradictions remain unresolved even after the 2021 amendments. I review the judgment in *Muhammad Imran v. State and Another* and the dissenting opinion[71] here to emphasize the lack of clarity about consent in jurisprudence on sexual violence.

Before we consider the 2024 judgment, we should trace how feminists globally have influenced rape laws, particularly with respect to the definition and interpretation of consent to sex. Feminists have for several decades struggled against interpretations of rape laws that place high burdens on the survivor to prove that she resisted the sexual act or that she was subjected to force or an objectively reasonable threat of force that made it impossible for her to resist. This high burden led to very few convictions. From the 1970s onward, a strand of legal feminist thought sometimes referred to as radical feminism, spearheaded by legal theorist Catherine MacKinnon, argued for rethinking the meaning of consent to sex.[72] Radical feminists argued that consent to sex must be viewed against the background of patriarchy. According to this view, while women are living in a state of pervasive subordination by men, one must assume that sex for women is unwanted unless it is positively desired. As MacKinnon says, "If sex is normally something men do to women, the issue is less whether there was force and more whether consent is a meaningful concept."[73]

The meaning of consent in the 2021 Criminal Law Amendment Act reflects a move toward the radical feminist position. It asserts that consent must be affirmative and communicated in some way (verbal or nonverbal). The Explanation of consent in the amended statute could be interpreted to mean that even a good-faith assumption of consent on the part of the accused is not sufficient to disprove rape. The 2021 law, however, is unclear as to *how* the absence of affirmative consent is to be proven.

In *Muhammad Imran v. The State*, the complainant alleged that she was raped in her home by Muhammad Imran who entered her house one night in 2016. Tests conducted on vaginal swabs of the complainant and the semen of the accused person showed that the DNA profile matched. The accused was convicted of rape by the trial court and sentenced to ten years of imprisonment. On appeal, the majority of the Supreme Court bench noted that, while DNA evidence establishes "illicit intercourse" between the parties, the question was whether the incident was that of rape or fornication. The majority concluded that the evidence before it did not established that the sex was nonconsensual. It stated that there were no marks or bruises detected in the complainant's medical report or evidence of torn clothes to indicate physical resistance. The majority also considered that both parties were previously arrested under Section 294 of the Pakistan Penal Code, for singing "obscene songs" in public, and were subsequently released. According to the majority, this indicated that the parties knew each other prior to the incident, and this made it likely that sex between them was consensual.

The majority concluded that, since sex between the parties was consensual, the accused person's conviction for rape should be overturned and that instead he should be convicted under fornication (Section 496 of the Pakistan Penal Code) and sentenced to five years of imprisonment. The complainant was not sentenced to imprisonment in spite of the finding of consensual sex, because, according to the Supreme Court majority, she was never charged with the offence and had no opportunity to defend herself.

In her dissent, Justice Ayesha Malik stated that the Supreme Court should have upheld the conviction based on the complainant's testimony and the DNA report. The dissent referred to Supreme Court precedent that the "solitary statement of the victim is sufficient to award a conviction in a rape case if that statement is trustworthy consistent and reliable."[74] Evidence of violence should not be required to prove absence of consent. The assumption that a woman must physically resist rape is one of the "influential myths in rape trials" and it denies "the realities of women's experiences," which prevent them from fighting back in ways that would be recognized by men. Citing American legal scholar and radical feminist Catherine MacKinnon, Justice Malik says that, when the law ignores the different experiences and reactions of women to sexual violence in patriarchal contexts, it "tends to conclude that rape did not happen." Her opinion strongly opposes the finding of consensual sex and the conclusion that the parties committed fornication punishable under the Pakistan Penal Code.

The Supreme Court majority opinion and the dissenting opinion convey competing understandings of how the burden of proof is to be satisfied in rape cases. In criminal cases, the burden of proof is on the prosecution to establish each element of the crime beyond a reasonable doubt. There are two elements of the crime of rape: 1. the occurrence of the sexual act, and 2. the absence of consent. To obtain a rape conviction, the prosecution must prove beyond a reasonable doubt that the sexual act occurred and that it was nonconsensual. The majority and the dissenting opinions in *Muhammad Imran v. The State* fundamentally differ on how the burden of proof to satisfy the second element of the crime—lack of consent—is to be met.

The majority opinion says that, after the prosecution establishes that the sexual act occurred, the burden is on the complainant to prove *through objective evidence* that she did not consent to sex. On the other hand, the dissenting opinion implies that, in rape cases, the *subjective frame of mind* of the complainant is sufficient to prove that she did not consent. The dissent implies that we should take her word for it as she is the best authority on her own frame of mind and that, once she testifies that she did not consent to the act, the burden shifts to the defendant to establish that she consented. The 2021 amendments, by explaining consent to mean an "unequivocal voluntary agreement" that must be communicated, entail that the defense must produce evidence of verbal or nonverbal behavior that shows that the complainant affirmatively consented. Evidence that the complainant did not resist, verbally or nonverbally, or just quietly succumbed to the sexual act, is insufficient for the defendant to prove consent.

The majority and the dissenting opinion fundamentally differ on whether objective evidence of nonconsent is required or whether the court should deem the complainant's account of her subjective frame of mind sufficient to sustain a conviction (unless the defense proves that the complainant is lying about her subjective frame of mind). The statutory amendments and jurisprudence in Pakistan have not resolved this difference of opinion. On the one hand, long-standing Supreme Court jurisprudence concluding that the trustworthy and reliable statement alone is sufficient to sustain a conviction of rape suggests that the subjective approach has been upheld at times. On the other hand, in some cases (such as the Mukhtaran Mai case) the Supreme Court has imposed such a high standard to establish the trustworthiness and reliability of the complainant's statement that, effectively, a complainant's account of her own frame of mind cannot be sufficient.

In contrast, the 2013 criminal-law amendments in India quite clearly entail that in certain cases of aggravated rape the complainant's statement about her subjective frame of mind is sufficient to create a presumption of absence of consent. The 2013 law made an amendment to the Indian Evidence Act, which states that, for the prosecution of certain types of rape offences, "where sexual intercourse by the accused is proved and the question is whether it was without the consent of the woman alleged to have been raped and such woman states in her evidence before the court that she did not consent, the court shall presume that she did not consent."[75] There is no such provision in Pakistan's law.

A rigorous debate, not only between judges and legal experts but also among feminists and human-rights activists, is needed to assess the competing views on how consent and lack thereof is to be proved in rape cases. The underlying values that each position represents as well as the impact of each interpretation should be articulated and assessed. One view asks that the interpretation of consent be sensitive to the context of unequal gender relations in which women often do not resist unwanted sex in ways that would be easily recognized as resistance by men. This view, espoused by radical feminists, such as Catherine MacKinnon, was endorsed by Justice Ayesha Malik in her dissenting opinion. On the other hand, proponents of the position that objective evidence is necessary to prove lack of consent would say that their approach is more consistent with the principle that a defendant is "innocent until proven guilty." To avoid the risk of wrongful conviction, the burden should not be placed on the defendant in a criminal case to prove that a key element of the crime of rape does not exist.

Each position above yields benefits and costs, and women's-rights activists should attempt to identify these costs and benefits and who will bear them. The criminalization of adultery and fornication in Pakistan raises the stakes in this debate. If a woman does not prove the absence of consent after sex is established, she could open herself up to a charge of fornication or adultery. And, if an accused person raises consent as a defense, he opens himself up to the charge of fornication or adultery and the possibility of incriminating himself. These scenarios present strong arguments for repealing the criminal prohibition on fornication and adultery, but any such attempt would be strongly resisted by the religious right and conservative forces. The majority opinion and the dissenting opinion in the *Muhammad Imran* case shows the importance of having an open discussion that carefully considers the possible impact of law reform around sexual violence as well as an assessment of the legacy of previous legal changes made to "Islamize" criminal laws.

RAPE IN TRIAL COURTS

Two case studies are discussed below to show how trial courts adjudicate sexual-violence cases in the aftermath of legal changes made by legislatures and judicial pronouncements in the Supreme Court and high courts. These case studies exemplify the stickiness of biases and prejudices against survivors in sexual-violence cases and the difficulty of downstreaming high-level legal reform to trial courts and the police—the institutions that make the first point of contact with survivors and their families.

Rape at Quaid-e-Azam's Shrine

In 2008 a woman (RK) travelled to Karachi with her family from Punjab for sightseeing. She and her husband went to the popular tourist destination, the tomb of Pakistan's founder (Quaid-e-Azam's Mazar). The husband told his wife to wait at the gate of the premises while he went to collect other family members. While she was waiting for her husband, one man grabbed her and put a handkerchief on her mouth. Another man pointed a pistol at her and they dragged her to a room. Three other men came to the room, and all five of them raped her. Meanwhile, RK's husband and the rest of her family searched for her for several hours but were unable to find her. The next day they filed a complaint with the police. Three days after she went missing, RK was found by the gates of the Mazar in a "semi-conscious" state. She was taken to the hospital, and a medical examination confirmed that she was raped.

The police arrested three men as suspects. Samples for DNA testing were collected from the rape survivor and the three accused persons. The DNA samples collected from the victim's clothes and body matched with those of all three accused persons. The three suspects were also identified by RK as the perpetrators.

The trial court acquitted all three persons in a judgment announced in April 2013—five years after the rape took place.[76] Surprisingly, the court characterized rape as an offence of Zina, invoking the Zina Ordinance, and ignoring the fact that the offence of rape had been placed back in the Pakistan Penal Code as the offence of "Rape" under Section 375 and that, in their current form, the Zina Ordinance covered only the offence of adultery. The legal development of 2006 seems to have escaped the attention of the trial-court judge entirely; he noted that the "Offence of Zina is specific to the Islamic jurisprudence and lays down the standard of proof and the punishment." He further noted that the "purpose" of the law is to "check licentiousness, lewdness, adultery or vulgarity committed at public places where four or more persons could witness the same." The judge's reasoning shows how the conflation of adultery and rape, introduced in the laws through the Zina Ordinance, persists. Courts continue to perceive rape as a crime that promotes "lewdness" and "vulgarity"—much like adultery in their minds—rather than as an offence that constitutes physical harm and violence and that is rooted in gender inequality. The trial court went on to note that in cases of "Zina," DNA evidence is irrelevant as the offence can be proved only upon the testimony of four witnesses. The trial court mischaracterized the burden of proof entirely, equating it with the burden of proof required to impose the maximum punishment or *hadd* under the erstwhile Zina Ordinance. Not only did the trial court ignore that the offense of rape can be proven through circumstantial evidence (like other offenses in the Pakistan Penal Code) but also the trial court seemed unaware that, even under the erstwhile Zina Ordinance, circumstantial evidence could be used to support a lesser punishment (or *tazir*).

The acquittal was appealed, and the Sindh High Court ordered that the case be remanded, noting that the Sessions Court mischaracterized the burden of proof required to prove rape, conflating it with the burden of proof required in adultery cases. On remand, however, the Zina Ordinance resurfaced again, and another judge ignored the admonition of the Sindh High Court. The second trial-court judge again rejected DNA evidence, noting that it was insufficient to implicate the accused.[77] The second judge also asserted that DNA evidence cannot be considered in "a case falling under the penal provisions of Zina punishable under the Hudood laws having its own standard of proof." After rejecting the admissibility of DNA evidence entirely in rape cases, the court noted other "material contradictions" in the case, including the delay between the collection of DNA samples and their delivery to the chemical examiner, concluding that the delay casts doubt on the credibility of the samples.

The trial court also affirmed the archaic notion that there must be evidence of physical force and resistance in rape cases. The court emphasized that the medico-legal report about the survivor noted that there were "no marks of violence" on her body and that there were no signs of "injury" on the body of the accused person. These considerations led the trial court to conclude that the "accused persons are entitled for benefit of doubt."

There was widespread outrage following the second acquittal. *Dawn*, a leading daily newspaper, published an editorial expressing dismay about the outcome and the fact that DNA evidence was ignored by the trial court.[78] Senator Sherry Rehman, a prominent politician and a defender of women's rights, tweeted that the acquittal constituted a "shocking selective application of the law."[79] The second acquittal was also appealed to the Sindh High Court, where the matter is pending.

The adjudication of this case is emblematic of a number of trends in sexual-violence cases in Pakistan. One, they show the pernicious effects a bad law—the Zina Ordinance—long after these were amended. The purported Islamic justification for the Zina Ordinance seems to have developed deep roots and continues to be invoked to create an extremely high burden of proof for rape survivors. Second, the two rounds of acquittal demonstrate the persistence of stereotypes regarding the necessity of physical force and resistance to demonstrate nonconsensual sex. Both trial courts found that the absence of physical injury to the accused persons as well as to the survivor cast doubt on the prosecution's case. Third, the trial-court decisions show how doctrinal law reform through legislative amendments and judicial pronouncements fail to influence trial-court adjudication of sexual-violence cases. In 2013, the Supreme Court declared that DNA evidence is admissible in rape cases. The 2016 amendments to the Code of Criminal Procedure require the collection of DNA evidence in rape cases. Nonetheless, trial courts refused to consider DNA evidence. Lastly, the case highlights the traumatising impact of trials on sexual-violence survivors and their families. It has been almost sixteen years since the crime was committed. The rape survivor has been subjected to lengthy police investigations and court proceedings only for her testimony to be disbelieved and the accused persons to be acquitted—not once but twice.

Julie's[80] Case

In 2021, a young Christian girl (ten or eleven years old) was sexually molested in the home of her tutor in the predominantly Christian neighborhood of Eesa Nagri in Karachi.[81] The accused is a Muslim man who was the brother of her tutor and lived in the next lane from Julie's home. She says that, as she was leaving the tutor's house, the accused took her to an empty room, pulled town her pants and started to molest her. She screamed and ran out of the house. Right outside his house, men from the neighbourhood saw a frightened Julie running out. They asked her what happened, and she told them. She then ran to her own house, which was nearby, where she told her mother what happened. The men started to beat the accused person when he came out to stand at his door. Someone in the neighborhood called the police. The police arrested the accused, who was then charged with sexual abuse and attempted rape.

At trial, the court recorded Julie's statement. Julie also identified the accused from a lineup presented to her in court. During cross-examination, she was aggressively questioned by the defense lawyer, who kept repeating questions that the ten-year-old did not understand, trying to force an answer. Julie's counsel raised objections, but the judge allowed the defense to continue the improper line of questioning. The defense lawyer kept insisting that the girl answer "yes" or "no," although it was clear that she did not understand the question! For example, she was asked if the police recorded her "161 statement." Section 161 is a CrPC provision under which the police reports witness statements during investigation. Obviously the ten-year-old did not know what a "161 statement" was, but the lawyer forced an answer out of her. She was also repeatedly asked about her faith, whether her parents disliked Muslims, and whether they wanted Muslims to leave the neighbourbood. Julie's mother also presented testimony, and she was also subjected to aggressive questioning about her faith, her perceptions of Muslims, and whether she wanted to evict them from her neighborhood. Two men who were standing in the lane when Julie came running out of the accused person's house also testified.

In his final argument, the main line of defense offered by the accused was that Julie and her parents had fabricated this story because as Christians they do not like Muslims and they want to drive all Muslims away from their neighbourhood. It was this argument that seemed to have resonated with the judge, who acquitted the accused. The judgment notes that animosity between religious communities is "normal" and so it is plausible that the family concocted a case of sexual violence against a Muslim.

The trial court did not consider that Julie's family belonged to a low-income background (both her parents worked as sweepers), that she and her family lived in a deprived neighborhood, and that Christian minorities are highly vulnerable and subjected to systematic discrimination in Pakistan. That they would collude with the police (all of whom involved in this case were Muslim) to frame a criminal case against a Muslim neighbor by putting forward their ten-year-old daughter as a sexual-abuse victim and making her testify before the police and courts would seem quite fantastical to the objective observer but seemed "normal" to the trial-court judge. The trial court also ignored Supreme Court precedent stating that due weight must be given to the statements of sexual-violence survivors and their credible testimony alone may support a conviction.

Julie's case highlights the intersectional discrimination faced by women and girls belonging to marginalized communities. It also shows the unjust treatment meted to minors in sexual-violence cases. In her study of rape trials in India, scholar Pratiksha Baxi observes that in "a statutory rape trial spoken law inserts questions which feign ignorance that the victim is really a child, and in the ultimate analysis it is her childhood that is on trial."[82] She goes on to note that "[i]t is not surprising then despite repeated guidelines issued by the Supreme Court, rape trials continue to display a child's body to a sexualized gaze, forcing her to recount the trauma repeatedly in adult ways, challenging her everyday knowledge about the world and inscribing blame on her for being raped."[83] Pratiksha Baxi's characterization, based on her study of rape trials in the state of Gujarat in India, maps well onto the treatment of Julie in her sexual-abuse case. She was not treated as a child by police, courts, and lawyers, her testimony was subjected to the skepticism and disdain that adult women's statements are made to face, and she was eventually disbelieved by the court.

LIMITS OF CRIMINAL-LAW REFORM

Activism for reform of laws relating to sexual violence in Pakistan has certainly come a long way since the early 1980s, when women's-rights activists mobilized against the Zina Ordinance. That law has been debilitated through amendments introduced in 2006 that also re-established rape as a criminal offence in the Pakistan Penal Code. Subsequent law reforms strengthened criminal penalties for rape, criminalized sexual offences other than rape, and introduced criminal procedures to facilitate prosecution. The impact of these laws, however, leaves much to be desired.

From the 1980s leading up to the cases of Mukhtaran Mai and Shazia Khalid, protests against sexual violence had profound political and social goals. Women's-rights activists, including members of the WAF (Women's Action Forum), combined their advocacy for repeal of Zia ul Haq's laws with resistance to his dictatorial and antisecular politics. Advocacy around the Mukhtaran Mai case was geared toward highlighting the prevalence of cultural attitudes and social practices that perpetuate sexual violence. Shazia Khalid's rape brought to light the impunity with which armed forces exercise control over not only women's bodies but also resources in the province of Balochistan, where the rape took place in a heavily militarized gas facility. In subsequent years, however, as NGOs promoting women's rights and legislators became increasingly concerned with criminalization, political activism around sexual violence gave way to advocacy for changes to formal laws and legal accountability in specific instances. It is worth asking whether this trajectory has limited the political potential of activism against sexual violence.

Upendra Baxi's categorization of law reform, which was mentioned in the first chapter, is relevant to the trajectory of reform of laws concerning rape in Pakistan. The 2016 and 2020–2021 legislative interventions on rape in the Pakistan Penal Code and the Code of Criminal Procedure and the judicial pronouncements on sexual-violence adjudication constitute regulatory reform. The regulatory reform, however, has limited impact on governance institutions. Implementation of regulatory reform is contingent on law-enforcement and judicial actors being aware of the legal change and then changing their behavior in accordance with these changes. Structural weaknesses across government departments in Pakistan do not permit this. Corruption and inefficiencies in the police force means that the investigation of rape cases will be compromised and that the institutional changes required to improve investigation will be de-prioritized, regardless of the stipulation of new investigation bodies such as the special sexual-offences investigation units. Judges, at the trial-court as well as the appellate level, will continue to ignore progressive jurisprudence or to interpret precedent restrictively.

The move from regulatory reform to social reform is similarly fraught. Social norms and mindsets strongly influence how government actors respond to regulatory reforms that aim to prevent and punish gender-based violence. Patriarchal values permeate in the police, the medico-legal system and the judiciary, and these influence whether a victim is believed, whether

her complaint is prioritized, and whether "character" is considered relevant in trials.

Feminists have their work cut out for them even after the passage of stronger criminal laws and progressive jurisprudence. They must continue to advocate for implementation of laws and attitudinal changes among government actors. Meaningful advocacy requires that feminists critically assess proposals for law reform, grasp the workings of the criminal-justice system, especially with respect to sexual violence, and also develop an understanding of the broader legal context, especially the role of laws justified by reference to Islam. In other words, feminists should develop strategies to critically engage with regulatory reform in the area of sexual violence. Critical engagement is especially desirable with respect to criminal legislation, which can have unintended and counterproductive consequences, as we will see in the next chapter on child marriages.

NOTES

1. Sheh-e-Azam and Haider Kaleem, "Massive Protests in Karachi & Lahore in the Aftermath of Motorway Rape Incident," Voicepk.net, Lahore/Karachi, September 13, 2020, <https://voicepk.net/2020/09/womenprotests/>, accessed August 15, 2024.

2. Geo News, "Lahore CCPO Blames Motorway Rape Victim for Choice of Route, Travelling Late at Night," *Geo News*, September 10, 2020, <https://www.geo.tv/latest/307200-ccpo-lahore-blames-motorway-rape-victim-for>, accessed August 15, 2024.

3. Haroon Janjua, "Protests and Fury at Pakistan's 'Rape Epidemic' after Woman Attacked in City Park," *The Guardian*, Islamabad, February 9, 2023, <https://www.theguardian.com/global-development/2023/feb/09/pakistan-rape-epidemic-woman-attacked-park-islamabad>, accessed August 15, 2024.

4. *Dawn*, "Two Killed in 'Encounter' Were Involved in F-9 Park Rape Case: Police," *Dawn*, Islamabad, February 17, 2023, <https://www.dawn.com/news/1737527/two-killed-in-encounter-were-involved-in-f-9-park-rape-case-police>, accessed August 16, 2024.

5. *Dawn*, "F-9 Rape Case: Victim's Lawyer Demands Inquiry into Suspects' 'Extrajudicial Killing," *Dawn*, February 17, 2023, <https://www.dawn.com/news/1737649>, accessed August 16, 2024.

6. Prabha Kotiswaran, "Governance Feminism in the Postcolony: Reforming India's Rape Laws," in *Governance Feminism: An Introduction*, eds. Janet Halley and others (University of Minnesota Press, 2018), 83.

7. Ibid.

8. Offence of Zina (Enforcement of Hudood) Ordinance 1979, Sections 5,6,7. Sections 6 and 7 were repealed by the Protection of Women (Criminal Law Amendment) Act 2006.

9. Ibid., at Section 5.

10. Ibid., at Section 8.

11. Ibid., at Section 10.

12. Asma Jahangir and Hina Jillani, *Hudood Ordinance, A Divine Sanction?* (Rhotas Books, 1990), 55.

13. Ibid., 58.

14. Martin Lau, "Twenty-Five Years of the Hudood Ordinance—A Review," *Washington and Lee Law Review* 64, no. 4 (2007): 1291, 1298.

15. Protection of Women (Criminal Laws) Amendment Act 2006, Section 10.

16. Offence of Zina (Enforcement of Hudood) Ordinance 1979, Section 8(b).

17. Protection of Women (Criminal Laws) Amendment Act 2006.

18. https://www.aljazeera.com/news/2011/4/21/pakistani-court-upholds-gang-rape-acquittals.

19. Ayesha Khan, Women's Movement in Pakistan, *Activism, Islam and Democracy* (I. B. Tauris, 2018), 219.

20. *The State vs Abdul Khalique* (2011) PLD Supreme Court 554.

21. Ibid., para 7.

22. Ibid., para 27.

23. Ibid., para 20, 21.

24. Ibid., para 20.

25. Ibid., para 12.

26. Ibid., para 24, 25.

27. Ayesha Khan, *The Women's Movement in Pakistan: Activism, Islam and Democracy* (I. B. Tauris, 2018), 222.

28. See, e.g., *Mushtaq Ahmed v. the State* (2007) SCMR 473; *Habibullah v. the State* (2011) SCMR 1665.

29. *State v. Abdul Khalique & Others*, n 20, para 33.

30. *New York Times*, "Rape Victim Can Travel, Musharraf Says," *New York Times*, Islamabad, June 30, 2005, <https://www.nytimes.com/2005/06/30/world/asia/rape-victim-can-travel-musharraf-says.html>, accessed August 16, 2024.

31. Terence McKenna, "Land, Gold and Women Part 2: The Case of Shazia Khalid," CBC News, February 28, 2006, <https://www.cbc.ca/news2/background/pakistan/mckenna_pakistan-pt2.html>, accessed August 16, 2024.

32. Ibid.

33. Ibid.

34. Ibid.

35. Glen Kessler, "Musharraf Denies Rape Comments," *The Washington Post*, September 18, 2005, <https://www.washingtonpost.com/archive/politics/2005/09/19/musharraf-denies-rape-comments/5f2e0d4c-5ff2-4273-81e5-878cd59a1744/>, accessed August 16, 2024.

36. Pratiksha Baxi, *Public Secrets of Law: Rape Trials in India* (Oxford University Press, 2014).

37. Criminal Law (Second Amendment) Act 2016.

38. Criminal Law (Amendment) (Offences Relating to Rape) Act 2016.

39. *Salman Akram Raja v. Government of Punjab* (2013) SCMR 203.

40. Associated Press of Pakistan, "CII Rules Out DNA as Primary Evidence in Rape Cases," *Dawn*, Islamabad, September 23, 2013, <https://www.dawn.com/news/1044879>, accessed August 15, 2024.

41. Ahmed Saeed, "Conviction Rate in Sexual Crimes Cases Stands at 3.6% in 2022," Voicepk.net, Lahore, March 27, 2023, <https://voicepk.net/2023/03/conviction-rate-in-sexual-crimes-cases-stands-at-3-6-in-2022/>, accessed August 15, 2024.

42. *The Express Tribune*, "DNA Testing Lab in Sindh," *The Express Tribune*, August 4, 2019, <https://tribune.com.pk/story/2027474/dna-testing-lab-sindh>, accessed August 15, 2024.

43. Fatima Yasmin Bokhari, "Accountability for Rape: A Case Study of Lodhran" (case study report, Centre for Human Rights University College Lahore, 2018), 50.

44. Ibid.

45. Ibid., 18.

46. Ibid., 3.

47. Hafiz Muhammad Azeem, Muhammad Sohail Thaheem, and Muhammad Ramzan Kasuri, "Exploring Factors Contributing to the Low Conviction Ratio of Rape Cases in Punjab, Pakistan," *Annals of Social Science and Perspective* 4, no. 2 (2023): 341–42.

48. Criminal Law (Amendment) Ordinance 2020, s 2.

49. Ibid.

50. Ibid., s 4.

51. Anti-Rape Investigation (Investigation and Trial) Ordinance 2020.

52. Ibid., Section 13.

53. Ayaz Gul, "Pakistan Drops 'Un-Islamic' Chemical Castration as Penalty for Rapists," *Voice of America*, Islamabad, November 19, 2021, <https://www.voanews.com/a/pakistan-drops-un-islamic-chemical-castration-as-penalty-for-rapists-/6320005.html>, accessed August 15, 2024.

54. *The News*, "18 Major Flaws Identified in Anti-Rape Criminal Law Ordinance," *The News*, May 6, 2021, <https://www.thenews.com.pk/print/830972-18-major-flaws-identified-in-anti-rape-criminal-law-Ordinance>, accessed August 15, 2024.

55. Kotiswaran, n 6, 98.

56. Kotiswaran, n 6, 102–3).

57. The "Explanation" of the meaning of "consent" is almost identical to the language used in India's Criminal Law Amendment Act of 2013, which amended the rape provision in the Indian Penal Code. The Delhi High Court has in at least one case interpreted the Explanation of "consent" in the amended provision to mean affirmative consent. In *Mahmood Farooqui v. State (Govt of NCT of Delhi) 2017* (Delhi High Court), the Delhi High Court noted that consent has to be an "affirmative one in clear terms." At the same time, however, the Delhi High Court stated that whether or not consent is affirmative is context-dependent and does not always require clear words or gestures indicating "yes." The *Mahmood Farooqui* case concerned a rape allegation made by an international graduate student against the accused, who is a writer and performance artist. According to the Delhi High Court, when persons are "intellectually/academically proficient and if, in the past, there have been physical contacts . . . it would be really difficult to decipher whether little or no resistance and a feeble 'no'

was actually a denial of consent." It goes on to say that "there can be an affirmative consent, or a positive denial, but it may remain underlying/dormant which could lead to confusion in the mind of the other." This is a contradictory interpretation of an affirmative consent standard. Based on the evidence before it, the Delhi High Court concluded that it could not determine if the sexual act, if it had taken place, "was without the consent/will of the prosecutrix and if it was without the consent of the prosecutrix, whether the appellant could discern/understand the same." The Delhi High Court placed the burden of proof on the prosecution to show that there was an absence of consent.

58. See, e.g., Janet Halley, "The Move to Affirmative Consent," *Signs: Journal of Women in Culture and Society*, 42, no. 1 (2016): 257.

59. *The News*, "18 Major Flaws Identified in Anti-Rape Criminal Law Ordinance," *The News*, May 6, 2021, <https://www.thenews.com.pk/print/830972-18-major-flaws-identified-in-anti-rape-criminal-law-Ordinance>, accessed August 15, 2024.

60. Imtiaz Ali, "Pakistan's First Anti-Rape Crisis Cell Set Up at Civil Hospital Karachi," *Dawn*, August 4, 2023, <https://www.dawn.com/news/1768385>, accessed August 15, 2024.

61. Punjab Commission on Violence Against Women, "Special Mechanisms to Address Violence Against Women in Punjab: A Study of Model Gender-Based Violence Court in Lahore & Violence Against Women Centre in Multan" (study report, Punjab Commission on Violence Against Women, 2019), 5.

62. Maliha Zia Lari, Associate Director, Legal Aid Society, interview by Sara Malkani and Farieha Aziz, Karachi, January 17, 2023.

63. Maliha Zia, interview by Sara Malkani and Farieha Aziz, Karachi, January 17, 2023.

64. *The State v. Abdul Khalique & Others*, n 20, para 29.

65. Zainab Z. Malik, "Call for Reform: Pakistan Must Ban Two-Finger Test for Rape—and Now," Scroll.in, December 25, 2017, <https://scroll.in/article/862310/call-for-reform-pakistan-must-ban-two-finger-test-for-rape-and-now>, accessed date.

66. *Atif Zareef & others v. The State* (2021) PLD Supreme Court 550.

67. Ibid.

68. Sadaf Chaudry, "'The Pain Was Unbearable': Thousands of Women Subjected to Banned 'Virginity Tests,'" *Vice*, Karachi, September 17, 2021, <https://www.vice.com/en/article/93y4v3/pakistan-virginity-tests-the-pain-was-unbearable-thousands-of-women-subjected-to-banned-virginity-tests>, accessed August 15, 2024.

69. Rana Yasif, "LHC to Initiate Contempt for 'Two-Finger Test,'" *Dawn*, Lahore, October 13, 2023, https://tribune.com.pk/story/2440899/lhc-to-initiate-contempt-for-two-finger-test, accessed August 15, 2024.

70. Bukhari, n 43, 45.

71. *Muhammad Imran v. The State and Another* (2024) Criminal Petition No. 725 of 2023 Supreme Court of Pakistan, decided on June 26, 2024.

72. Catherine MacKinnon, "Feminism, Marxism, Method and the State: Toward Feminist Jurisprudence," *Signs: Journal of Women, Culture and Society* 8, no. 4 (1983): 635.

73. Ibid., 650.

74. *Muhammad Imran*, n 70, para. 7.

75. Criminal Law (Amendment) Act (India) 2013, s 26.

76. Sessions Case No. 179 of 2008 (April 6, 2013) Judgement of Court of II Additional District and Sessions Judge (district) Karachi.

77. Sessions Case No. 179 of 2008 (October 5, 2021) Court of II Additional District and Sessions Judge Karachi.

78. *Dawn*, "DNA Evidence for Rape," *Dawn*, October 13, 2021, <https://www.dawn.com/news/1651746>, accessed August 16, 2024.

79. Sherry Rehman (@sherryrehman), "In a shocking selective application of the law; a session court in Karachi refused to consider DNA tests as evidence in the Mazar-i-Quaid gang-rape case." Twitter (now X), October 13, 2021, https://x.com/sherryrehman/status/1448186279351435271?lang=en.

80. The name has been changed to protect the identity of the minor.

81. The author represented the girl's family before the trial court. Case documents are available in file.

82. Baxi, n 36, xli.

83. Ibid., xlii.

Chapter 3

Child Marriage and the Pitfalls of Protection

Child marriage has been on the feminist agenda for activists and policymakers for decades in Pakistan. South Asia as a whole has high rates of child marriage, and, while these rates are steadily declining overall, the number of girls entering into marriage at a young age remains very high throughout the region. Ending child marriage is also a priority in the sphere of international human rights and development: one of the Sustainable Development Goals (Target 5.3) is to end child marriage by 2030.

Girls are disproportionately victims of child marriage. Patriarchal norms that devalue girls and deny any sexual autonomy to women and girls perpetuate child marriage, which leads to other rights violations: it exposes young girls to nonconsensual sex and leads to pregnancy at an early age and corresponding health complications. It also forecloses opportunities for education and formal employment. According to UNICEF data from 2022, 18 percent of women in Pakistan are married before they reach the age of eighteen. Four percent of women are married before they reach the age of fifteen.[1] Child marriage rates for boys are significantly lower: 5 percent of men are married before they reach the age of eighteen.[2] The rates, while still high, are steadily declining: in 1990–1991, the incidence of child marriage was 54 percent among women of childbearing age, defined as between fifteen and forty-nine.[3]

Child marriage was criminalized across India while it was a British colony, with the passage of the Child Marriage Restraint Act of 1929. The 1929 law, with its subsequent amendments, remains the applicable law in most of Pakistan. It sets the minimum ages for marriage as sixteen for girls and eighteen for boys. It carries criminal penalties for an adult male who enters into a child marriage, parents who coerce minors into a child marriage, and a religious authority who solemnizes child marriages. Sindh is the only province that passed child-marriage legislation in 2013, replacing the 1929 law. The law reform in Sindh followed many years of advocacy by prominent NGOs, including the Aurat Foundation and Shirkat Gah, for legal interventions to end child marriage.[4] In 2009, the Sindh government constituted a Committee for Standardization of Female Age of Marriage.[5] The Committee delivered a set of recommendations that included raising the minimum age for marriage of girls to eighteen.[6]

While the laws criminalise child marriage, they remain silent regarding the legal validity of a child marriage. In other words, the laws do not explicitly state that child marriages are void. Courts in Pakistan have stepped in to fill this gap and have interpreted child marriages to be valid in light of interpretations of Shariah law, according to which marriage of a child who has reached puberty is valid. In a 1970 decision, the Supreme Court of Pakistan declared that a marriage of a fifteen-year-old girl is valid by relying on interpretations of Shariah law, which permit marriage of persons who have reached puberty.[7] In this case, a fifteen-year-old girl entered into a *nikahnama*, or marriage contract, after which her mother filed a police complaint, accusing her daughter's husband of kidnapping. When the girl appeared in court, she stated that she married of her free will and wished to live with her partner. The Supreme Court found, "It is true that the said Act does not permit the marriage of a girl below the age of 16 years . . . the marriage itself does not become invalid on that score, although an adult husband contracting the marriage or the persons who have solemnized the marriage may be held criminally liable."[8]

Child-marriage legislation in Pakistan is underenforced due to entrenched cultural norms and endemic weaknesses in the criminal-justice system. Among the many barriers to the implementation of the law are low rates of birth and marriage registration, cultural practices that condone child marriages, lack of access to criminal-justice mechanisms, and poor child-protection mechanisms. Legislators for the last two decades in national and provincial legislatures have attempted to update child-marriage legislation to promote more effective implementation. The only province, Sindh, with its own child-marriage law has set the minimum age of marriage for both girls and boys to eighteen. It also set higher criminal penalties than the 1929 law. Other than these differences, the scheme of the Sindh law is similar to that of the older legislation: it sets forth criminal penalties for adult males, parents and "*nikahkhwans*," and remains silent regarding the legal status of a child marriage.

Attempts by other provincial legislatures to raise the minimum age for child marriage in Pakistan encounter resistance, primarily from conservative religious forces who believe that restrictions on child marriages should reflect Shariah law, which permits marriage of persons who have reached puberty. In

2016, a bill proposed to amend the child-marriage law at the federal level was withdrawn due to opposition from the Council of Islamic Ideology. In 2019, a bill raising the minimum age for child marriage to eighteen for girls passed in the Senate "amid a noisy protest by the members of religious parties."[9] When it was moved before the other house of parliament—the National Assembly—it failed to pass, with the Minister for Religious Affairs labelling the bill un-Islamic.[10]

IMPLEMENTATION CHALLENGES

The paradigmatic child marriage involves a forced marriage imposed on a girl by parents and community members. Child-marriage legislation in Pakistan and, indeed, in much of South Asia primarily aims to target such cases. The underenforcement of the law in Pakistan suggests that child-marriage legislation in Pakistan is not particularly effective in tackling these cases. Data received from Sindh police in response to an information request say that, between 2018 and 2024, 272 criminal cases of child marriage were registered in Sindh.[11] Of these, only 30 led to conviction, and 23 of these were in one division only, Hyderabad. In some large divisions, including Karachi and Sukkur, there were no convictions over a period of six years. The data do not reflect which of these cases were initiated by parents to stop a "free will" marriage of an underage girl and how many of these were filed by the police against parents or community members who arranged an underage marriage.

In recent years, however, a large proportion of child-marriage cases that are reported in the media and make their way to courts involve self-arranged marriages—those that the minors have voluntarily entered into, often in the face of opposition from family and community members. Cases before the high courts as well as cases reported in the media therefore seem to suggest that the child-marriage law is used by parents against girls who choose relationships without their parents' consent. Staff at the Panah Shelter Home in Karachi, where courts send married minor girls when they decide that the girls should not be permitted to live with their parents, reported to the author in May 2023 that all girls sent to this shelter home are those who run away from homes to marry their partners. The shelter home has not admitted through court order any girls whose marriages were forcibly arranged by parents or community members.

Self-arranged marriages pose a challenge to the implementation of criminal legislation prohibiting child marriages. Enforcement of laws in these circumstances entails going against the preferences of girls and also imposing criminal penalties on their male partners. The absence of social-welfare services and protection mechanisms for minors poses a particular challenge to the regulation of such marriages since the state has little to no capacity to address the needs of minor girls who do not wish to live with their parents after they have left their home to marry their partners.

Complicating the implementation of the law further is the fact that many cases of underage marriages reported in the media and highlighted by human-rights activists involve girls from non-Muslim minority communities—communities that are vulnerable to systemic persecution in Pakistan. Activists and representatives from minority communities claim that underage girls are abducted by Muslim men, forcibly converted to Islam and then made to marry their abductors. Multiple layers of human-rights violations are alleged in these cases—kidnapping and child marriage as well as persecution of religious minorities by majoritarian elements.

I go on to discuss some prominent child-marriage cases that received significant attention from the media, human-rights activists, and child-rights activists. While these cases became flashpoints in advocacy for strengthening child-marriage legislation, they also highlighted the limitations of legal intervention in solving complex social and cultural dilemmas. I discuss these cases to highlight the tensions between child-marriage laws and advocacy efforts to strengthen criminal prohibitions on the one hand, and on the other hand the complex social realities experienced by minors who marry. The challenges posed by child-marriage cases exemplify the difficulty of applying criminal laws to address structural human-rights violations.

Dua Zehra

Dua Zehra, a girl living in Karachi, Pakistan, was reported missing by her parents in April 2022. Dua's parents filed a first information report with the police, alleging that Dua was kidnapped.[12] The case was picked up by the media and covered intensively as an abduction. Soon after parents reported the matter to the police, Dua Zehra appeared before reporters in the city of Lahore and stated that she had left her parents' home and married Zaheer Ahmed of her free will. She also filed an application before a court in Lahore, seeking protection from her parents.[13]

Dua Zehra's father filed a petition before the Sindh High Court, asking the court to direct the police to "recover" the minor and hand her over to the parents. Around this time Dua Zehra and her partner, Zaheer, went missing again, and the police informed the Sindh High Court that it was were unable to locate them. With intense media pressure around the case, the senior-most police officer in Sindh, the Inspector General of Police, was summoned before the Sindh High Court, where he submitted that seven teams had been dispatched to different parts of the country to locate Dua Zehra.[14]

Finally, on June 6, 2022, Dua was produced before the Sindh High Court, and she made a statement that she had not been not kidnapped and had left her home of her free will to live with Zaheer Ahmed. Dua's parents claimed that she was in fact fourteen years old and that they had the documentation to prove it.[15] The Sindh High Court passed an order that a bone ossification test be conducted to determine Dua Zehra's age. In the meanwhile, Dua Zehra was ordered to go to Panah Shelter Home. The bone ossification test concluded that Dua Zehra was sixteen to seventeen years old.[16]

On June 7 2022, the Sindh High Court observed that it could not finally decide the factual allegations raised before it regarding abduction and forced marriage in a habeas petition. It ordered the police to submit its investigation reports before the trial court so that the criminal case alleging that Dua Zehra had been kidnapped by Zaheer and his family could proceed. Meanwhile, the Sindh High Court concluded that Dua Zehra was at liberty to decide with whom she wished to go.[17] Dua Zehra chose to go to Lahore with Zaheer Ahmed.

Dua Zehra's parents appealed against this order to the Supreme Court. They maintained that Dua was under the age of the eighteen and therefore her marriage to the Zaheer Ahmed must be deemed illegal and void. They maintained that, since she was a minor, they, her parents, must be deemed her guardians and that, therefore, the Sindh High Court was incorrect to conclude that Dua Zehra was free to live with Zaheer Ahmed if she so chose.

The twists in this intensely watched case continued. On July 19, 2022, Dua submitted an application before a court in Lahore, requesting to be shifted to a shelter, saying that she faced "constant threats" from her parents and was also "not on good terms" with Zaheer Ahmed.[18] On July 21, 2022, the Sindh High Court ordered that Dua could not stay in Lahore while the criminal case in Karachi against Zaheer Ahmed was pending. Dua was brought to Karachi and placed under the care of a child-protection bureau.[19] After several months in a child-protection institute, Dua made a statement before the Sindh High Court, stating that she wished to go with her parents. Finally, Dua's parents successfully took possession of her.

With the Dua Zehra case, there emerged divisions between activists and civil society on the approach to the layers of human-rights violations involved. Proponents of stringent enforcement of child-marriage laws insisted that the marriage between Dua and Zaheer be deemed void. Some went further and insisted that Zaheer be charged with kidnapping and rape since any sexual relations between the parties while Dua Zehra was under the age of sixteen must be deemed statutory rape.[20] They also maintained that Dua's statements in court, indicating that she chose to marry Zaheer and wanted to live with him, were the products of her grooming by Zaheer and therefore should not be given any credence.

Others pointed out that Dua Zehra's statements in court, indicating that she feared violent backlash from her parents, must be taken seriously and that she should not be compelled to go to her parents.[21] Given Dua's statements that she chose to marry Zaheer Ahmed, it seemed grossly unfair to charge him with rape of a minor, a crime punishable by death.[22] The submissions made by and on behalf of Dua Zehra's parents in court denied her capacity to have opinions about her own well-being and also violated her right to be heard. Dua's parents insisted that, since she was under the age of eighteen, courts should not recognize her statements and that they, as her parents, had the sole right to make decisions on her behalf.

The Dua Zehra case exposed the limits of criminal legislation that prohibits child marriage. It highlighted the difficulties of enforcing the law when it comes to self-arranged marriages that are initiated by adolescents. It illustrated the problematic consequences of invalidating child marriages when there is possible threat of retaliation by family members and the absence of any appropriate protection mechanisms for minors. It also shows how criminal legislation aimed to protect young people can be deployed to undercut the agency of young people.

Arguments submitted on behalf of Dua Zehra's parents in the petition before the Sindh High Court included a claim that, under the law of the Muslim Shia sect, to which Dua Zehra's parents belonged, a woman's male guardian's consent is essential for marriage, regardless of her age.[23] This is a particularly reactionary claim in light of the fact that activists struggled long and hard for the legal recognition of a woman's right to choose her spouse in Pakistan. The marriages of many women who married without their parents' consent have been challenged in courts by their fathers. In the 1990s women's-rights activists galvanized to defend the rights of women to marry without the consent of their male guardian, and one case in particular, that of a young woman, Saima Waheed, whose marriage was challenged by her father, gained widespread public and media attention. It was not until 2003 that Pakistan's Supreme Court conclusively recognised the right of an adult Muslim woman to marry without her male guardian's consent.[24] The fact that this right was challenged on behalf of Dua's parents before the Supreme Court, avowedly in defense of human rights of girls, shows the extreme nature of some protectionist positions advanced in child-marriage cases.

Aarzoo Raja

Aarzoo Raja was a Christian girl who was living in Karachi with her parents. In October 2020, her father complained to the police that she had been kidnapped. The police arrested a forty-four-year-old Muslim man and his brother. When produced before the court, Aarzoo Raja claimed that she converted to Islam and married of her free will. She also claimed that she was eighteen years old. Arzoo Raja filed a petition before Sindh High Court, seeking protection for herself and her husband against her family members.[25]

By the time Aarzoo Raja's petition was heard by the Sindh High Court, several leaders of Christian minority communities and prominent human-rights activists became involved in the case. Media coverage of the case was intense. Christian groups and human-rights activists framed it as a case of forced religious conversion.[26] Before the Sindh High Court, Aarzoo's parents claimed that she was thirteen years old and therefore her marriage was illegal. To resolve the dispute regarding Aarzoo's age, the Sindh High Court ordered the formation of a medical board. The medical board concluded that Aarzoo's age was fourteen to fifteen.[27]

Aarzoo Raja appeared before the Sindh High Court in person and maintained that she chose to marry the much older man. The Sindh High Court however determined that, because of her young age, her so-called consent could not be accepted and that she could not be allowed to live with the man she said she married.[28] The Sindh High Court remained silent on the validity of the marriage itself, most likely because it was bound by Supreme Court precedent, according to which the marriage of a minor is valid so long as the minor has reached puberty. At the same time, the Sindh High Court rejected the challenge that was posed in the petition to the constitutionality of Sindh's child-marriage law, which claimed that the law is inconsistent with Islam as it not does not permit a marriage of a person who is below the age of eighteen but has reached puberty.[29]

Aarzoo told the court that she did not want to go to her parents' home. The court ordered that she go to Panah Shelter Home, a facility for adult women who are battered and need to escape abusive situations. The Sindh High Court further noted that, during this period, Aarzoo Raja should ponder over her life choices[30]—a statement that seems to assume that she is capable of making some choices even though the court deemed that she may not have the capacity to consent to marry. Aarzoo Raja stayed at the shelter for several months. For a long time, she refused to meet her parents. Aarzoo's parents and leaders of the Christian community claimed that Arzoo was brainwashed by her adult husband. Aarzoo's parents also demanded that the criminal charges for violation of the child-marriage law as well as rape be added to the charge sheet against Aarzoo's husband/abductor.[31] Eventually, Aarzoo agreed to return to her parent's home, after spending almost a year in the shelter home.[32]

Aarzoo Raja's case follows a pattern that is not very different from that of other cases involving underage marriages of girls from minority communities to Muslim men. The basic facts alleged by parents are contested by the girl. She claims she was not forced into conversion or into marriage. Legal arguments are advanced to challenge her claims on the basis that she is incapable of consent or free will because she is a minor. Her parents and community leaders claim that the girl is brainwashed into saying that she wants to stay married. Little effort is made by neutral authorities, such as the courts or police, to resolve these competing claims. An inquiry to understand what really transpires in the cases would involve collecting and analyzing complex facts. It would involve understanding the circumstances that may motivate an adolescent girl to elope and the constraints, including fear of reprisal, that prevent her from returning to her parents. Law-enforcement officials and courts would have to understand the family life and community pressures on the girl, her constraints due to poverty and patriarchy, and influences of and coercions by all adults involved. Unfortunately, there is little impetus to engage in complex and contested inquiries, especially when cases become highly publicized in the media and instigate protests among minority and human-rights communities.

Raveena and Reena

In March 2019, the father of two Hindu girls—Raveena and Reena—in the Ghotki district in Northern Sindh claimed that his daughters were kidnapped. A video of the father, Lal, crying out helplessly and slapping himself outside a police station in Ghotki went viral, and "over 2000 Hindu men and women from neighboring villages and towns had joined him in demanding justice for Reena and Raveena, blocking the highway for three consecutive days."[33] The girls filed a petition in the high court in Islamabad, saying that they moved to Punjab, converted to Islam, and married Muslim men of their free will. They sought protection from their family who, they claimed, was likely to retaliate against them for their decision.

The girls' father claimed that they were sixteen and fourteen years old, that their cases therefore were subject to Sindh's child-marriage legislation, and that their marriages were illegal. He claimed, with the support of large sections of the Hindu minority community in Pakistan, that the girls were forcibly converted to Islam and forced to marry Muslim men to preclude permanently any chance of their return to the Hindu faith and community. Members of the Hindu minority community also claimed that this was one instance of a systematic project organised by powerful Muslim leaders to target and exploit religious minorities in Pakistan.[34] This case became politically charged at the highest levels. Then Prime Minister Imran Khan took notice of the incident, and PPP Chairman Bilawal Bhutto Zardari met with Lal, the father of Raveena and Reena.[35] The Indian mainstream press also covered the case closely as a litmus test for Pakistan's willingness to protect the Hindu minority.[36]

The chief justice of the Islamabad High Court acknowledged the seriousness of the issue for girls and religious minorities. Recognising the existential threats faced by the Hindu community in Pakistan, the chief justice appointed amicus curiae or "friends of the court" to provide recommendations on how courts should deal with such cases. He also ordered that medical tests be conducted to determine the ages of the girls and that in the meanwhile they should be placed in shelter homes.

A medical board eventually concluded that the ages of the girls were eighteen and nineteen years. In light of this report, the Islamabad High Court concluded that, as adults, Reena and Raveena had the capacity and the right to consent to conversion to Islam and marriage to Muslim men. With that, the Islamabad High Court declared that Reena and Raveena were free to live with their Muslim husbands. Because the medical board concluded that Raveena and Reena were adults, the Islamabad High Court did not consider these to be cases of child marriage and therefore avoided any further inquiry into whether minors had the capacity to consent to marriage or whether their marriages should be deemed valid.

Many advocates for the Hindu community were deeply dismayed by this result. They claimed that vulnerable Hindu girls are targeted by influential Muslim leaders, made to convert to Islam, forced to marry Muslim men, and then coerced to say that they have acted of their free will. One culprit identified as a schemer and facilitator of these conversions is Mian Mithu, a guardian or pir of a shrine in Sindh known as Bharchundi Sharif Dargah.[37] A former member of the National Assembly, Mian Mithu has been accused for many years of intimidating and coercing Hindus to convert to Islam. The accusations are so severe that the political party to which he belonged, the PPP, has distanced itself from him entirely, and other political parties, including Pakistan Tehrik-i-Insaaf, also denied him their party ticket for elections.[38] Mian Mithu however claims that he only facilitates the conversion of those who voluntarily wish to become Muslims.

Because a majority of the cases alleging forced conversion of Hindu girls end up like those of Raveena and Reena, where the girl herself claims to the police and court that she converted and married of her free will, hard proof against Mian Mithu and others of systematic forced conversions that will stand in a court of law is hard to come by. Courts, police, and even members of minority communities are unwilling or unable to probe deeper to determine the extent of coercion, if any, faced by the girls. A report in the daily newspaper *Dawn* succinctly summed up the complexity:

> 'Forced conversions' of young girls is an emotive issue within the Hindu community of Sindh. Those accused claim that 'young love' is being misrepresented by the community, the media and activists. But those who know the whole truth are often not speaking.[39]

In his research on forced conversion of women and girls in Sindh, Jurgen Schaflechner notes that "cases of forced conversion reveal many layers of complexity, which thwart simple mono-causal explanations offered by both sides—either the liberal groups or the religious right."[40] His research shows how forced-conversion cases trigger "male identity politics" with majority Muslim population and minority communities claiming ownership over the woman or girl while making it dangerous for her to freely express and exercise her agency.[41] He notes that "most of these cases are only possible due to a rigid moral authority which orchestrates female agency in Sindh."[42]

CHILD MARRIAGES AND FORCED RELIGIOUS CONVERSIONS

Human-rights activists say that a law prohibiting forced conversions is required to prevent cases such as those of Raveena and Reena and many other minority girls like them. They say that the law should regulate the manner in which religious conversions are legally accepted. One way to evade murky questions about girls' consent and factual inconsistencies regarding whether the girls have been abducted by Muslim men or have eloped with them willingly is to enact a law that deems invalid any conversion of a person below the age of eighteen. Such a law would nullify the marriage of a non-Muslim child with an adult Muslim.

Numerous bills have been proposed before the National Assembly and the Sindh provincial assembly to curb forced conversions, but none has been enacted into law due to opposition from the Muslim religious right. The bills propose that conversion of minors below the age of eighteen be deemed void and that coerced conversions be subject to criminal penalties. In December 2016, the provincial assembly in Sindh passed a bill criminalizing forced religious conversions. Shortly after it was passed, religious leaders and the Council of Islamic Ideology conveyed their opposition to the leadership of the PPP, which formed the government in Sindh.[43] According to news reports, the PPP leadership asked the governor of Sindh to refrain from assenting to the bill so that it would not be enacted into law.[44] The governor of Sindh then asked the provincial assembly to reconsider the bill, particularly the provision that invalidated the conversion of persons under the age of eighteen. Reportedly his objection was that "[w]hen Hazrat Ali [the fourth caliph and successor to Prophet Muhammad] can convert to Islam at a young age, why can't Hindu girls?"[45] Another bill introduced in the National Assembly in 2020 to prohibit forced conversions was rejected by the Senate Standing Committee on Religious Affairs.[46]

Proponents of a law seeking to declare invalid all religious conversions of persons below the age of eighteen will contend not only with the Muslim religious right but also with international human-rights law. The Convention on the Rights of the Child, an international human-rights treaty to which Pakistan has acceded, recognizes that children have the right to form their own beliefs regarding religion. Article 14 of the Convention requires that state parties "respect the right of the child to freedom of thought, conscience and religion." Article 14(2) goes on to say that state parties shall "respect the rights and duties of the parents and, when applicable, legal guardians, to provide direction to the child in the exercise of his or her right in a manner consistent with the evolving capacities of the child." The Committee of the Rights of the Child, an expert body in charge of authoritative interpretations of the child-rights convention has stated that "it is the child who exercises the right to freedom of religion, not the parent, and the parental role necessarily diminishes as the child acquires an increasingly active role in exercising choice throughout adolescence."[47] Claims of persons under the age of eighteen regarding their religious belief should not therefore be dismissed outright, and the evolving capacities of children should be considered when determining whether an underage person had the capacity to knowingly change his or her religious belief.

Advocacy around forced religious conversion in Pakistan is linked closely to child marriages and raises similar questions regarding capacities of young girls to consent. The proposed legislation is driven by an assumption that forced marriage of young minority girls is a tool through which coerced conversions are carried out. Curiously, the forced conversion of minority boys has very little place in the discourse. Overwhelmingly, religious minorities complain about conversions of girls, not boys. Whether it is because conversions of girls take place more frequently or because minority communities are more concerned about girls than boys is difficult to glean from available data. Perhaps accounts of manipulation and sexual violence against young girls are more likely to evoke sympathy among paternalistic elements in Pakistan's Muslim majority and are therefore highlighted with much greater frequency and concern. Whatever the explanation, it appears that patriarchal sentiments over communities' ownership of girls are closely entangled with advocacy by minorities against forced religious conversions and girl child marriages.

HIGH COURTS INTERVENE

In February 2022, the Islamabad High Court stepped in to resolve the ambiguities in the law on child marriage. It addressed perplexing questions arising repeatedly before courts in child-marriage cases about the validity of child marriages and the capacity of persons under the age of eighteen to consent to marriage.[48] Under Shariah-based Muslim personal laws, a marriage is valid so long as both parties to the marriage have attained the age of puberty. The reliance on Muslim personal law is the reason why courts refrained from invalidating the marriage of Dua Zehra and Arzoo Raja, which was discussed in the case studies presented above. Validating a child marriage also means validating sexual relations with a minor within that marriage.

For many child-rights activists, this rendered the law toothless when it came to underage marriages involving persons who have reached puberty (puberty itself being an ambiguous standard). In its 2022 decision, the Islamabad High Court, through detailed reasoning that relied on constitutional rights, international human-rights law, and related criminal laws, declared that child marriages must be found void (invalid from the outset) and that sex within a child marriage must be deemed rape. Since the jurisdiction of the Islamabad High Court is limited to the federal capital territory of Islamabad, this decision has limited applicability. It was nonetheless hailed by human-rights activists across the country because it affirmed the primacy of child rights in the interpretation of child-marriage legislation.

The Islamabad High Court referred to the Convention on the Rights of the Child to conclude that a child must be deemed to be a person under the age of eighteen and explained that this is reinforced in other laws in Pakistan, including the Majority Act 1875 and the National Commission on the Rights of the Child Act. The court rejected previous judicial precedent that validated underage marriages on the basis of Muslim personal law, stating that the latter cannot be invoked "in the presence of clear statutory provisions addressing the subject matter."[49] The statutory provisions that the court relied on included criminal-law provisions related to sexual assault. Interpreting Section 375 of the Pakistan Penal Code, which says that sex with a person under the age of sixteen is rape, with or without the person's consent, and Section 377A, a Pakistan Penal Code provision prohibiting sexual abuse of persons under the age of eighteen, the court concluded that Pakistan's legal framework cannot deem permissible any act of a sexual nature involving a child, regardless of whether the child claims to have consented to the act.

In addition to statutory provisions, which the court interpreted to vitiate any likelihood of capacity and consent in the context of sexual relations for persons under the age of eighteen, the Supreme Court relied on an international human-rights treaty, the Convention on the Rights of the Child, noting that its ratification was a significant legal development subsequent to the Supreme Court case law from the 1970s and that it requires the overruling of previous precedent. The court reasoned that the statutory provisions and international human-rights treaty must mean that all persons under the age of eighteen lack the capacity to consent to marriage and to sexual activity: "Children, on the other hand, are not assumed to have complete agency and the law therefore acknowledges that they might neither understand the consequences of their actions nor can be held completely responsible for such actions."[50]

On this basis, the court concluded that all child marriages involving a person under the age of eighteen have no legal effect whatsoever as they run contrary to rights guaranteed in the Constitution and Pakistan's treaty obligations. It further concluded that "neither a child under the age of 18 can consent to engage in sexual conduct in any form, nor can a parent or guardian of a child contract a child out to engage in sexual conduct."

In its well-intentioned spirit to protect children (and possibly religious minorities who claim to be strongly affected by child marriages), the Islamabad High Court adopted a strong protectionist stance without considering the danger its reasoning poses for adolescents in consensual sexual relations. The court's interpretation of the Convention on the Rights of the Child was highly selective as it ignored those provisions of the treaty that recognize the "evolving capacities" of children as they grow older. The Committee on the Rights of the Child has noted that adolescence "is a unique defining stage of human development characterized by rapid brain development and physical growth, enhanced cognitive ability, onset of puberty and sexual awareness and newly emerging abilities, strengths and skills."[51] The Committee on the Rights of the Child has noted that, while states should introduce minimum legal age limits, "the right of any child below that minimum age and able to demonstrate sufficient understanding *to be entitled to give or refuse consent should be recognized*."[52] In view of these principles of international human-rights law, the statement by the Islamabad High Court that there is no room in our legal framework to "deem permissible any act of a sexual nature involving a child even if it is with the explicit consent of such a child" is inconsistent with the rights of the child.

The most disturbing aspect of the Islamabad High Court judgment is that it criminalizes consensual sexual activities between adolescents by concluding that a person under the age of eighteen cannot consent to sex. The Islamabad High Court ignored international human-rights law principles that adolescent sexual behavior *should not be criminalised*. The Committee on the Rights of the Child, the human-rights body responsible for interpreting and monitoring the implementation of the Convention on the Rights of the Child has stated that nonexploitative, consensual sexual behavior among adolescents of similar ages should not be criminalised.[53] The Committee has reaffirmed the call for decriminalisation of adolescents who engage with one another in consensual sexual acts in its General Comment No. 24 on *Children's Right in Juvenile Justice*.[54]

While the Islamabad High Court's judgement aims to clear ambiguities in the law on child marriage, it creates more knots in the already-entangled questions about adolescent liability for sexual activity under Pakistan's criminal laws. One example of a knotty question is that posed by 2021 amendments to the Pakistan Penal Code that state that any person—male, female, or transgender—may be held liable for rape. The age of criminal responsibility in the Pakistan Penal Code is ten years. The Islamabad High Court reasoning therefore entails that even a girl who is ten or older may be held liable for rape if she engages in consensual sex with a boy under the age of eighteen.

In 2024, the Lahore High Court, the highest appellate court in the province of Punjab, followed the footsteps of the Islamabad High Court when it passed judgement on a constitutional petition challenging the disparate minimum age restrictions on child marriage in the 1929 Child Marriage Restraint Act. In a brief five-page judgment, a single judge of the Lahore High Court declared that the differing definitions of "child" in the 1929 law (a female under sixteen and a male under eighteen) is unconstitutional as it impermissibly discriminates between males and females.[55] The judgment states that "[e]qual opportunities for females means equal restraint on marriage as the males." The court invoked Article 25(2) of the Constitution, which says that there shall be no discrimination on the basis of sex. It concluded, with little further reasoning, that the difference in minimum age between males and females in the 1929 law is "without lawful authority and of no legal effect."[56] The Lahore High Court did not make any observation regarding the validity of child marriage or the legality of sexual relations within a child marriage.

Typically, a court judiciously exercises it power to declare legislation invalid and confers sufficient respect to the legislative branch of government. The Islamabad High Court, for example, engaged in detailed reasoning comparing child-marriage legislation to other statutory provisions related to protection of children and sexual violence as well as to international human-rights law. In contrast, the Lahore High Court engaged in very little factual or legal analysis to support its conclusion that the law is void. There is long-standing precedent that discriminatory laws may be constitutionally permissible if they are based on "intelligible differentia" that have a rational nexus to a desirable policy outcome. The Lahore High Court did not reason as to whether there may be any rational basis for permitting a distinction in minimum age between girls and boys for child marriages. Nor did it consider any evidence from Sindh, where the age of marriage for girls and boys was made uniform at eighteen more than a decade earlier, in 2013. Surely it would have been relevant to consider whether the legal development in Sindh had an impact on the incidence of forced marriages of girls under the age of eighteen before concluding whether the minimum age should be raised in other parts of the country. It is perhaps a testament to the effectiveness of child-rights advocacy in Pakistan and globally, which has focused intensively on the age of marriage, that the Lahore High Court felt comfortable invalidating long-standing law without offering detailed reasons for doing so. As we see with reform of laws concerning rape, however, legal changes that attempt to settle social controversies without rigorous discussion and debate are unlikely to gain acceptance, and this poses a barrier to their implementation.

CHILD MARRIAGE LAWS AND SOCIAL REALITIES

If the Islamabad High Court paid attention to the facts of the child-marriage case before it, its 2022 judgement might have reflected the social context in which these marriages occur. The Islamabad High Court judgment was passed on a petition filed on behalf of the mother of a fifteen-year-old girl who said her daughter had gone missing. A habeas corpus application was filed in a criminal court, after which the girl informed the criminal court that she was married and living with her husband and was unwilling to live with her mother. On that basis the criminal court dismissed the habeas corpus application. That order was challenged before the Islamabad High Court, and that is how the appellate court was seized of a case that led to pronouncements regarding the validity of child marriage. The case before the Islamabad High Court followed a familiar pattern in child-marriage cases: a minor girl elopes with her partner to marry, and her parents approach the police and criminal courts for her "recovery."

Prior to passing a final order on the petition, the Islamabad High Court directed that the girl be moved to a shelter home and that she undergo a physical and psychological examination. In its judgment declaring that her marriage cannot be deemed valid and that she should be released from the shelter home to go with her parents, the court stated that it "has not determined the age of the Minor definitively, nor has it made any observations regarding the liability of the 'husband'"[57] as that factual determination is to be made by a criminal court. The Islamabad High Court's ruling regarding the applicability of the Pakistan Penal Code rape provision to consensual sex engaged in by minors meant that the male partner could be tried and convicted for rape for engaging in sexual relations with the minor. The age of the male partner was not mentioned in the Islamabad High Court judgment.

The facts before the Islamabad High Court seem consistent with the trend of self-arranged marriages of adolescents. In light of this trend, a relevant inquiry for those interested in curbing child marriages in Pakistan should be as follows: *why do girls run away to marry?*

Very little work, however, has been done in Pakistan to attempt to answer this question. I visited Panah Shelter Home in Karachi in May 2023. I was told by staff at Panah that, of the thirty-seven women in the shelter home at the time, thirteen were minors. All minors were sent to Panah Shelter Home by courts, and they had entered into marriages against their parents' wishes. The author interviewed some of the girls at the facility, and below are some of their stories.

Jihan's[58] Story

Jihan grew up in Karahi and is the second oldest of ten siblings. She never went to school and said that, in her family, children are "put to work" as soon as possible. She said that from the age of nine, her mother sent her to people's homes to work. Her father works as a driver, and her mother is also a domestic worker. When she was about thirteen or fourteen, her parents arranged her engagement to her uncle's (mother's brother's) son. Jihan did not want to marry him, and she told them that. Soon after, she met her partner, Imran, who used to sell vegetables on a cart in the neighborhood of the house where she went to work. She would buy vegetables from him before going to the house where she would prepare food, and she started talking to him. Jihan said she had no one to talk to at home—her mother would scold her constantly. They would constantly quarrel about her impending marriage to her cousin. One day, Imran asked her if she would marry him. She said he was around twenty-two years old at the time. After the *nikah*, she moved to his village in Rajanpur district to live with him and his family.

A few months later, the police raided her husband's family home and took them both to Karachi. Jihan's parents had filed a police complaint against her husband. She was then made to appear in court where the judge ordered that a medical examination be conducted to determine her age. The medical examination concluded that her age was approximately sixteen. The judge ordered that that, since she was sixteen, she could not live with her husband as her marriage was unlawful under the child-marriage law. Since she did not want to go to her parents, the judge ordered that she be sent to Panah Shelter Home where she would have to live until she was eighteen. The court ordered that, once she turned eighteen, she would then decide whether or not she wanted to live with her husband. In the meanwhile, her husband was charged with the criminal offense of abduction and released on bail. At the time we spoke to Jihan, his criminal trial was ongoing. Jihan says she hopes that Imran is acquitted so she can be with him when she is allowed to leave the shelter. She does not want to return to her parents as she believes she will be unhappy with them.

Hania's Story

Hania, who says she is around fifteen years old, lived in Karachi with her parents. She ran away from her parent's home one day to marry a young man in her neighborhood. She says that she left her home to get married because her mother arranged her marriage with a fifty-year-old man.

Soon after she left her home to get married, her mother filed a criminal complaint, saying she had been abducted. Hania and her partner, Amin, were apprehended by the police. Hania made a statement before a judicial magistrate, saying that her mother was forcing her to marry a much older man. She also said that her mother would take her to the home of the older man and he would rape her. Hania stated that she did not want to return with her parents and wanted to live with her partner.

Since Hania was under eighteen, the judicial magistrate did not permit her to stay with Amin or his family. The judicial magistrate determined that, in light of the "serious allegations" leveled by Hania against her parents, she should not be made to live with them and ordered that she be sent to Panah Shelter Home instead.[59] When the author spoke to Hania at the shelter, she was concerned about the criminal case against Amin and wanted him acquitted. We asked Hania if the judicial magistrate or police initiated any investigation against the much older man who raped her and her mother for taking Hania to the man. Hania said that no such investigation was initiated in spite of her statement in court.

Amna's Story

Amna lived in Karachi with her parents. She says she is around fifteen or sixteen years old. Her father worked as a driver in Saudi Arabia. Her mother stitches clothes at home. Amna was engaged to her cousin when she was eight years old. A few years later the engagement broke off as the boy said he did not want to marry her. Soon after, Amna met a boy, Amir, in her building who was around twenty years old. Her family refused to allow her to marry him. Instead, they fixed a marriage date with the same cousin that had broken off the engagement earlier. She told Amir she did not want to marry her cousin, and they decided to elope a few days before the wedding date. They got married soon after the elopement and went to Hyderabad to stay with some of Amir's family members. When they reached Hyderabad, they learned through Amir's family that Amna's family members lodged a police complaint against Amir for abduction of Amna. The family made Amir and Amna go back to Karachi. Amna went to court to record a statement that she had not been abducted and had married voluntarily. The court however determined that she was a minor and could not be permitted to live with her husband and in-laws. She was sent to Panah, and in the meanwhile Amir got bail.

Amna said that she wants, in her next appearance before court, to ask the court to allow her to go live with her parents. She wants to convince them to accept her marriage and to drop their criminal complaint against Amir. In the meanwhile, she said she will try to continue to meet Amir and her in-laws. She plans to start living with Amir when she turns eighteen.

The stories conveyed here are similar to those of the dozens of other cases referred to Panah Shelter Home, based on our conversations with its senior staff. The girls are from low-income backgrounds and are put to work at a very young age—either at home, where they are responsible for domestic chores, or outside the home, as domestic workers. The common belief that a child marriage puts a stop to a girl's education is challenged by these facts, since the girls entering into these marriages have already been taken out of school by their parents or never attended school in the first place. The parents of all the girls we spoke to had arranged their marriages to boys or men against their wishes. The existence of laws prohibiting child marriages did not seem to deter parents from forcing a marriage on minor girls, and apparently parents do not fear criminal penalties. The girls who decide to elope tend to be adolescents, under the age of eighteen, while their male partners tend to be older.

Often the decisions of girls and young men to elope is to avoid a forced marriage imposed by parents and community members. The boys or young men who face criminal charges of child marriage, abduction, and sometime even rape are not necessarily the ones imposing force or constraint on the girls. Rather, for girls in highly patriarchal societies, these males offer the only option of escape from constraints and, sometimes, serious abuse, imposed by parents and family members. The relationships must be placed in the context of social and cultural restrictions in Pakistan on adolescents, especially adolescent girls, who have limited options to escape such constraints. Adolescents are also unable to explore romantic relationships that are socially acceptable outside the bounds of marriage. In order to legitimise a romantic relationship, especially after it is discovered by parents or family members, they have no option but to enter into a marriage.

Implementation of child-marriage legislation should be consistent with the evolving capacities of adolescents. The Committee on the Rights of the Child has emphasised that, during adolescence, children develop "evolving capacities," which is "an enabling principle that addresses the process of maturation and learning through which children progressively acquire competencies, understanding and increasing levels of agency to take responsibility and exercise their rights."[60] While the Committee affirmed that the minimum age for marriage should be eighteen years, it also emphasises that states should "avoid criminalizing adolescents of similar ages for factually consensual and non-exploitative sexual activity."[61]

Unfortunately, recent jurisprudence by courts as well as advocacy by activists for child rights and minority rights in Pakistan undermines the evolving capacities of adolescents and ignores the social and cultural realities faced by young people. Demands that all child marriages be declared *void ab initio* do not take into account the impact that this would have on young people who have consummated marriages and on girls who may be pregnant. Calls that all sex within a child marriage be deemed rape also ignores the consensual nature of relationships among young people and the fact that they chose to enter into a marriage due to social and cultural constraints imposed on their romantic relationships.

Particularly in high-profile cases of child marriages, such as that of Dua Zehra and Arzoo Raja, discussed above, child-rights activists in Pakistan insist that girls below the age of eighteen cannot consent to sexual relationships and therefore their claims that they are in consensual relations cannot be taken seriously. This assumption violates the Convention on the Rights of the Child that recognizes that persons under eighteen may have the capacity to consent to sexual relations. It also violates the crucial principle that adolescents have the right to be heard. The Committee on the Rights of the Child has emphasized that states should guarantee adolescents the right to "express views on all matters of concern to them, in accordance with their age and maturity, and ensure they are given due weight, for example, in decisions relating to their education, health, sexuality, family life and judicial and administrative proceedings."[62]

A common response to girls' claims that they chose to marry their partners is that they have been groomed by their male partners. While the possibility of grooming should be taken very seriously, particularly when there is evidence of highly unequal power between the girls and their partners (for example, when considerable differences exist in age, financial status, etc.), the presumption that all girls in these cases are manipulated and incapable of expressing the truth is incorrect. Consistently girls explain in clear and articulate terms the family circumstances that led them to elope and offer good reasons why they do not wish to return to their parents' home. While the state as well as human-rights activists should always be vigilant to manipulation and coercion—both overt and subtle—of girls by men, they should also take seriously the claims, views, and preferences of young people before brushing them aside on the basis that people under eighteen do not know any better.

Policy discourse on child marriage is overwhelmingly focused on the age of marriage and imposition of criminal penalties. Far less attention is paid to protection and welfare mechanisms to support persons vulnerable to child marriage or those wishing to escape forced marriages. Until 2023, courts referred all girls who had entered into child marriages in Karachi to Panah Shelter Home, which is intended for adult women. Welfare officers and counselors trained to deal with the needs of minors do not exist there. Girls who are victims of forced child marriages or who have entered into self-arranged marriages have no meaningful options other than going back to their parents or to their marital home with their partners. The girls that we spoke to at Panah Shelter Home were frustrated by the constraints imposed on them, the restrictions on their freedom of movement, and the absence of educational or recreational activities to keep them engaged.

Our findings about the social circumstances under which girls enter into self-arranged marriages are mirrored in a study conducted in India by the NGO called Partners in Law in Development, published in 2019. The study, titled "Why Girls Run Away to Marry: Adolescent Realities and Socio-Legal Responses in India," found that girls under the age of eighteen often exercise the choice to marry as the only form of escape from economic, social, and cultural restrictions placed on them. It notes that poverty, marginalisation, and lack of opportunities for girls and boys push adolescents and youth into early adulthood. The report concludes that "typically the girls in the study opted for running away to marry or live with their boyfriend than face the prospect of confinement and forced marriage."[63]

The following conclusion reached by Partners in Law and Development in its report is noteworthy for lawmakers and policymakers in Pakistan as well:

> The evidence of self-arranged marriages, with its surrounding complexities, prompts questions regarding the policy solutions that promote punitive measures that treat underaged marriages as a homogenous forced practice and all underaged parties to marriage as lacking agency in relation to their future. Such assumptions lay the basis for proposals that deny the legal validity to all marriages, without seeking the views of the involved underaged parties or, indeed, a focus on "age of marriage", without equal attention to the intersecting concerns, like the criminalization of sexual consent.[64]

NOTES

1. UNICEF, "Child Marriage Country Profile—Pakistan," March 9, 2022, <https://www.unicef.org/pakistan/media/4151/file/Child%20Marriage%20Country%20Profile.pdf>, accessed August 8, 2024.
2. Girls Not Brides, "Child Marriage Atlas: Pakistan," 2020, <https://www.girlsnotbrides.org/learning-resources/child-marriage-atlas/atlas/pakistan/>, accessed August 8, 2024.
3. Rashid Javed and Mazhar Mughal, "Girls Not Brides: Evolution of Child Marriage in Pakistan" (GLO discussion paper no. 731, Global Labor Organization (GLO), 2020), <https://www.econstor.eu/bitstream/10419/226830/1/GLO-DP-0731.pdf>, accessed August 8, 2024.
4. Population Council and United Nations Fund for Population, "Child Marriage in Sindh: A Political Economy Analysis" (Population Council, November 2021), 48.
5. Ibid., 52.

6. Ibid.
7. *Bakhshi v. Bashir Ahmed* (1970) PLD Supreme Court 323.
8. Ibid.
9. Amir Wasim, "Child Marriage Restraint Bill Sails through Senate," *Dawn*, Islamabad, April 30, 2019, <https://www.dawn.com/news/1479317>, accessed August 8, 2024.
10. Amir Wasim, "Bill against Child Marriages Divides Parties in NA," *Dawn*, Islamabad, May 1, 2019, <https://www.dawn.com/news/1479444>, accessed August 8, 2024.
11. Data received from Sindh Police on June 10, 2024.
12. Aaj News, "Timeline of the Dua Zahra Case," Aaj News, July 22, 2024, https://english.aaj.tv/news/30293228/timeline-of-the-dua-zahra-case, accessed August 8, 2024.
13. Ibid.
14. Ishaq Tanoli, "FIA Chief Told to Cooperate with Sindh Police to Recover Dua Zehra," *Dawn*, Karachi, June 4, 2022, https://www.dawn.com/news/1692944, accessed August 8, 2024.
15. Shafi Baloch, "SHC Sends Dua Zehra to Shelter Home, Orders Medical Test to Determine Age," *Dawn*, June 6, 2022, https://www.dawn.com/news/1693439, accessed August 8, 2024.
16. Ishaq Tanoli, "Dua 'Free to Decide' Where She Wants to Go," *Dawn*, Karachi, June 9, 2022, https://www.dawn.com/news/1693895, accessed August 8, 2024.
17. Shafi Baloch, "'She Is Completely Free': SHC Allows Dua Zehra to Decide Who She Wants to Stay With," https://www.dawn.com/news/1693769, accessed August 8, 2024.
18. Ishaq Tanoli, "SHC Rules Dua Zehra Can't Be on Her Own in Lahore, Police Empowered to Move Her to Karachi," *Dawn*, July 21, 2022, https://www.dawn.com/news/1700838/shc-rules-dua-zehra-cant-be-on-her-own-in-lahore-police-empowered-to-move-her-to-karachi, accessed August 8, 2024.
19. Ibid.
20. *The Friday Times*, "'A Minor Cannot Consent To Marriage': Sensational Reporting Of Dua Zehra Case Condemned," *The Friday Times*, April 25, 2022, https://thefridaytimes.com/25-Apr-2022/a-minor-cannot-consent-to-marriage-sensational-reporting-of-dua-zehra-case-condemned, accessed August 8, 2024.
21. Naya Daur TV, "Dua Zahra Case—And The Harsh Realities | Sara Malkani on Syaapa," June 12, 2022, https://www.youtube.com/watch?app=desktop&v=oqbO-Jaqmm1s, accessed August 8, 2024.
22. Pakistan Penal Code, Section 376(3).
23. A copy of the petition is on file with the author.
24. *Hafiz Abdul Waheed v. Mrs. Asma Jehangir and another* (2004) PLD Supreme Court 219; *Dawn*, "Girls Can Marry of Their Own Will: SC," *Dawn*, Islamabad, December 20, 2003, https://www.dawn.com/news/130393/girls-can-marry-of-their-own-will-sc, accessed August 8, 2024.
25. *Arzoo Fatima v. Province of Sindh and Others*, C.P. No. D-5364 of 2020 (High Court of Sindh).

26. Madeeha Syed, "The Case of Missing Arzoo," *Dawn*, December 27, 2020, https://www.dawn.com/news/1598113, accessed August 8, 2024.

27. Aaj News, "Arzoo Case: Medical Board Declares Girl Underage," Aaj News, November 9, 2020, https://english.aaj.tv/news/30247528/, accessed August 8, 2024.

28. Ishaq Tanoli, "Aarzoo Refuses to Go Home after SHC Finds Her Marriage 'Not Legally Valid,'" *Dawn*, November 10, 2020, < https://www.dawn.com/news /1589502>, accessed November 11, 2024.

29. *Ali Azhar v. Arzoo Fatima and 5 Others* (2022) PLD Sindh 1.

30. *Dawn*, "SHC Orders Social Welfare Official to Look after Arzoo at Shelter Home," *Dawn*, November 24, 2020, https://www.dawn.com/news/1592050, accessed August 8, 2024.

31. Zubair Ashraf, "Main Suspect to Be Tried for Rape in Arzoo Underage Marriage Case," *The News*, December 10, 2020, https://www.thenews.com.pk /print/756222-main-suspect-to-be-tried-for-rape-in-arzoo-underage-marriage-case, accessed August 8, 2024.

32. Ishaq Tanoli, "Underage Marriage: SHC Allows Arzoo to Leave Shelter Home, Return to Her Parents," *Dawn*, December 22, 2021, https://www.dawn.com/ news/1665223, accessed August 8, 2024.

33. Naeem Sahoutara and Ali Ousat, "The Strange Case of the Silent Women," *Dawn*, November 10, 2019, https://www.dawn.com/news/1515863, accessed August 8, 2024.

34. Ibid.

35. Ibid.

36. See, e.g., Yudhvir Rana, "Two Pakistani Hindu Girls Being Falsely Proved Adult," *Times of India*, April 2, 2019, < https://timesofindia.indiatimes.com/world/ pakistan/two-pakistani-hindu-girls-being-falsely-proved-adult-pakistan-hindu-body/ articleshow/68691659.cms>, accessed November 11, 2024.

37. Ibid.

38. Atika Rehman, "UK Sanctions Controversial Sindh Cleric," *Dawn*, London, December 10, 2022, https://www.dawn.com/news/1725577, accessed August 8, 2024.

39. Sahoutara, n 33.

40. Jurgen Schaflechner, "'Forced' Conversion and (Hindu) Women's Agency in Sindh," *South Asia Chronicle*, 2017, <https://edoc.hu-berlin.de/server/api/core/ bitstreams/194bc6db-594c-4178-a9e9-b187f34f5d6a/content>.

41. Ibid.

42. Ibid.

43. Ahmad Tariq, "Pakistan: Sindh Province Rejects Bill Against Forced Conversions," *Library of Congress*, November 15, 2019, https://www.loc.gov/item/global -legal-monitor/2019-11-15/pakistan-sindh-province-rejects-bill-against-forced-conversions/, accessed August 8, 2024.

44. Ibid.

45. Ibid.

46. *The Express Tribune*, "Senate Panel 'Turns Down' Bill on Minorities Rights." *The Express Tribune*, Islamabad, February 2, 2021, https://tribune.com.pk/story

/2282277/senate-panel-turns-down-bill-on-minorities-rights%3Famp=1, accessed August 8, 2024.

47. UN Committee on the Rights of the Child (UNCRC), "General Comment No. 20 (2016) on the Implementation of the Rights of the Child during Adolescence," December 6, 2016, UN Doc CRC/C/GC/20.

48. *Mumtaz Bibi v. Qasim and 4 Others* (2022) PLD Islamabad 228.

49. Ibid., para 16.

50. Ibid., para 11.

51. UNCRC, n 47, 4.

52. UNCRC, n 47, 11.

53. UNCRC, n 47, 11.

54. UN Committee on the Rights of the Child (UNCRC), "General Comment No. 24 (2019) on Children's Rights in the Child Justice System," September 18, 2019, UN Doc CRC/C/GC/24 4.

55. W.P. 32798 of 2023 in Lahore High Court, decision dated April 9, 2024, para 11.

56. Ibid.

57. *Mumtaz Bibi*, n 48, 40.

58. Names have been altered to protect confidentiality.

59. A copy of Hania's statement before the judicial magistrate dated April 18, 2023, is on file with the author.

60. UNCRC, n 47, 6.

61. Ibid., 11.

62. Ibid., 7.

63. Ibid.

64. Ibid., 69.

Chapter 4

Domestic Violence

Enforcement and Backlash

After failed attempts to enact a federal law on domestic violence, Sindh became the first province to adopt domestic-violence legislation in 2013. The other three provinces followed, and, by 2021, all provinces in Pakistan had passed laws on domestic violence. Prior to the push for domestic-violence laws, several policy initiatives were made in Pakistan to address violence against women. Women's shelters, known as Dar-ul-Amans, were established in the 1960s.[1] Police stations staffed by women police officers, known as women's police stations, designed to receive and investigate complaints of violence and abuse of women, were established during the 1990s under Benazir Bhutto's government.[2] A law to establish a Women in Distress and Detention Fund was passed in 1996 to provide financial assistance to women in distress for a range of reasons, including spousal abuse. In response to frequent acid attacks on women by spouses and family members, a law criminalizing violent use of acid was passed in 2011.[3] Implementation of these measures was poor and inconsistent, and women's-rights activists and civil-society organisations persistently advocated for stronger legal and policy measures to address violence against women.

Endemic domestic violence in Pakistan gives rise to the need for strong legal and policy frameworks. According to the latest demographic and health survey, Pakistan Demographic and Health Survey 2017–2018, one in four married women have experienced physical violence.[4] The survey notes that 56 percent of women who have experienced physical or sexual violence have not told anyone or sought help. Of the ones that do reach out for help, the most common sources of support are their family or their husband's family. These numbers point not only toward the widespread incidence of violence but also to poor availability and accessibility of state resources for prevention and protection of vulnerable people.

The implementation of domestic-violence laws in Pakistan has been very slow and inconsistent. In the few years following the passage of the laws in Sindh and Punjab, there were very few cases filed in court and there was very little implementation of required protection mechanisms. This chapter shows how domestic-violence laws encounter resistance from law-enforcement officials, courts, and government bureaucracies, making it very cumbersome for women to use these laws for protection. The impact of domestic-violence legislation in Pakistan is evidence that formal legal changes by themselves have limited impact on gender-based violence that is rooted in deeply embedded patriarchal social and cultural structures, especially when the state apparatus is incapable or unwilling to take meaningful and consistent enforcement measures. At the same time, however, the laws create some openings and opportunities for women as well as feminist activists and lawyers to pursue some protection against and accountability for domestic violence.

FIRST DOMESTIC-VIOLENCE LAW

Before the first domestic-violence law was passed in the province of Sindh in 2013, the federal legislators made attempts to pass domestic-violence legislation and failed. The first domestic-violence bill was introduced in 2009 by a member of the PPP. While the bill passed in the National Assembly (the lower house of the parliament), it failed to go through the Senate (the upper house of the parliament) and therefore could not become law. The Council for Islamic Ideology, a constitutional body that advises lawmakers about the consistency of proposed legislation with Islamic injunctions, objected to the bill. The council stated that the bill would promote family feuds and increase divorces.[5] The bill was re-tabled by women legislators again in 2012 but could not pass due to opposition from the religious right. The JUI-F (Jamiat Ulema-e-Islam) leader Maulana Fazlur Rehman declared that the bill promoted Western values and therefore his party would not tolerate it.[6]

With the stalemate at the federal level, provincial legislators worked toward the passage of domestic-violence legislation before the Sindh provincial assembly, where the influence of religious right was significantly weaker. The overwhelming majority in the Sindh assembly was that of the PPP. The law was drafted with the assistance of women's-rights NGOs, primarily the Aurat Foundation. It drew considerable inspiration from India's Prevention and Protection Against Domestic Violence law, passed in 2005. The passage of the law in Sindh in 2013 was hailed by women's-rights groups, locally and internationally, as landmark legislation that demonstrated the willingness of the PPP to promote progressive women's-rights legislation.

The law passed in 2013 defines domestic violence very broadly, introduces new criminal offenses, and sets forth a range of remedies. It has a strong feminist underpinning with its conceptualisation of domestic violence as gender-based violence. The law defines domestic violence to include all forms of gender-based violence, including physical, sexual, psychological, verbal, and economic abuse. The law cross-references provisions in the Pakistan Penal Code that penalize various degrees of "hurt." It also creates new criminal offenses: "emotional, psychological and verbal abuse," "sexual abuse," and "economic abuse."[7] The creation of the offence of "sexual abuse" is especially significant since the Pakistan Penal Code provisions on rape have barely been utilised for convictions for marital rape, and it was not until 2024 that a husband was convicted for nonconsensual relations with his wife.[8] At the same time, family laws in Pakistan recognize that men have "conjugal rights" over their wives, and suits in which men seek to assert their right to have sexual relations with their wives are entertained in courts. The inclusion of the provision of "sexual abuse" therefore provides an opportunity to obtain some accountability for sexual violence within a marriage as well as other domestic relations.

Other remedies offered under the law include protection orders, residence orders, which may order restoration of residence to a person who has been forced out of her home due to domestic violence, as well as monetary relief as compensation for the harm suffered as a result of domestic violence. The law provides that a person may directly approach the judicial magistrate to file a petition to initiate criminal action or to attain protection orders or other remedies provided under the law. It also establishes a mechanism to facilitate the implementation of the law by providing for district-level protection committees to oversee implementation of the law as well as the appointment of protection officers in each district to assist complainants.

The law, with its conceptualisation of domestic violence firmly rooted in feminist theorizing of violence as an expression of, and a tool to maintain, gender hierarchy, directly challenges the values of a conservative and patriarchal society. How did such a law pass in Sindh after similar legislation encountered such strong opposition from legislators in the federal parliament? The alliance among women's-rights NGOs, progressive lawyers, and a receptive provincial government made this possible. By strategically working with a sympathetic political party that was firmly in power in the province of Sindh, the feminist coalition was able to sidestep majoritarian tolerance for domestic violence in deeply patriarchal societies.

The law was prepared by feminists in consultation with civil-society members who directly lobbied the Ministry of Law to approve the legislation. Lawyer Maliha Zia Lari, one of the lead drafters of the law, says that it incorporates the work of many women's-rights activists and lawyers over the years, with the NGO the Aurat Foundation being a key advocate since the early 2000s.[9] The Aurat Foundation hosted consultations with lawyers, activists, and parliamentarians that led to various draft versions of the law. Key legislators across political parties were identified as champions of domestic-violence legislation. The Sindh government at the time was led by the PPP with its relatively progressive agenda on gender issues, and so the domestic violence legislation was introduced in the Sindh Assembly as a government bill. Maliha Zia, affiliated with the Aurat Foundation at the time, worked for months with the secretary of the Law Department to secure the support of the Sindh government for the draft legislation. The bill sailed through the PPP-dominated legislature, with no debate on the floor on the contents of the law.

Implementing Legislation: First Domestic-Violence Conviction

Unfortunately, the law was forgotten soon after it was passed. The women's-rights groups and legislators who played a crucial role in passing the law could not make a direct impact on the institutions and actors responsible for its implementation, namely the courts, police, and government bureaucracy. From 2013 to 2017, no cases were filed under the law. In the initial years, there was little to no attempt to share the contents of the law with police officials, with members of the judiciary, or among lawyers through bar associations; nor were trainings of key actors conducted. As a result, the law had no impact in the initial years. While it was celebrated among women's-rights activists and human-rights organisations at the time of its passage, there was little to no effort to push for its implementation.

In 2017, the first case that led to a conviction was filed on behalf of a woman living in Karachi who was physically and sexually abused by her husband. One reason why this case went to court is that the woman was personally known to one of the main drafters of the 2013 law. Rabia[10] was abused repeatedly during her brief marriage. When her husband beat her severely on February 11, 2017, she decided she couldn't tolerate the abuse anymore. Rabia went to the police station with her mother. The police insisted that she needed to get a medico-legal report before they could register the complaint. On the same day, Rabia went with her mother to the medico-legal department at a public hospital in Karachi and obtained a medical report. The police still refused to register a first information report (FIR). Rabia engaged me as a lawyer, and we petitioned the court under Sindh's domestic-violence law. She prayed that her husband would be found guilty of "hurt" under the Pakistan Penal Code as well as of sexual and economic abuse. She also requested the court to grant protection and residence orders.

The judge before whom the petition was filed was not aware of the existence of a domestic-violence law. I presented the law to him, and he walked through it for the first time. The judge recorded Rabia's statement and then framed a charge against the accused. The charge included the offences of physical and sexual as well as emotional abuse. The judge also granted a protection order to Rabia, based on her statement as well as the evidence in the medical report. The trial then commenced and continued for almost two years. During the trial, her husband repeatedly violated the protection order by trying to contact her and coming to her parents' house. When Rabia and her father approached the police for enforcement of the protection order, they were turned away, and the police refused to take action.

Eventually, Rabia succeeded, and her ex-husband was convicted for committing physical abuse as well as emotional, psychological, and verbal abuse, and he was sentenced to six months in prison. This was the first conviction under Sindh's domestic-violence law. Rabia's ex-husband appealed the conviction before the sessions judge, who was also unaware of the law. When provisions of the law were brought to his attention, he was quite surprised to learn that wife-beating had been criminalised. He encouraged Rabia to forgive her ex-husband, but she refused to do so. The primary argument by the defendant's lawyer on appeal was that the 2013 Act was against the values of Islam and an "eastern society," and therefore the conviction must be set aside. He said that the defendant beat his wife because she was denying him sex, and therefore he was justified in doing so.

Eventually, the sessions judge upheld the conviction. When announcing the judgment, however, he verbally stated in court that, while he was bound to follow the law, he did not agree with it and found it incredible that a man should have to go to jail for beating his wife.

For Rabia, obtaining a conviction was an uphill task in spite of the fact that she had many things going for her: a supportive network of lawyers and activists who assisted her pro bono, the support of her family, and strong medical evidence. At the trial stage, the judicial magistrate eventually understood the spirit of the law, which was reflected in his decision. The conviction was possible primarily because of Rabia's courage and support from family and friends that enabled Rabia to overcome the obstacles imposed by law-enforcement officials and courts.

More Domestic-Violence Cases Filed

After the first conviction, the number of cases filed under the 2013 domestic-violence law began to increase. Orders passed by the Sindh High Court, discussed in detail later in this chapter, calling for implementation of the law, also created a more enabling environment for domestic-violence cases.

Data received from the registrar of the Sindh High Court shows that from 2017 to 2023, 415 cases under the 2013 Act were filed in courts across Sindh.[11] Of these, 374 cases have concluded, while 41 remain pending. The data received do not clearly indicate which specific provisions of the Act the cases are filed under (i.e., which specific offenses are alleged) or which specific remedies (for example, protection orders, residence orders, or monetary relief) were requested by complainants/petitioners. Nor do the data reveal the nature of the relationship between the complainant/petitioner and the person against whom the case is filed.

The data received show that a significant majority of the cases (192) concluded so far end up being "withdrawn," "compromised," or "dismissed for non-prosecution." A small number of cases (three) ended in a conviction. Eighty cases ended in "acquittal" or "dismissal." The label ascribed to some cases is ambiguous: thirty-four cases are described as being "allowed" or "granted," and the precise meaning of these outcomes is unclear.

Why are a majority of cases "compromised," "withdrawn," or "dismissed for non-prosecution"? This is so for several reasons, including the failure of courts and law-enforcement officials to enforce the law in its true spirit and the absence of protection mechanisms that would allow women to pursue lengthy cases in courts.

Courts are often reluctant to enforce the law in a manner that would facilitate its implementation. The failure of the police to swiftly enforce protection orders severely undermines their effectiveness. The gravest difficulty is faced by women who face imminent violence, including threats to their lives, and need immediate protection. In such cases, delays on the part of the court to grant interim protection orders place women in serious danger. Even when courts grant interim protection orders, they prolong hearings for final protection for days, sometimes weeks, which for many women defeats the purpose of a protection order.

Courts are even more reluctant to grant residence orders, a crucial remedy that could enable a woman to obtain a court order allowing her to stay in the house and preventing the abuser from removing her from the residence. One factor preventing many women from taking any kind of recourse against their

Table 4.1 Domestic Violence Cases in Sindh, 2017–2023

Outcome	Number of Cases
"Compromised," "withdrawn," "dismissed for nonprosecution"	192
"Acquitted," "dismissed"	80
"Allowed," "granted"	34
"Convicted"	3
"Disposed of," "dormant," "proceeding stopped," etc.	65

abuser is the threat of being thrown out of their house and rendered homeless. In Pakistan, a man may unilaterally divorce his wife by pronouncing *talaq* (divorce) and submitting a notice of the divorce before the relevant local government authority. Such divorce becomes effective in three months unless revoked by the husband. The unilateral power to divorce makes women quite vulnerable, especially when they are financially dependent on the spouse. The remedy of residence orders is very significant in this context as, if and when enforced, it allows a woman to stay in the home and forbids the husband from throwing her out. This remedy is underutilised, however. In one case that I pursued in court, the woman obtained a residence order that affirmed her right to remain in the house and restrained the husband from disturbing her right to peacefully enjoy her home. However, in this case the judge asked to see the title documents of the house, and the house happened to be owned by the woman. In the absence of the fact of ownership, it is likely that the judge would not have passed this order.

My experience in bringing domestic-violence cases to court shows that judges and practitioners are confused by the scheme of the law that provides both civil remedies in the form of protection and residence orders and monetary relief as well as criminal penalties. Judicial magistrates tend to believe that the civil remedies and criminal penalties are intertwined. When applicants approach the court for protection or residence orders, judicial magistrates ask why they are not at the same time pressing criminal charges against the perpetrator. When informed that the victim at this stage seeks only to secure her physical safety in her home and does not wish to participate in criminal proceedings nor seek criminal sanctions for her partner, judges sometimes find it incredulous and begin to doubt her credibility.

In one case in which I represented the complainant in an application seeking protection and residence orders, the accused's lawyer insisted that no order can be passed unless it be proven in a criminal trial that the defendant was in fact violent against the applicant. Even though the law contains no such requirement, the judicial magistrate agreed with this view. The applicant told the court that she was not interested in pursuing a criminal case and in fact did not want to see her former spouse behind bars. In spite of this, the court framed a criminal charge against the defendant and ordered that summons be served upon him to defend himself in a criminal trial.

Unsuccessful outcomes in domestic-violence cases are sometimes the result of confusion among judges about the procedure for hearing applications for protection and residence orders. Because the law contains provisions regarding criminal penalties and also provides that, unless otherwise specified, proceedings under the Act will follow the Code of Criminal Procedure, judicial magistrates are confused about whether they should follow the process of a trial before granting protection and residence orders. They are also confused about the burden of proof required to pass protection and residence orders. In some cases where the defendant seeks both criminal penalties as well as protection orders, judicial magistrates maintain that granting a protection order will be tantamount to deciding the criminal case. They do not understand that protection orders may be granted on proving a prima facie case and there's nothing in the law that precludes the grant of protection orders independent of criminal remedies. As a result, hearings for protection orders can last several weeks, requiring the applicant to appear in court several times to plead her case.

A sensible reading of the law should not give rise to such confusions, as it is very much possible to distinguish between the criminal sanctions and other remedies provided in the law. Absurd readings of the law, however, are not at all uncommon. This can be attributed to the poor analytical abilities of lawyers and judicial magistrates that make them unable to properly apply a law that is somewhat complex. Absurd interpretations also reflect an inherent discomfort with a law that is contrary to patriarchal societal norms and values and a consequent reluctance to facilitate complainants and interpret the law in a way that is beneficial to vulnerable people. Any procedural ambiguity or complexity therefore makes the law difficult to enforce for the survivor. These experiences are significant deterrents for survivors.

Another significant procedural gap in the law is silence regarding whether an offence is "cognisable" or "noncognisable." Under Pakistan's Code of Criminal Procedure, criminal offences that are cognizable are those for which the police may arrest without a warrant from the magistrate. Noncognisable offences are those for which the police may not arrest a suspected perpetrator without a warrant from the judicial magistrate. Sindh's domestic-violence law is silent with respect to whether criminal offences specified in the law are cognizable, and, therefore, when a survivor approaches the police to complain about domestic violence, the police does not make an arrest. This significantly weakens the effectiveness of the law in situations where women require immediate police intervention for protection. In order to pursue a criminal case, the survivor must file a petition directly before the judicial magistrate, a process that takes time and typically requires her to engage a lawyer. With the procedural barriers and the reluctance of judges to grant speedy relief, it isn't difficult to see why a majority of domestic-violence cases filed end up in compromise or withdrawal.

It is not necessary, however, that all cases that end up in compromise reflect a complete failure of the law. In some cases, survivors are able to achieve some positive practical outcome for themselves through the compromise. Two cases that I dealt with directly as a lawyer illustrate this. In one case, Asha[12] faced physical and psychological abuse from her husband. Asha was raised in an orphanage as a small girl, and, when she grew older, the orphanage arranged her marriage. She had four children. In 2020, she reached out to me through her orphanage. She conveyed that her husband had married another woman and had brought her to their house. Since this marriage, he stopped spending time with Asha and his children and did not support them financially. When Asha complained, he would verbally and physically abuse her.

When Asha approached me, she said that on the one hand she wants to leave her husband but on the other hand does not know how she would financially support herself and the children. She also feared that, if she left her husband, he would take custody of her children and separate her from them. Asha was not interested in pursuing a criminal case against her husband but what she wanted was immediate protection from violence for herself and her children as well as monetary support for h er children from her husband. For some respite from the ongoing abuse, she wanted to leave her home with the children, and the only option available to her was Panah Shelter Home.

We filed a petition under the domestic-violence law on her behalf before a court in Karachi in which we asked the court to grant a protection order, a monetary order, and a custody order allowing her to keep her children with her. The court granted her an interim protection order and ordered that Panah Shelter Home admit her and her children. After spending a few days in the shelter, Asha wanted to leave, primarily because it was not a suitable place for children for an extended period of time. Asha wanted to go and live with her relatives in another city instead. She had to get permission from the court to leave the shelter, which the court granted reluctantly. She went to her relatives, but in the meanwhile she, her relatives, and husband talked about the situation and her husband agreed to make some changes. He promised to begin supporting her and her children financially. With very limited financial options available to her, Asha believed that this was the best option as she could not stay separated from her husband and keep her children with her. Asha's husband submitted an undertaking in court stating that he would take these measures and in return Asha submitted a statement that she would not press the case further.

Asha's case is one example of the dozens of domestic-violence cases that have been compromised or withdrawn according to the data discussed above. Her reasons for the compromise are probably fairly common, especially for women who pursue domestic-violence cases against their husbands. Asha lacked the means to financially support herself and her four children and was therefore compelled to return to her husband. The domestic-violence case that she filed, however, was not all in vain, at least in the short run. She was able to get some immediate respite from the volatile situation at her home through the protection order. She was also able to was use the "threat" of the case to motivate her husband to make important concessions to her. Even though

Asha compromised and effectively terminated the proceedings against her husband within a few weeks, she was able to impose some accountability on her husband and to disrupt the unequal power relations to some extent. As her lawyer, I also made it clear in court that she would return with a contempt application if Asha's husband were to renege on any term in his undertaking. We do not know how long Asha's husband's behavior improved after the court proceeding, but, several months after this case, I received a phone call from a woman who had been referred through Asha. The woman said that she was facing abuse from her husband and that Asha told her to contact me, the lawyer who would "speak to her husband and make things alright." This suggests that Asha perhaps saw the legal process as part of a dialogue or negotiation with her husband in which both the court and the lawyers were mediators. This is indeed one way in which domestic-violence litigation can be viewed.

This point is illustrated in another case, this one involving a twenty-six-year-old woman whom we'll call Rahma.[13] Rahma's father passed away, and her mother married a man with two daughters. Rahma lived with her mother, stepfather, and stepsisters. Her mother and stepfather placed too many restrictions on her movement and pressured her to get married. They also wanted her to stop working. On one occasion, after her mother beat her, Rahma called the police. They came to her house and took her to the police station, and she told the police that she would rather go to a shelter home than return to her parents. She was taken to the shelter, and the next day the police took her to the court. Her maternal aunt was present in court at the time, and Rahma said that she would go and live with her. A few weeks after this incident Rahma wanted to leave her aunt's house and live independently, but she was afraid that if she did so her mother and stepfather would harass her and force her to live with them. She approached me for legal options, and we decided to file a protection order in court to restrain her mother and stepfather from harassing her if she wanted to live on her own. The court sent notice to the stepfather, and, when he appeared in court on the next day with the mother, they were very eager to reconcile with Rahma. They told the court that they would give an undertaking stating that they would not harass Rahma or prevent her from pursuing a job and living independently. Rahma agreed not to pursue the case further.

This case was withdrawn after a compromise, but the very act of filing the case enabled Rahma to get a sworn statement from her mother and stepfather that they would halt their physical and emotional abuse. It created circumstances that enabled her to move out of her toxic home situation, live independently, and pursue her job. The law therefore, even when invoked briefly, helped Rahma to break out of patriarchal constraints.

Neither Rahma nor Asha sought criminal convictions in their cases. Nor did they obtain permanent protection orders from the court. But the immediate relief they got from the court, in the form of an interim protection or a custody order, was of help to them. Their cases illustrate that not every case of compromise or withdrawal should be seen as a complete failure.

Absence of Protection Mechanisms

Effective enforcement of domestic-violence legislation requires functioning protection mechanisms. Vulnerable persons will pursue the legal remedies offered by the law while they feel physically safe, have financial support if needed, and are able to access counseling. The underutilisation of domestic-violence legislation is partly due to the absence of functioning protection mechanisms, as a result of which vulnerable persons, most often women, have to bear all the social and financial burdens of pursuing domestic-violence cases.

Shelter homes, known as Dar ul Amans, were established decades ago, but their utility is very inconsistent. In the province of Sindh, there are four shelter homes, but they remain underutilized in general. According to the Social Welfare Department of Punjab, there are a total of twelve crisis centres in the province.[14] In addition to these crisis centres or shelter homes, there are Dar-ul-Falahs, or transitional homes, which house women with children for a longer duration.[15]

Activists and NGOs working with survivors consistently observe that women are reluctant to go to shelter homes and, once they do go, they are keen to leave soon. One factor identified is the lack of mobility of women once they are inside a shelter. Women are generally not permitted to leave the shelter without court permission. Sometimes courts place restrictions on meetings between women and family members, and women are also not permitted to keep mobile phones on them. Shelters are also not supportive environments for children, and so women with children are unable to stay in shelters for any extended period of time. Effectively, shelters become jails.

Very disturbing reports of abuse of women in shelter homes surface from time to time. In 2011, sixteen women escaped from a Dar ul Aman shelter in Quetta in Balochistan by climbing out after breaking windows due to degrading conditions.[16] In 2021, a staff member at a Dar ul Aman in Sukkur in Sindh was accused of raping women in the shelter.[17] An inquiry conducted by a sessions judge found that he had assaulted several women at the shelter. The Sindh High Court took notice of the incidents and summoned the director of the Social Welfare Department to explain whether any accountability or prevention measures had been taken in response to the incident. The Social Welfare Department director said that the person accused had been transferred but had not been removed from service and that no criminal complaint had been initiated against him. On the order of the Sindh High Court, a criminal case was initiated,[18] but it was apparent that the Social Welfare Department itself was not concerned with accountability for such a grave incident in its institution. It is then little wonder that women often report that shelter homes are hostile and at times very dangerous spaces.

Although a policy to establish police stations staffed by women police officers was announced in 1994, only a handful exist and the ones that do are under-resourced. There are only ten functioning women police stations staffed by women police officers currently in Sindh.[19] The rationale behind these stations is that women police officers would be more receptive to complaints from women and that they would offer safer spaces for women looking to escape abusive situations. Since very few of these police stations are functional, women still largely encounter male police officers when they report domestic violence. While women activists working with survivors perceive attitudes of senior police officials improving over time, attitudes of officials who make the first point of contact with women complainants remain by and large judgmental and unhelpful. Police officials consistently refuse to register criminal complaints against abusers and encourage women to compromise with their families. Even though availability of qualified medico-legal officers is limited, especially in rural areas, police require women to obtain medico-legal services before registering a domestic-violence complaint, adding to the obstacles in the way of women seeking protection and accountability.

During emergency or crises, such as the COVID-19 pandemic, protection facilities and services become even more scarce and inaccessible.[20] During the pandemic, women were locked in with their perpetrators. Their access to communication devices even ordinarily tends to be limited and controlled in any case; during the pandemic, due to lockdowns and lack of public transport, reaching out to neighbors or traveling to family members also became a challenge. Those who did manage to seek legal help had to contend with stringent protocols and delays vis-à-vis courts and shelter requirements, such as COVID-19 testing, which, in the initial days, was not as accessible or broad-based as it later became.

When women are trying to escape immediate life-threatening situations in their homes, rescue services are generally inadequate.[21] Helplines set up for domestic-violence complaints are of little help to women who do not have access to phones. Activists report that police often refuse to act unless the complaint of violence comes directly from the person impacted—complaints of observers, relatives, and friends are not taken seriously by the police. This is a real obstacle as often vulnerable persons in the midst of volatile and dangerous situations are unable to reach the police directly. Even when the police respond to a domestic-violence complaint reported on a helpline and come to the homes of complainants, they are not properly trained to respond appropriately to the situation. A common approach of the police is to remove the woman from the house and take her to the police station along with the perpetrator. In the police station, the officers try to facilitate a "compromise," which sometimes results in a written undertaking on the part of the perpetrator stating that he will not be violent in the future.

In some cases that I have encountered, police do inform women of the option of going to a shelter home instead of returning to her home. Police will take the woman to the shelter home and the next day will take her to court, where she records a statement saying that she has chosen to leave her family home and live in the shelter. Effectively, this procedure confines the woman to the shelter home, and she becomes "court dependent." She can then only leave the shelter home with the permission of the court. In the meanwhile, there is typically no investigation against the perpetrator of violence, who is free to live in the home and continue with his daily life. The approach of the police and courts therefore creates a highly perverse situation where a woman is effectively detained for complaining about domestic violence, but the abuser goes free.

The Sindh High Court Steps In

Almost six years after the law was passed, the Sindh High Court passed a judgment calling for the implementation of Sindh's 2013 domestic-violence law.[22] A judge of the Sindh High Court, Justice Salahuddin Panwhar, noted in 2018 that a large number of petitions were filed in the Sindh High Court, requesting the court to order the police to provide protection to persons facing violence and harassment from family members. The judge observed that these cases should not be filed before the high court, which is primarily an appellate court, if alternative and effective remedies are available. Even the office of the Advocate General, the legal counsel for the government of Sindh, was unaware of the 2013 Act.[23] Eventually, Justice Panwhar became aware that a law had been passed years previously to provide protection to persons facing family violence. The Sindh High Court ordered that aggrieved persons, instead of approaching the high court directly in a writ petition, should approach the judicial magistrate for protection orders, residence orders, and other remedies. The Sindh High Court noted that, even though the law had been enacted years ago, protection committees and protection officers had not been appointed under the law. He ordered that the Women Development Department take immediate steps to notify the committee and fill the positions of protection officers. He also ordered that the administrative branch of the high court monitor the enforcement of the law by judicial magistrates and maintain records of cases filed under the law.

In 2019, the Sindh High Court formed a committee to develop recommendations to address violence against women. The committee comprised a senior police official, a member of the Women Development Department, a representative of the Social Welfare Department, and a lawyer. Over the course of several months, the committee developed a set of recommendations for policy measures, including the establishment of one-stop protection centres in each district that would provide various services required by a survivor under one roof. The final recommendations submitted by the committee to the court noted that the "absence of integrated services for women seeking protection from violence and accountability for violence has been identified by the committee as a key issue."[24] The committee recommended the establishment of "one-stop facilities" that "provide support services for survivors of sexual and gender-based violence." These facilities were to include a short-term shelter; provisions for medical examination, legal consultation, and psycho-social support; police protection; and services relating to initiation of complaints. The detailed recommendations of the committee included the following:

- Each district in Sindh should have either a police station staffed by women police officers or a woman and child protection cell (WCPC), which should become the home of the one-stop relief centre.
- These women's police stations and WCPCs should be scaled up and their facilities enhanced to include the following: a temporary shelter facility; counseling; legal-aid services; transportation, including transportation to court and medical facilities where required; and registration of FIRs.
- The one-stop protection centre shall be under the direct supervision of a senior superintendent of police, and at least one woman police officer not below the rank of assistant sub-inspector must be posted at each station.
- The one-stop protection centre must have the authority to register an FIR of any case involving violence against women (including murder, rape, and domestic violence) that has taken place anywhere in the province. The FIR may then be transferred to the relevant jurisdiction.
- These facilities must be made available twenty-four hours a day and seven days of the week.
- All officers present at the facility must be notified that women escaping violence are not to be considered detainees and that the one-stop protection centre is not to be viewed as a jail or sub-jail for women who are seeking temporary shelter. Women must be permitted to leave the temporary shelter in accordance with their free will, without the requirement of a court order.

Although the recommendations were endorsed across key government departments and then incorporated in an order of the Sindh High Court, as of 2023 they remained largely unimplemented. In 2023, the police submitted in court that ten women's police stations were established in Sindh. This number did not increase since the last submission in 2020. In 2023, the Home Department submitted a report to the court, stating that a budget amounting to Rs. 740 million (Pakistani rupees) has been allocated and sanctioned, which includes funds for the construction of one-stop protection centres.[25] However, there was no evidence of measures taken to establish these facilities after this budget allocation.

In spite of detailed directions from the Sindh High Court, the wheels of bureaucracy moved at a snail-like pace so that, even after two years, there was no meaningful progress toward implementation. Key government departments are not staffed with proper personnel required to enforce the law, rules, and regulations; recruitment of key personnel seems to be a highly cumbersome process, requiring a government department to get approval from the Finance Department. There are long time lags in this process, and the secretary leading each department blames secretaries of other departments for the delays. The setting up of facilities, such as one-stop protection centres and women's police stations, requires the approval of budget allocations from more than one department. Once the budget is approved, it is released to the relevant government department in phases, based on the pace with which the budget is utilized. In order to utilize the budget at a reasonable pace, personnel are needed to complete all the tasks on schedule. Often this is not possible, and therefore budget utilization also becomes very slow.

The implementation of domestic-violence legislation and policies requires a degree of bureaucratic coordination and competence that, in Pakistan's governance context, is very difficult to accomplish. The result is the piecemeal

Table 4.2 Timeline of Implementation of Domestic-Violence Laws in Sindh

Year	Key Milestones
2013	Sindh Domestic Violence (Prevention and Protection) Act is passed
2016	Rules under Sindh Domestic Violence Act are framed
2018	Sindh High Court takes notice of nonimplementation of Sindh Domestic Violence Act
2019	First conviction under Sindh Domestic Violence Act
2019	Sindh High Court passes order on nonimplementation of domestic violence legislation
	Sindh High Court orders the formation of a committee to propose policies to address violence against women
2020	Sindh High Court–appointed committee makes its recommendations
2021	Sindh High Court orders the implementation of recommendations made by court-appointed committee
2023	Sindh government makes submission to court detailing the measures taken to implement court orders; submits the budget allocated toward one-stop protection centers but the centers are not yet functional

introduction of protection measures, many of which are not functional on a long-term basis. In the absence of these protection measures, few vulnerable people will avail themselves of the remedies offered under domestic-violence legislation.

DOMESTIC-VIOLENCE LEGISLATION IN PUNJAB

The pace of implementation of domestic-violence law in the province of Punjab has been similarly slow. In contrast to Sindh's law, however, some aspects of the law's language itself creates significant hurdles in the way of enforcement. The Punjab Protection of Women Against Violence Act was enacted in 2016. One unique and rather strange aspect of the law is a provision that says that it will not come into force immediately; rather it would only come into force in "areas" in the province after a notification issued by the provincial government. Initially, a notification was issued only for the division of Multan.[26] It was not until 2022 that the Protection of Women Against Violence Act became applicable in all of Punjab.[27] Rules to set up a framework of implementation have not yet been notified.

The government in Punjab at the time, the Pakistan Muslim League Nawaz (PML-N), was more conservative than that of the PPP in Sindh, and this is reflected in the definitions and the range of relief provided in the law. The definition of "domestic violence" in the Punjab law does not reflect a structural understanding of the phenomenon. It says that "domestic violence" means the violence committed by the defendant with whom the aggrieved person is living or has lived in a house or visits the house when they are related to each other by consanguinity, marriage, adoption or in terms of employment."[28] The law defines "violence" to include "domestic violence, sexual violence, psychological abuse, economic abuse, stalking or a cybercrime."[29] Unlike the Sindh law, however, it does not include emotional or verbal abuse.

The definition of "psychological" violence is highly restricted, and it covers only "psychological deterioration of aggrieved person which may result in anorexia, suicide attempt or clinically proven depression resulting from defendant's oppressive behaviour or limiting freedom of movement of the aggrieved person," and that these conditions must be "certified by a panel of psychologists appointed by District Women Protection Committee."[30] The limited scope of psychological abuse evinces an intent to restrict claims under this provision. Like the Sindh law, it provides for a range of remedies, such as protection and residence orders, to protect and provide redress to persons facing domestic violence. The law also provides for the establishment of protection centres and a district protection committee that is to supervise the work of the protection centres and women protection officers in each district who would coordinate a protection system in each district. Significantly, the Punjab law does not include criminal penalties for domestic violence.

In 2017, the Punjab Women Protection Authority Act was passed to create a legal framework for the establishment of protection centres. This authority overlaps with district protection committees to be set up according to the 2016 law. The year 2017 also saw the establishment of a large Violence Against Women Center in Multan that garnered much publicity. It was to serve as a "one-stop" centre for processing domestic-violence cases. The centre was to comprise a shelter facility, a medico-legal facility, a gender-based violence court and a police station. The centre brought all the required services under one roof to minimize the running from "pillar to post" that a woman has to do to file and pursue a case.

Challenges before the Federal Shariat Court

A significant obstacle in the way of the law's implementation came through petitions filed in the Federal Shariat Court, challenging the validity of the law on the basis that it violates Islamic injunctions. These challenges, filed in 2016, were dismissed by the Federal Shariat Court in 2022, but, during the pendency of the petitions, the validity of the law remained uncertain.[31]

The petitions were filed by lawyers and a charitable foundation, objecting to the 2016 Act on the ground that the law is "based upon the famous NGO vision rather slogan that 'male is always guilty.'"[32] This objection reflects the widespread belief that laws on violence against women are driven by malicious agendas of westernized NGOs. The petitioners objected to the fact that only women are entitled to relief under the law. The petition goes on to present its own analysis of domestic violence: "That in many cases it has been observed that in conflict and debate between the spouses, the wife abuses the husband and his family which again results in violence by the husband because the male is master of physical violence while the female is master of oral violence."[33] This can be summed up as a common patriarchal justification for gender-based violence: "she was asking for it."

One of the Quranic injunctions that the petition relies on is a verse in Surah An-Nisa, which says,

> So righteous women are devoutly obedient, guarding in [the husband's] absence what Allah would have them guard. But those [wives] from whom you fear arrogance—[first] advise them; [then, if they persist], forsake them in bed; **and [finally], strike them.** But if they obey you [once more], seek no means against them. Indeed, Allah is ever Exalted and Grand [emphasis added].

This verse is commonly cited by Muslims who maintain that domestic violence is justified in Islam.

The Federal Shariat Court reasoned that Islam permits a woman to lodge a complaint against her husband for mistreatment or his failure to perform his duties toward her, including financial maintenance. The court noted that widespread violence faced by women in Pakistan is no reflection of Islamic values but is rather the result of a "false sense of male chauvinism and unjustified sense of male patriarchy" and that "Islam took all the positive steps to eliminate such a misogynist attitude of men as a policy from society more than fourteen centuries ago."[34] This recognition by the Federal Shariat Court of the scourge of "male patriarchy" and "misogynist attitude" is significant and perhaps an indication of the effectiveness and wide reach of feminist activism around gender-based violence in Pakistan. It could also be a reaction to the continuous daily stream of reports in the media about violence against women and girls, including incidents of rape and murder, that have provoked some sense of urgency, even among the members of a typically conservative court.

Regarding the verse in Surah An-Nisa in the Quran, which has been translated to mean that a husband may "strike" or "beat" a woman, the Federal Shariat Court asserted that it "should not be read independently and out of context" and "it is not to be used to form a generalized principle."[35] Referring to interpretations by well-known scholars, the court said that such a measure is only permissible in "very exceptional situations" and the act should be avoided and "in a worst case scenario if it happens, then it should be in a manner that it will not leave any mark on her body."[36] The court goes on to say that a husband can never be permitted to beat his "wife black and blue" and that, if someone does that, then he can be held culpable under the 2016 Act.[37]

On the one hand, the court rejected the argument that the 2016 Act is inconsistent with injunctions in the Quran, but on the other hand it concluded that there are exceptional circumstances that may permit a man to beat his wife lightly as long as he does not leave her "black and blue." This does not reflect a "zero tolerance" approach to domestic violence. Predictably, the Federal Shariat Court adopted a strong protectionist approach in its reasoning. It did not disrupt the paradigm that the husband is the caretaker of his wife, she should be obedient to him, and, while he cannot beat her severely, there are certain circumstances in which he has the right to strike her.

The Federal Shariat Court also emphasized that differences between a husband and wife should be reconciled through mediation and noted with approval that the 2016 Act provides for the creation of protection centres and district protection committees that have the roles of mediation and reconciliation spelt out as among their responsibilities. The court found that a report from the Violence Against Women Center established in Multan on the progress of cases showed that a majority of cases were "successfully mediated/reunited/resolved" through the intervention of mediators at the centre. The report noted that the centre received complaints of 4,979 cases of domestic violence and, of these, 4,351 were mediated. On this basis, the Federal Shariat Court concluded that the mechanism is "quite satisfactory" and that the performance of the centre is "positive."[38]

The fact that a vast majority of cases lead to reconciliation led the Federal Shariat Court to conclude that the apprehensions of abuse of the law by the petitioners are not well-founded. The court concluded that the law was working effectively without considering whether the remedies provided in the law in the form of protection orders, residence orders, and monetary relief, were being utilized or how many court proceedings had been initiated under the law. The perception that the law and Violence Against Women Center was being used to facilitate reconciliation presented a stronger justification for the law, whereas the absence of accountability under the law helped to refute the petitioner's claim that the law will be misused. This perception of the Federal Shariat Court is in contrast to the impressions of civil-society actors and lawyers working with survivors of domestic violence, who as we will see below believe that the strong drive toward reconciliation in the Violence Against Women Center in Multan undermined the effectiveness of the centre as well as the 2016 legislation.

Implementation Challenges

The protection measures required under the 2016 and 2017 laws adopted in Punjab have encountered serious implementation challenges, similar to those experienced in Sindh. Although the construction of the facility was completed by 2017, the government of Punjab did not immediately allocate the required funds and personnel to make it fully functional.[39] The centre was built before the Woman Protection Authority designated to oversee the facility was established, which added to the problems with administration. Years elapsed before a police station was established at the premises. After elections were held in 2018, leadership of the Punjab government was taken over by PTI, which did not allocate sufficient funding to the centre in Multan or set up such centres in other districts in Punjab. As of 2022, the facility did not have a court or a functional health facility. The location of the centre—in the outskirts of the city of Multan—made it difficult to access the facility.

According to a report by the news website Lok Sujag, the manager of the centre in 2022 (who also served as senior psychologist and the woman protection officer for the district of Multan) says that a reason behind the poor functioning of the centre is a "lack of coordination among various government departments required to assist it in its working."[40] She notes that since "the employees of these departments are answerable only to their own superiors, they do not take our referrals seriously."[41] This is paradoxical since the main purpose behind establishing the centre was to solve coordination problems by bringing these services under one roof. Unfortunately, however, the creation of a physical facility that houses the required services did not lead to coordination among the departments responsible for these services. This indicates that the problem of fragmentation and noncoordination cannot be solved simply with the creation of a physical facility—even a state-of-the-art Violence Against Women Center at that—but requires transformations in working methods of the personnel inside the departments and their willingness and ability to cut through bureaucratic red tape to actually provide services to survivors. Bringing personnel performing different functions together under one roof will not improve services in practice if the personnel themselves do not work competently, are poorly resourced, and fail to coordinate with each other.

Lawyers with years of experience in working with domestic-violence survivors in Punjab say that while a one-stop location for women and vulnerable persons is a very useful measure in theory, the facility in Multan has fallen short of its potential largely due to the inability of the personnel stationed at the centre to handle cases effectively and provide the required services.[42] Senior lawyers at the Lahore-based NGO and access-to-justice centre Dastak say that, in the years after the centre was established, its primary role was mediation and its staff's priority in dealing with complaints was to bring about a compromise.[43] Staff at the centre made no use at all of the 2016 Protection of Women Against Violence Act and did not inform women of their options to seek any remedy under the law. Lawyers say that often women become disillusioned upon approaching the centre as its staff strongly encourages them to reconcile, even in instances of grave physical abuse when women clearly want accountability and an end to the relationship. Due to refusals of personnel at the centre to register criminal complaints or provide other adequate remedies, those who can turn to other lawyers or organizations offering pro bono legal help.

By 2023, public prosecutors were appointed to the Multan centre to provide legal support. That did not, however, lead to any significant increase in the utilization of the law, in large part because the prosecutors—whose primarily role is criminal prosecution—did not understand how to make use of a law that does not prescribe criminal penalties for violence. They did not see how they could approach courts for protection, residence orders, or monetary relief without simultaneously pursuing criminal charges against defendants. In a consultation organized by Dastak and Lahore University of Management Sciences on the implementation of the 2016 Act, the prosecutors insisted that the law was ineffective because it did not contain criminal penalties and there was not much they could do to enforce it.[44] In fact, the law does not require a person seeking the remedies of protection orders, residence orders, and monetary relief to simultaneously pursue criminal charges, but, because the prosecutors have such rigid notions about their role as criminal lawyers, they cannot conceive of any remedy in the absence of criminal prosecution. It also appears that they have little guidance or motivation from their supervisors in the prosecution department to file and pursue cases under the law, and this adds a layer of apathy to the confusion. Without meaningful training and mindset shifts, it is unlikely that staff appointed to the centre will have an effective impact.

The few cases that have been taken to court under the 2016 law have encountered serious hurdles.[45] The courts designated to hear cases under the law are confused by the scope of the law and apathetic about its enforcement. In Punjab's capital city of Lahore, the court of a senior civil judge in the family courts division was initially designated to hear cases under the law, but when Dastak's lawyer approached the court to file a case, the judge assigned to that court was not aware that she had jurisdiction. It took some time to convince the judge to assume jurisdiction, and then it took even more time to explain the terms of the law to the judge, who had never seen it before and was not aware of its existence. Eventually the lawyer obtained a protection order on behalf of her client, but it took three court hearings to achieve this result. For many women seeking immediate protection, waiting this long to get an order defeats its purpose entirely.

The appointment of the senior family judge to hear these cases is also ill-advised because the court is overburdened with family cases and does not have the capacity to bear the additional caseload.[46] It is likely that in order to avoid hearing a case and thus to limit their burden, courts would try to devise some procedural obstacle to avoid accepting jurisdiction over a case. For example, the senior family judge in Lahore insisted that only cases referred by government-designated women protection officers could be heard by the court and that cases brought directly by women through their lawyers were not admissible. It took some time for a lawyer to convince the judge that there is no such requirement under the law.[47]

Lawyers also say that one significant omission in Punjab's law is that it does not criminalize domestic violence.[48] The only criminal penalties set forth in the law are for violation of a protection, residence, or monetary order, for filing a "false complaint," or for obstructing the work of a protection officer. Domestic violence itself does not carry criminal penalties. According to some lawyers this has severely curtailed the deterrent effect of the law, and, in the absence of criminal convictions for domestic violence, the law will fail to make an impression. They believe that the law in Sindh, which specifically criminalises domestic violence, should have been adopted as a model. Experiences with the Sindh law, however, show that criminal convictions are very difficult to attain, and, according to lawyers and activists working with domestic violence survivors in Sindh, most women who seek remedies under the law do not wish to pursue criminal trials. Therefore, it is unclear whether the absence of criminal penalties in the Punjab legislation is a significant barrier to its utilization. At the same time, however, the experience in Punjab shows that remedies that should be attained expeditiously (such as protection orders), by bypassing the procedural requirements of a criminal trial, are not quick or accessible.

As a result, the 2016 law has had very little to no impact on domestic violence in Punjab. Although the lawyers at the shelter Dastak deal with domestic-violence cases on a day-to-day basis, they find that the law has been of little help to the women who approach them. Relief from courts is hard to come by, and, even when it does come, it is after so many delays that it becomes worthless in many cases. NGOs and lawyers working with survivors are often unable to recommend that women use this law because the uncertainty of getting relief and delays in proceedings do not justify the costs in time and money, costs that are borne by women.

SUBTLE AND OVERT BACKLASH

Enforcement of domestic-violence laws in Sindh and Punjab is painstaking. While this chapter does not cover the state of implementation in Khyber Pakhtunkhwa and Balouchistan, it is likely to be just as, if not more, fraught. Once these laws were passed, it is clear that the burden of implementation shifted to a large extent onto survivors themselves, their lawyers, and civil-society organizations with resources to come to their support. The state bureaucracies largely absolved themselves of responsibilities. Some additional push toward enforcement in Sindh came from the judiciary, with the directions of the Sindh High Court to the district judiciary, the Women Development Department, and the police. In Punjab, while the government took an optically appealing measure with the establishment of a large Violence Against Women Center in Multan, it did not invest sufficiently in personnel to make the place an effective site for protection and accountability. Nor did the Punjab government take adequate measures to support implementation in other parts of the province.

How this law is actually experienced by survivors of domestic violence, mostly women, is at best bewildering and at worst oppressive and humiliating. Even the more fortunate women, who were able to obtain remedies such as protection or residence orders, or even a conviction, were compelled to make multiple appearances in court and overcome skepticism and often hostility from law-enforcement officials, all while trying to keep their heads (and often those of their children) above water financially. Lawyers and activists assisting women with the police and before the courts must also repeatedly overcome obstacles imposed by the very authorities that are responsible for implementation of the law.

One obvious interpretation of the nonimplementation of domestic-violence laws is that the state lacks resources and capacities to provide effective services. Another, perhaps equally illuminating, explanation is that the nonimplementation is a subtle form of backlash against the legislation.

An analysis of the weak and inconsistent implementation of domestic-violence legislation in Bangladesh as "subtle backlash" by Maheen Sultan and Pragyna Mahpara, in their research for the Institute of Development Studies, provides a lens through which we can view experiences with laws in Pakistan.[49] The government in Bangladesh passed the Domestic Violence (Prevention and Protection) Act in 2010, but the implementation of the law remains lax. Service delivery in the form of shelters and trained counselors is weak. There is also a lack of "conceptual and technical understanding" among judges and lawyers, who are uncomfortable using the law.[50] Implementation also faces "bureaucratic resistance," with delays in the formation of rules and trainings of enforcement officials.[51] Analyzing these trends, Sultan and Mahpara propose that "there are deliberate efforts by the actors responsible for implementing the act to delegitimize the issue of domestic violence and deprioritize it by not allocating sufficient financial or human resources."[52] They note that "'[r]esistance' in some accounts includes processes that preserve the status quo such as institutional inertia and lack of support in the form of non-engagement understaffing, under-budgeting, insufficient gender training, and so on."[53] Resistance in times of "progressive change" is "manifested by the members of privileged groups (advantaged by the status quo) to restore, maintain, and increase their power position in contexts of inequality and injustice."[54] Even when backlash does not take the form of overt hostility, "it can take the form of trivializing gender issues through the demonstration of lack of interest, inaction, and non-participation."[55]

This resonates very well for those who work with domestic laws in Sindh and Punjab and observe both overt and subtle backlash to their implementation. At the federal level, there was an overt backlash against proposed domestic-violence legislation that prevented the passage of a law. In Punjab, the threat of backlash led to a relatively watered-down law—one that did not criminalize domestic violence and also did not become automatically effective in the absence of an additional bureaucratic step in the form of a notification. The unique provision in the law that said that it will be made effective in an "area" only upon notification indicates a reluctance even on the part of the legislature to fully implement legal guarantees. Overt backlash against the Punjab law came in the form of petitions challenging the validity of the law before the Federal Shariat Court, which were eventually dismissed. The more "subtle" forms of backlash in both Sindh and Punjab come in the form of poor investments in service delivery. The discomfort with domestic-violence legislation among key institutional actors is reflected in the deprioritization of government departments responsible for implementation of the legislation (women development departments and social welfare departments), underfunding of key mechanisms, and shortage of key personnel. It took six years for the Punjab law to be made applicable across the province. The lack of sustained support for the Violence Against Women Center in Multan is also evidence of the deliberate deprioritization of protection mechanisms.

This chapter's discussion on courts' attitudes shows that their lackadaisical response is not merely the result of poor understanding of the law but also a reflection of disagreement and discomfort with a law that provides for accountability for gender-based violence. This discomfort may not always be expressed in written orders, but it is present in the attitude toward survivors and their lawyers in court as well as the delays in hearings and the refusal to grant urgent relief. The conceptual confusion expressed by judges and prosecutors regarding procedures partly reflects a discomfort with the law.

What would happen if the subtle backlash was overcome and the law in Pakistan began to be more vigorously implemented, actually leading to accountability for perpetrators and more freedom for women to escape violent and abusive situations in their homes? Chances are that more overt and openly hostile forms of backlash would become stronger. The ongoing resistance to domestic-violence legislation in India perhaps helps us to predict reactions to domestic-violence legislation in Pakistan were it to more seriously implemented.

Section 498A was introduced to the Indian Penal Code in 1983, and, under this provision, any husband (or his relatives) who inflicts "cruelty" on his wife could face a criminal fine and imprisonment for up to three years. This is a cognizable (which means that the police may make an arrest without a warrant) and nonbailable offense. As noted by prominent women's-rights lawyers in India, Section 498A has been given a "bad name by constructing the image of a scheming wife"[56] who misuses the penal provision to blackmail her spouse. Section 498A of the Indian Penal Code has been criticised as a "poorly and vaguely formulated law that allows women to fake frivolous lawsuits that lead to innocent men and their relatives being arrested without investigation."[57] A "male rights" movement has coalesced around the perceived victimization of men under this law.[58]

In 2005, the Protection of Women from Domestic Violence Act (PWDVA) was passed, providing a range of civil remedies for domestic violence, including protection, residence, and monetary relief orders. The law was the first of its kind in India to recognize the concept of a "shared household and the right to residence of a woman in a shared relationship."[59] While PWDVA has been widely used by women in India to assert their rights in domestic relationships, there have also been criticisms of the law for including vague and overbroad provisions that are harmful for men and make them vulnerable to malicious prosecution and frivolous litigation. One criticism of PWDVA is that it defines domestic violence broadly and includes "insults" and "ridicule."[60] A complaint against the provision for residence orders in favor of men is that it could potentially render a man homeless.[61]

The constitutional validity of Section 498A of the PPC was challenged before the Indian Supreme Court on the basis that it has a propensity to be misused. The Indian Supreme Court held that mere possibility of misuse could not render the provision invalid. It warned, however, that a "legal terrorism can be unleashed" due to the misuse of the provision: "If cry of 'wolf' is made too often as a prank, assistance and protection may not be available when the actual 'wolf' appears."[62] Domestic-violence laws in India were also criticized by the Malimath Committee, which was formed in 2003 to propose reforms of the criminal-justice system. The committee concluded that Section 498A helps neither the wife nor the husband in a domestic-violence situation.[63] The report claimed that "[s]ince it makes "cruelty" both a nonbailable and noncompoundable offense, innocent individuals are regularly arrested and imprisoned, leading to stigmatization and both mental and physical hardships."[64] According to the Malimath Committee Report, reconciliation or return to the marital home becomes practically impossible as a result. However, the committee provided no data to show how frequently Section 498A is misused.[65]

This scale of overt backlash to the domestic-violence law in India is not seen in Pakistan, most likely due to the fact that it has not had a strong impact on patriarchal hierarchy due to poor implementation. If and when it is more widely used, however, it is quite possible that similar campaigns will be launched against the legislation.

INCREMENTAL IMPLEMENTATION?

The discussion in this chapter shows that implementation of domestic-violence laws in Sindh and Punjab is slowly taking place, even though it is moving at a snail's pace. This suggests that ambitious laws that may not have broad societal and cultural support in the short term can be implemented on an incremental, gradual basis. But the enforcement of the laws has been driven primarily through efforts and energies of survivors, activists, civil-society organisations, and lawyers who push reluctant state actors to comply with their legal duties.

Laws and the implementation mechanisms that they provide are not, by their very nature, sufficient to make a dent in the endemic problem of gender-based violence. The problem of gender-based violence is so intertwined with social attitudes and cultural norms that an imposition of laws and rules from government institutions will remain inadequate. The laws rely on existing institutions—the police, the judiciary, and the civil bureaucracy—to implement laws that are tackling very deeply ingrained, socially and culturally sanctioned practices. The law's reliance on committees comprising bureaucrats and district-level officers to implement the law reflects faith in top-down bureaucratic structures to monitor and promote enforcement of the law. This poses a serious challenge because the gender biases existing in society as a whole permeate all state institutions, and they filter how these laws are viewed and enforced by state actors. Courts adopt a judgmental and even incredulous attitude toward domestic-violence complaints, and their encouragement of reconciliation and compromise over accountability undermines the effectiveness of the law. The bureaucracy does not fund or staff mechanisms required for effective implementation of the law.

Laws passed to regulate gender-based violence have symbolic value. The passage of domestic-violence laws signals the acceptance of the state of its responsibility to take measures against domestic violence. This chapter asks us to consider, however, whether the symbolic value of the law is undermined by backlash. The passage of progressive laws, even those based on rich understanding of the structural causes of gender-based violence, will by itself be inadequate to prevent domestic violence. Therefore, there must be parallel efforts to work toward reform of social structures and mindsets that promote domestic violence and, at the same time, empower survivors, with the help of their support networks, to advocate for themselves before unyielding state actors and institutions.

In the first chapter, I discussed three broad criticisms of the movement to end violence against women: it encourages an essentialist perception of women, especially women belonging to developing countries, as voiceless victims persecuted by rigid and timeless cultural values and traditions; this movement's advocacy tends to support and promote the punitive powers of the state; its agenda foregrounds gender hierarchy as the central cause of all oppression of women and girls, including violence, while obscuring the impact of structural economic inequalities in societies. The push to enact and implement domestic-violence legislation in Pakistan should be sensitive to these concerns.

Feminists should be mindful of the risk that domestic-violence laws reinforce tropes of women as perpetual, passive victims. We see this reflected in the application of certain protection mechanisms, such as shelters that severely restrict women's freedom of movement for the sake of their protection. We also see that support for domestic-violence laws from some institutions, such as the Federal Shariat Court, relies on stereotypical notions of men as benevolent protectors of women who must look after them and discipline them without being unnecessarily aggressive. Proponents of domestic-violence laws often push for strong criminal penalties, without reflecting on the extent to which such advocacy legitimises the punitive powers of the state. While police intervention and incarceration may be necessary in some situations—particularly given the absence of noncarceral forums for effective accountability—feminists should critically engage with the real and potential consequences of their advocacy for carceral interventions.

This chapter discusses how remedies offered in the law are inaccessible to women who do not have the economic resources to access legal institutions and are also stuck in violent family relations because they are unable to financially sustain themselves or their children. Domestic-violence legislation in Pakistan assumes that all women are able make use of the law equally, when in reality women from poor or low-income backgrounds will often be unable to escape violence due to financial constraints and the absence of state-supported welfare mechanisms. Women activists who wish to see enforcement of domestic-violence law must consider the differential impact of domestic violence and varying utility of legal options on differently situated women as they work toward implementation.

NOTES

1. Punjab Commission on the Status of Women, "Sheltering Women from Harm: Dar-ul-Amans of Punjab," 2016, <https://pcsw.punjab.gov.pk/system/files/ShelteringWomenfromHarmDarulAmansofPunjabAchievementsandChallenges2016.pdf>, accessed August 12, 2024.
2. Hassan Shehzad, "'The Female Warriors," *The News*, January 25, 2022, <https://www.thenews.com.pk/magazine/you/926944-the-female-warriors>, accessed August 12, 2024.
3. Criminal Law (Second Amendment) Act 2011.
4. National Institute of Population Studies (NIPS) and ICF, *Pakistan Demographic and Health Survey 2017-18* (NIPS and ICF, 2019).
5. *Dawn*, "Domestic Violence Bill to Push Up Divorce Rate: CII," *Dawn*, Islamabad, August 25, 2009, https://www.dawn.com/news/855084/domestic-violence-bill-to-push-up-divorce-rate-cii, accessed August 12, 2024.
6. Zahid Gishkori, "Domestic Violence Bill a Copy of Indian Law: Fazl," *The Express Tribune*, Islamabad, April 7, 2012, https://tribune.com.pk/story/360999/domestic-violence-bill-a-copy-of-indian-law-fazl, accessed August 12, 2024.

7. Sindh Domestic Violence Act 2013, Sections 5(f), (l) and (o).

8. "The IBAHRI Commends Pakistan's Landmark Ruling in Marital Rape Case," International Bar Association, February 15, 2024, https://www.ibanet.org/The-IBAHRI-commends-Pakistans-landmark-ruling-in-marital-rape-case, accessed August 12, 2024.

9. Maliha Zia Lari, Associate Director, Legal Aid Society, by Sara Malkani, Karachi, January 17, 2023.

10. The name has been changed to protect identity.

11. The data were received by the author from the registrar of Sindh High Court on November 30, 2023.

12. The name has been changed to protect confidentiality.

13. The name has been changed to protect confidentiality.

14. "Shaheed Benazir Bhutto Human Rights Centers for Women (Crisis Centers)," Social Welfare & Bait-Ul-Maal Department Government of Punjab, https://swd.punjab.gov.pk/crisis_centres, accessed August 12, 2024.

15. "Mother and Children Homes (Dar-ul-Falah)," Social Welfare & Bait-Ul-Maal Department Government of Punjab, https://swd.punjab.gov.pk/mother_and_children_homes, accessed August 12, 2024.

16. Nazish Brohi, "Gap Analysis of Service Providers for Gender-Based Violence in Punjab and Sindh," Oxfam and Legal Aid Society, 2020, 5.

17. *Dawn*, "SHC Wants Darul Aman Employee Booked for Rape of Inmates," *Dawn*, Karachi, May 4, 2021, <https://www.dawn.com/news/1621937>, accessed August 12, 2024.

18. *Dawn*, "SHC Wants Probe Report in Darul Aman Rape Case Submitted in Time, Offenders Tried," *Dawn*, Karachi, May 16, 2021, <https://www.dawn.com/news/1623789>, accessed August 12, 2024.

19. Submission by Sindh Police to the Sindh High Court, October 9, 2023, in C.P. S-728 of 2016.

20. Dr. Asha Bedar and Farieha Aziz, "Domestic Violence in the Time of COVID-19 and Beyond: A Situational Analysis," *Bayan Bi-Annual Socio-legal Journal* vol. VII (December 2021).

21. Farieha Aziz, "Dealing with VAW," *The News*, June 27, 2020, https://www.thenews.com.pk/print/678241-dealing-with-vaw, accessed August 13, 2024.

22. *Mst. Hina v. Province of Sindh and 4 Others* (2019) PLD Sindh 363.

23. Ibid.

24. Recommendations submitted by a court-appointed committee in C.P. 728 of 2016 before the Sindh High Court on October 12, 2020.

25. Constitutional Petition No. S-728 of 2016 before the Sindh High Court, Order dated September 19, 2023.

26. Nadeem Shah, "Pakistan's First 'Violence Against Women Center' Inaugurated in Multan," *The News*, Multan, March 29, 2017, <https://www.thenews.com.pk/latest/195270-Pakistans-first-Violence-Against-Women-Center-inaugurated-in-Multan>, accessed August 13, 2024; Xari Jalil, "Punjab Domestic Violence Act: Black and Blue But Nowhere To Go," Voicepk.net, Lahore, August 22, 2022, <https://

voicepk.net/2022/08/punjab-domestic-violence-act-black-and-blue-but-nowhere-to-go/>, accessed August 13, 2024.

27. Social Welfare and Bait-ul-Maal Department, Government of Punjab Notification No. SO(D)1-56/2017(P-VI), dated November 18, 2022; *The Friday Times*, "Punjab Protection of Women Against Violence Act 2016 Notified Across Punjab," *The Friday Times*, December 12, 2022, <https://thefridaytimes.com/12-Dec-2022/punjab-protection-of-women-against-violence-act-2016-notified-across-punjab>, accessed August 13, 2024.

28. Punjab Protection of Women Against Violence Act 2016, Section 2(h).

29. Ibid., Section 2(r).

30. Ibid.

31. *Professor Muhammad Ibrahim Khan and others v. Province of Punjab and Others* (2023) PLD Federal Shariat Court 1.

32. Ibid., para (a).

33. Ibid., para (b).

34. Ibid., para 14 (ii).

35. Ibid., para 22.

36. Ibid., (23).

37. Ibid., (24).

38. Ibid., para 34, 37.

39. Fatima Razzaq, "Victim of Neglect: Multan's Center for Helping Women in Distress Fails to Achieve Its Objective," *Lok Sujag*, March 24, 2022, https://loksujag.com/story/violence-against-women-centre-multan, accessed August 13, 2024.

40. Ibid.

41. Ibid.

42. Saba Sheikh and Sabahat Riaz, senior staff at the NGO and shelter, Dastak, interview by Sara Malkani and Farieha Aziz, November 24, 2023.

43. Ibid.

44. Lahore University of Management Sciences (LUMS), Dastak, and Punjab Women Protection Authority, "Legal Experts Consultation on the Implementation of the Punjab Protection of Women Against Violence Act 2016," Lahore, June 5–6, 2023.

45. Interview, n 42.

46. Interview, n 42.

47. Interview, n 42.

48. LUMS, n 44.

49. Maheen Sultan and Pragyna Mahpara, "Backlash in Action? Or Inaction? Stalled Implementation of the Domestic Violence (Prevention and Protection) Act 2010 in Bangladesh," vol. 2023, no. 590 (working paper, Institute of Development Studies, 2023).

50. Ibid., 23.

51. Ibid.

52. Ibid., 11.

53. Ibid., 17.

54. Ibid., 16.

55. Ibid.

56. Indira Jaising and Pinki Mathur Anurag, eds., *Unscrambling the Images: Conflict in the Shared Household in Conflict in the Shared Household* (Oxford University Press, 2019), 4.

57. Rehan Abeyratne and Dipika Jain, "Domestic Violence Legislation in India: The Pitfalls of a Human Rights Approach to Gender Equality," *American University Journal of Gender, Social Policy & the Law* 21, no. 2 (2013): 333, 355.

58. Ibid.

59. Jaising, n 56, 19.

60. Abeyratne, n 57, 337.

61. Abeyratne, n 57, 349.

62. *Sushil Kumar Sharma v. Union of India and Others* (2005) 6 SCC 281 Supreme Court of India.

63. Abeyratne, n 57, 356.

64. Ibid.

65. Ibid., 357.

Chapter 5

Upholding Formal Justice

Activism against Honour Killings and Jirgas

A precursor to legislative advocacy around domestic violence in Pakistan was the widespread activism around honour killings. Honour killings are a particularly persistent form of gender-based violence. Over the last few decades a number of high-profile cases of honour killings have rocked Pakistan's state and society. One such honour killing was the murder of Samia Sarwar in her lawyers' office by her mother and her mother's attendant in 1999. Samia Sarwar, a young woman from Peshawar, had left her husband and planned to remarry against the wishes of her parents. Fearing that her parents would murder her for violating the family's honour, Samia Sarwar sought refuge in Dastak, a shelter run by renowned lawyer and human-rights defender, Hina Jilani. At her mother's insistence, Samia Sarwar agreed to a meeting in her lawyer's office. There she was shot dead by her mother's male attendant.[1] This incident triggered an uproar among women's-rights groups, who demanded accountability for the heinous crime, which was committed in front of witnesses in the office of a prominent lawyer and human-rights defender. No one was punished for the crime.

Almost seventeen years after this murder took place, one of Pakistan's most famous social media celebrities, Qandeel Baloch, was murdered at the age of twenty-six by her brother, who said that she brought shame to her family.[2] Qandeel Baloch's provocative social media posts scandalized viewers and garnered a huge following across Pakistan for their humor and innuendo. While media reports of murders of women by their family members in Pakistan are common, Baloch's murder struck a nerve. Qandeel Baloch was viewed by many feminists as an iconoclast who challenged stereotypes about the "good" Pakistani woman. Feminists, outraged that she was murdered because of her provocation to patriarchal morality, organized several protests and raised their voices in the media. Qandeel Baloch's brother was arrested for the murder, and he confessed to the crime. A trial court convicted him of murder, but, in 2022, the Lahore High Court overturned the conviction.[3]

The years between Samia Sarwar's unpunished murder and the acquittal of Qandeel Baloch's brother were years of intense advocacy by women's-rights activists on honour killings in Pakistan. They were also years of law reform. Amendments were made to the Pakistan Penal Code and the Code of Criminal Procedure in 2004 and then in 2016, with the goal of increasing the number of convictions for honour killings. But continuing incidents of murders of women by family members, followed by acquittal of those accused, show that impunity for these crimes persists despite legal changes.

This chapter will discuss the limitations of the legal interventions. Much of the advocacy around honour killings in Pakistan has focused on opposition to the Qiyas and Diyat amendments to the Pakistan Penal Code that were first introduced in an ordinance in 1990 and finally enacted in 1997. These amendments made it possible for legal heirs of murder victims to waive criminal punishments of perpetrators. I discuss the amendments in this chapter and explore why advocacy efforts to reverse these changes have not yet met with success. I also question whether the desired legal change, if achieved, will have a significant impact on honour killings in light of other causes of impunity that will persist in spite of reversals of the Qiyas and Diyat amendments. The chapter goes on to discuss a related cause taken up by the women's-rights movement in Pakistan: condemnation of informal justice processes (jirgas, panchayats, faislo). Advocacy against these processes is premised on a hope in the formal justice system. I suggest that experiences with advocacy around honour killings as well as informal justice forums raise questions about the extent to which reliance on formal justice systems is practical and desirable. These questions are similar to those raised in previous chapters about the effectiveness of criminal laws to address rape, child marriage, and domestic violence.

Honour killings in Pakistan are rooted in cultural practices, such as *karo kari* in Sindh, which literally means "black man, black woman." *Karo kari* is a "practice enforceable by any individual, specifically any man, whose *ghairat*—a timeless, natural and therefore unquestionable ideology of honour—has been violated."[4] The murder is an act of punishment by a male relative of a woman against a woman or man for engaging in sexual relations that violate patriarchal honour.

In her in-depth study of honour killings in Upper Sindh, scholar and legislator Nafisa Shah notes that, often, killings labeled *karo kari* are not in fact motivated by violations of *ghairat*, i.e., due to illicit sexual relations. Instead, men often use custom "strategically, whether for private gain, to harm their enemies, or to rid themselves of women they don't want."[5] Honour or *ghairat* is therefore a pretext to give cultural sanction to murders that have different motives. Outside of Sindh, the specific labels and particular cultural norms around these marriages may differ, but they are motivated by similar claims of patriarchal honour that are sanctified by culture.

One reason why honour killings do not result in convictions is that family members of the perpetrators and the victims reach settlements which effectively end the prosecution of the case. Often the process for arriving at the settlement involves community-driven "mediation," which has different names across the country. These community-based processes are typically led by groups of male elders known as jirgas in Khyber Pakhtunkhwa, as panchayat in Punjab, and as *faislo* in Sindh. These groups facilitate a compromise between family members that eventually leads to "forgiveness" and the withdrawal of any criminal complaint. These processes operate outside the formal justice system and prescribe certain terms for compromise between feuding parties. Such jirgas play an important role not only in honour killing but also in other crimes, including sexual violence against women, to facilitate a compromise in lieu of criminal penalties. Women's-rights activists have claimed that the role played by such institutions—sometimes called "parallel" or informal justice systems—is crucial toward perpetuating honour killings, among other crimes against women.

As Nafisa Shah has shown in her book, however, it is a mistake to consider the community-based dispute-resolution process as "parallel" to or operating in opposition to or even outside of the criminal-justice system. Instead, Shah writes that, due to amendments in Pakistan's criminal laws, specifically the Qisas and Diyat amendments, "homicides legally [become] private offences to be settled by kin" and "the dominant form of justice is self-help followed by mediations both through judicial officers and private mediators."[6] She states that so-called parallel or informal justice processes are incorporated in formal justice through the Qisas and Diyat amendments.

QISAS AND DIYAT AMENDMENTS

The Pakistan Penal Code is inherited from the colonial era. Prior to amendments from 1990 onward, the provision on murder was based on common-law definitions of the crime. Section 300 of the Pakistan Penal Code defined murder as an act by which a person causes the death of another person with the intention to cause death or with the intention to cause grave bodily harm that the offender knows is likely to cause death. The section set forth certain exceptions to "culpable murder." An exception to murder, framed by courts as "grave and sudden provocation," was used by courts to mitigate the offence of murders of women by husbands and family members where the motive for the murder was alleged sexual deviance by the woman.[7] Courts would consistently categorize such murders as manslaughter and thereby impose a lenient sentence on the husband. Women's-rights activists criticized this approach of courts, saying that it legitimized accusations of unchastity against women as a justification for violence and led to lenient sentences for husbands and family members who committed honour killings.[8]

Certain crimes in the Pakistan Penal Code are deemed to be "compoundable." This means that punishment for the offence could be mitigated or excused entirely if the victim of the offence does not press the criminal case and enters into a compromise with the accused. Prior to the Qisas and Diyat amendments, murder was not a compoundable offence, which meant that the state was required to prosecute the crime irrespective of whether the parties reached a compromise.

The move toward amending the Pakistan Penal Code provisions on bodily harm first came with a 1980 decision of the Shariat Appellate Bench of the Peshawar High Court.[9] A murder convict filed an appeal before the Shariat Appellate Bench on the ground that he was convicted under Pakistan Penal Code provisions that are contrary to Islam. The Peshawar High Court ruled that the Pakistan Penal Code provisions are contrary to Islam, based on interpretations of Shariah that require the option for a compromise between the heirs of the murder victim and the perpetrator. The court decided that Pakistan Penal Code, to be consistent with Islam, must permit compromise for murder and declared that the only forms of punishment that are allowed under Islamic law are retaliation (*qisas*), compensation (*diyat*), or a pardon.[10]

In 1980, Zia replaced Shariah benches in high courts with the Federal Shariat Court, which passed a judgment on several petitions tagged together for determination of the same point: the consistency of the Pakistan Penal Code provisions with Islamic law. The Federal Shariat Court declared that the murder provisions must be amended to allow for compromise between the parties. It agreed with the Shariah bench of the Peshawar High Court that, under Shariah law, the forms of punishment prescribed for murder are retaliation (*qisas*) or compensation to the heirs of the murder victim (*diyat*).[11]

Zia's government at the time was reluctant to make the required amendments. This is in contrast to his government's zeal to introduce other purportedly Shariah-based laws, such as the Hudood Ordinances. This reluctance can be explained in large part by the fact that the Peshawar High Court and Federal Shariat Court decisions came soon after Prime Minister Zulfiqar Ali Bhutto's execution following his conviction for murder and death sentence. Z. A. Bhutto, who had been removed from office and charged with murder after Zia's military coup, pled that he be tried under Islamic law.[12] The option of compromise or diyat was not offered to him, however. The execution of Z. A. Bhutto was condemned by large swathes of the population, and, in this environment, Zia was reluctant to make changes to the murder provisions in the Pakistan Penal Code that many would say should have been applied to Z. A. Bhutto. To stall amendments, his government appealed the Federal Shariat Court decision before the Shariat Appellate Bench of the Supreme Court.

The Shariat Appellate Bench of the Supreme Court did not reach its decision until 1989. By this time Zia had been killed in a plane crash and Prime Minister Benazir Bhutto's government was in office. The Supreme Court's Shariat Appellate Bench declared that all provisions related to bodily harm, including murder, in the Pakistan Penal Code were against Islam.[13] It affirmed that the punishment for murder under the Penal Code must be retaliation (*qisas*) or compensation as compromise (*diyat*). It also declared that the Code of Criminal Procedure must be amended to permit compromise or compoundability for murder at any stage in the criminal process. The Supreme Court noted that in some circumstances a lesser punishment (*tazir*) than retaliation for bodily harm may be imposed. It ordered that the Pakistan Penal Code provisions on bodily harm would cease to have effect from March 23, 1990 onward, giving the government a few months to make the required amendments to the Pakistan Penal Code.

The amendments were introduced as an ordinance in September 1990. By then, Benazir Bhutto's government had been removed, and an interim government was in power. The Qisas and Diyat amendments to the Pakistan Penal Code kept being renewed as an ordinance for seven years. They were not passed by a parliament until 1997, when Prime Minister Nawaz Sharif's party, the Pakistan Muslim League (PML), held a majority. In a session that was boycotted by the opposition due to the failure of the government to follow parliamentary procedure, the Criminal Law Amendment Act II of 1997 was passed swiftly with no debate.[14]

The Qisas and Diyat amendments to the Pakistan Penal Code were deemed highly controversial from the outset. In his richly detailed study of these provisions, Tahir Wasti has described the weaknesses in the reasoning underlying the court judgments, including the Supreme Court's Shariat Appellate Bench decision of 1989, that led to the introduction of the ordinances and finally the enactment.[15] The law drafted in compliance with the Supreme Court judgment was very vague and filled with lacunae. It entirely altered the chapter on bodily harm in the Pakistan Penal Code and introduced *qisas*, *diyat*, and *tazir* as punishments without clear definitions. The exceptions for murder incorporated in the erstwhile Section 300 of the Pakistan Penal Code, including that of a killing committed in a "sudden fight," were removed. No clear guidance as to how these punishments were to be administered was provided in the Pakistan Penal Code or the Code of Criminal Procedure. From a criminal justice lens, the courts' requirement that compromise be permitted between legal heirs of a murder victim and the perpetrator in lieu of punishment meant that murder would be treated as a private crime rather than as a violation of public peace and morality that must be punished by the state, regardless of the preferences of the victim's family members. From a Shariah-based perspective, the interpretations of Islamic jurisprudence made by the courts were not well founded and, according to scholar Tahir Wasti, ignored opinions of many Islamic jurists that punishments for murder under Shariah are not restricted to the categories set forth in court judgements.[16]

The amendments engendered confusion among law-enforcement officials and the judiciary as to how crimes involving bodily harm were to be tried and prosecuted. Soon after the amendment was introduced as an ordinance, compromise applications filed by heirs of murder victims began to flood the trial courts. Courts often allowed these applications without proper scrutiny as to whether the compromise was genuine and entered into without coercion and whether the terms of the compromise were actually executed.[17] Courts also allowed for exchange of a woman or girl as a bride as a compromise. The Supreme Court, in the case of *Yara v. State*,[18] permitted giving a daughter to a party as a bride as a valid term for compromise for murder. In 2005, the Pakistan Penal Code was amended to criminalize exchange of women and girls as a compromise to avoid criminal liability.[19] Since the law permits compromise at any stage in the criminal proceeding, a large number of cases are compromised even before a police investigation is initiated and the accused is formally charged.[20]

Courts were and to this day continue to be confused about the application of the new Section 311 in the Pakistan Penal Code. This section permits courts to overrule a compromise where the murder involves *fasad fil arz*, which means that the past conduct or criminal convictions of the accused or the "brutal or shocking manner" in which the crime had been committed could be considered by courts to overrule compromise and punish a murder.[21] Under the 1997 enactment, where *fasad fil arz* was applicable, courts could impose a penalty of up to fourteen years of imprisonment, irrespective of whether a compromise was reached between the accused and legal heirs.[22] Courts, however, adopted different criteria to determine whether or not they could overrule a compromise. In the case of *Ijaz Ahmed v. The State*,[23] the Lahore High Court overruled a decision of the trial court to convict an accused under *fasad fil arz* for a period of fourteen years. The convict murdered his sister after he discovered that she had not ironed his clothes by shooting her multiple times with a pistol. The heirs of the victim, who were also family members of the accused, informed the trial court that they forgave him, but the trial court found that the manner in which the murder was committed was brutal and that therefore it could sentence the perpetrator to prison under the principle of *fasad fil arz*. The Lahore High Court disagreed with the trial court's decision and ruled that *fasad fil arz* was not applicable because the accused did not have a record of conviction. Such rulings undermined the ability of courts to overrule compromises even in cases where they deem the murder to be a crime against the state and society as a whole, given its brutal and shocking nature.

The Qisas and Diyat amendments undermine the capacity of the state to punish perpetrators of murder. Women's-rights activists have observed that their impact on murders of women, especially murders in the name of honour, was particularly damaging. Given the difficulty of collecting accurate data on honour killings, it is difficult to determine the exact extent to which incidents of honour killings increased after the Qisas and Diyat amendments.[24] Nafisa Shah's analysis of crime records in Sindh covering the period from 1995 to 2004 show that approximately 3 percent of honour killings end in convictions at the trial-court level.[25] Women tend to be murdered by family members. Since their murderers are often related to their legal heirs, their murders are likely to be compromised. A major criticism of the Qisas and Diyat amendments therefore came from women's-rights activists who emphasised their role in perpetuating impunity for honour crimes. Their advocacy led to the first set of changes to the Qisas and Diyat laws with the Criminal Law Amendment Act of 2004.

Amendments in 2004

The Criminal Law (Amendment) Act of 2004 attempted to carve out exceptions for honour killings. It introduced a definition of honour killing[26] and provided that, in case the court determines that an honour killing has taken place, it has the discretion to impose a punishment, irrespective of compromise, and that punishment must be no less than ten years.[27] One problem with the application of these provisions is that they base the categorization of honour killing on the motivation of the perpetrator. To avoid falling under this caveat for honour killings, a perpetrator may claim that he had a motive other than honour, and there is likely to be little objective evidence to disprove this claim. The 2004 amendments also forbade the offering of a woman or girl as a bride as compensation to legal heirs of murder victims.[28]

The most significant limitation of these amendments is that they did not remove the possibility of compromise for honour killings and that discretion remained with the judge to accept such a compromise. The key demand of the women's-rights activists that the honour killings be made noncompoundable was not met. In large part, therefore, these changes were cosmetic. As noted in a report by the Aurat Foundation, the amendments did not make punishment for honour crimes mandatory, "which makes the purpose of introducing the legislation redundant."[29] Shahla Zia, lawyer and founder of the Aurat Foundation was one of the key drafters of the legislative bill that was handed to the Ministry of Women Affairs for vetting before it was introduced on the floor of the parliament. Her draft of the bill, however, was "severely 'mutilated' with the final outcome that its most vital clauses were dropped when it was passed by the National Assembly."[30] Even though the 2004 amendments were initiated in response to activists' objections to the option of compromise for murder, the law that was eventually enacted did not make any substantive changes to the Qisas and Diyat amendments. Acquittals for honour killings persisted.

Amendments in 2016

Activists continued to highlight impunity for honour killings over the years. In 2016, the Oscar-winning documentary by Sharmeen Obaid Chinoy, "Girl in the River: Price of Forgiveness," depicted the outcome of criminal laws that permit compromise for the crime of honour killing. The documentary followed the story of a woman whose father attempted to kill her for eloping with a man and depicted the pressures placed on her and the rest of her family to forgive and close criminal proceedings against him. The film highlighted how the Qisas and Diyat amendments create a legal basis for acquittal of perpetrators of honour crimes. Pakistan's Senate passed a unanimous resolution congratulating Sharmeen Obaid Chinoy for the Oscar win and declared, "[s]he has highlighted the issue of honour killing which has created awareness in the society and the determination to deter such killings."[31]

The international women's-rights organisation, Equality Now, went on to partner with Obaid Chinoy to advocate for law reform. In a press release, the organisation stated that the film "has re-invigorated a focus on 'honor' killings in Pakistan, and in February, the Prime Minister Nawaz Sharif publicly declared his intention to end them."[32] The press release said that the government will "advocate for a strong law in Pakistan that makes no allowances for compromise or forgiveness in 'honor' crime cases."[33] A few months after the much-celebrated Oscar victory, social media celebrity Qandeel Balouch was murdered by her brother.

The momentum generated by the Oscar win and protests surrounding Qandeel Balouch's murder provided impetus for further tinkering with the law, and another set of amendments were made to the Pakistan Penal Code and the Code of Criminal Procedure in 2016. The Criminal Law (Amendment) (Offences in the name or pretext of honour) Act 2016 was passed by the parliament in October 2016.

As with the amendments made in 2004, the 2016 legal changes did not in fact make honour killings noncompoundable. The 2016 law amended *fasad fil arz* to specifically include murders "committed in the name of or on the pretext of honour."[34] It also provided that, where the trial court exercises its discretion to award a punishment irrespective of a compromise or waiver for an honour killing, the punishment must be imprisonment for life and no less.[35] This provision did not, however, make it mandatory for the court to overrule compromise for honour killings. Further, this provision only applies where the "right of *qisas*" has been waived, and *qisas* is only applicable where the highest burden of proof under Islamic law is met. In all other cases, the lesser punishment of *tazir* will be applicable, which may be compounded by legal heirs at any stage in the criminal proceeding through the Qisas and Diyat amendments to the Code of Criminal Procedure.[36]

Therefore, the 2016 amendments, much like the 2004 amendments, made largely cosmetic changes to the Pakistan Penal Code and the Code of Criminal Procedure, which left the impact of the Qisas and Diyat amendments untouched. In contrast to the 2004 amendments, however, the 2016 law created an impression among the public and media that it made substantive changes to the law. Some NGOs that campaigned for legal changes celebrated the amendments. Media around the world reported that Pakistan's parliament has "closed the loophole" that enabled perpetrators of honour killings to go free.[37] The NGO, Global Citizen, that launched the hashtag Levelthelaw celebrated that the Pakistan government had "stepped up," saying that,

> Today, thanks to the new law, all perpetrators will receive a mandatory sentence of 25 years for those convicted of honor killings. Families can only pardon the murderer if he is facing a death sentence, but the pardon will not affect the prison sentence.[38]

This is incorrect, as the 2016 law does no such thing. The misplaced celebration around the 2016 law means that many in Pakistan, including activists and journalists, are surprised when they observe that compromise for murders, including honour killings, continue to take place. In May 2023, a man who killed his nineteen-year-old daughter in Karachi's city court because she married against her family's wishes was acquitted after his wife and other children forgave him.[39] After this incident was reported in the media, I was contacted by journalists and activists and asked to explain how the court allowed this compromise even after the 2016 amendments. I explained that the 2016 amendments did not prohibit compromise for murder, but this came as a surprise to many, including activists and experts who had been working on this issue for years.

Why do misconceptions about the 2016 amendments persist? One reason is that global organisations, such as Equality Now and Global Citizen, projected a wrong impression about the impact of the amendments and Pakistan-based

NGOs did not do much to dispel the impression. In contrast to the response to the 2004 amendments, where NGOs and women activists conveyed emphatically that the legal changes fall far short of the desired goal, the 2016 amendments were not met with the same degree of criticism.

Another reason for the ongoing misconceptions about the 2016 law is that lawmakers added another layer of complicated language to the already convoluted Pakistan Penal Code provisions, and this made it very difficult to understand their effect. I have mentioned that the Qisas and Diyat amendments, as they were introduced in 1990 in an ordinance and finally enacted in 1997, were ambiguous and ridden with lacunae. The 2004 amendments added more complexity by inserting definitions of honour killings and introducing new penalties. The 2016 amendments added yet more definitions, explanations, and cross-references to other provisions. The complexity and ambiguity of the 2016 amendments made it difficult to decipher their meaning, and so many people simply accepted the representations made about the law without reading it or understanding it themselves. Seasoned criminal lawyer, Asad Jamal, wrote after the amendments were passed in an article titled, *How Not to Legislate*,

> Notwithstanding the joy over the passage of the amended law, it is a classic example of how parliaments should not legislate. The fundamental issues have been left unaddressed. At the root of the problem lies a lack of understanding of, and training in, good legislative drafting skills and process. Besides, unlike what some people think, it does not make forgiveness or compromise—with or without monetary consideration—impossible.[40]

Statutory drafting must always aim for clarity to promote enforceability. Not only did the Qisas and Diyat amendments make murder a compoundable offence, they also created ambiguity in the Pakistan Penal Code provisions on murder and bodily harm, leading to difficulties in enforcement of the law by police and judges seeking to address these very serious offences.

TO WHAT EXTENT ARE THE QISAS AND DIYAT AMENDMENTS THE PROBLEM?

While activism around honour killings in Pakistan has paid much attention to the Qisas and Diyat amendments, it is useful to take a step back and ask to what extent are acquittals for honour killings a consequence of these provisions and, conversely, to what extent will the reversal of these amendments promote convictions for honour killings.

The opposition to the Qisas and Diyat amendments is that they impede successful criminal prosecution for honour killings. Before I assess this position, it is important to articulate that the claim presupposes that criminal prosecution will in fact prevent honour killings and promote gender justice. Successful criminal prosecutions could be a desired goals for two reasons. First, it is possible that the convictions would deter perpetrators of honour killings and therefore reduce the incidence of the crime. It should be acknowledged, however, that the assumption that convictions do in fact deter every crime is subject to some debate, but we will leave aside that debate for now.[41] Another reason for advocating against impunity for honour crimes is not that convictions would necessarily deter commission of the crime, but that convictions would send a message from the state to society that it deems honour killings to be a crime that it will prosecute. Even if this does not reduce the incidence of honour killings specifically, it would lead to an overall improvement in gender justice across state institutions and society as a whole. It is important to recognize that the criticism of the Qisas and Diyat amendments as being an impediment to gender justice is based on these two assumptions that may or not be correct, since we do not know for certain the impact of an increased number of convictions.

In this chapter, I do not assess the claims made in support of criminal prosecution for honour killings. But it is important for women's-rights activists to acknowledge that their support is based on certain assumptions that should not be accepted uncritically; rather, these assumptions should be assessed and debated. Setting aside this debate here, I will go on to consider the claim that the Qisas and Diyat amendments are a leading cause of acquittals for honour killings.

Honour killings are not typically a separate category in crime data, and therefore it is difficult to conduct a "before and after" analysis to assess the impact of the Qisas and Diyat amendments. We should, however, be skeptical of the claim that the Qisas and Diyat amendments are the main cause behind acquittals and the consequent claim that the repeal of these provisions would significantly improve the rate of convictions. This is because other factors may contribute as much, if not more, to the high rate of acquittals. One such factor is the inability of the prosecution to meet the burden of proof to sustain a criminal conviction.

The prosecution in any criminal case is required to prove its case beyond a reasonable doubt to sustain a criminal conviction. This requires collection of evidence and a clear presentation of this evidence in court. Due to poor quality of investigation and weak prosecution in courts, the state is consistently unable to meet this burden of proof. Acquittals for honour killings will therefore continue even if compromises are deemed irrelevant by courts because, as is the case with many other crimes, the prosecution will be unable to prove its case against the alleged murderer beyond a reasonable doubt.

Nafisa Shah's study of honour killings in Sindh concludes that the formal justice system enables the acquittal of perpetrators of honour crimes not only because it accepts compromises under the Qisas and Diyat amendments but also because of what she calls the principle of "benefit of the doubt."[42] Shah presents the case study of two cousins, Abida and Tehmina, who were killed after they left their parents' home to allegedly elope with two boys.[43] When the girls went missing and before their dead bodies were found, a police complaint was registered by Tehmina's brother, Fazaldin, who implicated their close relatives. Once the case went to trial at the lower court, the complainant Fazaldin denied having ever made the first statement, saying that he had not named the accused and that his supposed statement resulted from a police blunder. Hence, the main witness withdrew his statement, and the police investigation did not yield other evidence that could have sustained a conviction. There was no statement or application before the court regarding a compromise, and therefore the Qisas and Diyat amendments were not invoked. Instead, the perpetrators were acquitted because, in the absence of incriminating testimony by the complainant, the prosecution had no case. Shah notes that the complainant withdrew his statement after family and political pressures had forced the disputing sides to come to a compromise outside the court, with the help of mediators.

The case study of Abida and Tehmina shows how out-of-court compromises can shape the outcome of a criminal case even without the operation of the Qisas and Diyat amendments. Even though the out-of-court compromise was not officially recorded in court, it led to the acquittal of the accused because it resulted in the withdrawal of the crucial piece of evidence against the accused. The oral statement of the complainant is overwhelmingly the most crucial piece of evidence in criminal trials in Pakistan due to the inability and often unwillingness of law-enforcement officials to collect corroborating physical evidence.

Shah's evidence shows that, even when the Qisas and Diyat amendments are not invoked, perpetrators avoid accountability for honour killings due to the failure of the state to build a criminal case that can support a conviction. Shah says that the legal requirement that the prosecution meet its burden of proof in proving that the accused is guilty leads to the acquittal of many perpetrators of honour killings because the prosecution is so often unable to meet this burden. She asserts that the "low number of convictions is not due to problems in the law but because they are a product of the very law, making us conclude that the frequent acquittals show a law that is not inactive or weak but one that is active and operating."[44]

Whether in such acquittals the law may be considered active in that it imposes a high burden of proof for criminal convictions or weak and inactive in the sense that the legal system fails to build a case that meets its burden of proof is perhaps more of a semantic rather than a substantive question. While Shah lumps together both aspects of the law that, in her analysis, promote acquittal—the high burden of proof on the prosecution as well as the Qisas and Diyat amendments—the former legal principle is a desirable limitation on the power of the state and an important safeguard against the risk of convicting an innocent person. Activists concerned with social justice should therefore oppose a reduction of this burden even if would lead to an increase in the number of convictions. Instead, they should push for more efficient investigation and prosecution that satisfy all requirements of due process.

That such out-of-court compromises enable acquittals even in the absence of Qisas and Diyat amendments is evident in rape trials in Pakistan, which, largely, end in acquittal due to compromise between the rape survivor or her family and the perpetrator. Unlike murder after the Qisas and Diyat amendments, rape remains a "noncompoundable" offence, which means that a settlement between the parties cannot legally lead to a closure of the criminal case. In practice, however, out-of-court compromises shape the outcome of rape trials nonetheless. The study on rape trials in Punjab's Lodhran district in Punjab, discussed in Chapter 2, shows that a vast majority of rape complaints result in acquittal because the survivor retracts her statement against the accused after she or her family reaches an out-of-court settlement with the accused.

The comparison with rape acquittals indicates that the Qisas and Diyat amendments are one factor, but by no means a decisive factor, contributing to acquittals and impunity for honour killings. Efforts to reverse the Qisas and Diyat amendments, even if they ever achieve success, are therefore unlikely to have a significant impact due to structural flaws in the criminal-justice system, as reflected in the poor quality of investigation and prosecution, the attitudes of law-enforcement officials and the courts, and social pressures on family members of survivors to settle out of court.

The most recent high-profile acquittal in an honour-killing case in Pakistan, that of Qandeel Baloch, is further proof that the Qisas and Diyat Amendment are not the only obstacle to accountability for honour killings and that the inability of law-enforcement officials to build a strong criminal case obstructs convictions. Qandeel Baloch's brother, Muhammad Waseem, was arrested for her murder, and, on July 18, 2016, he confessed that he had killed his sister Qandeel Baloch because her social media posts brought shame on the family.[45] While the trial was pending, Qandeel's parents forgave their son and sought his exoneration. During the course of the trial, Muhammad Waseem stated that the confession was false and obtained forcibly after torture and therefore should not be admissible.[46] The trial court, however, exercised its discretion to ignore the compromise with the parents and convicted the brother, relying on his confession as the main piece of evidence. The trial court concluded that, based on Muhammad Waseem's confession, Qandeel Baloch's murder was an honour killing and that, therefore, the court could exercise its discretion to convict in spite of the compromise. The trial court imposed a sentence of life imprisonment.

On appeal, the Lahore High Court considered whether the trial court had sufficient evidence to conclude that the murder was an honour killing. According to the Lahore High Court, the trial court mainly relied on the confession to arrive at this conclusion, a confession that was subsequently retracted. The Lahore High Court referred to Supreme Court precedent that sets forth a detailed set of standards that must be followed when recording a confession for it to be deemed admissible. These standards include the following: the accused is to be provided full assurance that, in case he is not guilty or is not making a confession voluntarily, then he would not be handed back over to the police; all police officials must be kept outside the court and beyond the view of the accused; after observing all these legal requirements, if the accused person was willing to confess, then all required questions, as formulated by the high court rules and orders, should be put to him and the answers given should be recorded in the words spoken by him; and the statement of the accused should be recorded by the magistrate with his own hand. . . .[47]

While some of these standards appear very technical, they serve a purpose. The rationale behind imposing stringent standards for admission of a confession is that police torture is endemic in Pakistan, and there is a risk that any confession is forcibly extracted. In order to avoid the admission of a coerced and false confession, courts in Pakistan have mandated that strict procedural safeguards be in place before any such confession can be the basis of implicating a criminal defendant. The Lahore High Court observed that the magistrate had committed a number of "illegalities" when recording Muhammad Waseem's confession, including that the statement was silent as to whether handcuffs were removed; that, except for the confession, the proceedings were typed in English; that there was no oath made by the stenographer to show that he had typed all facts; and that the custody of the accused was handed over to the same investigation officer who produced him in court.[48]

Based on these and some other procedural irregularities, the Lahore High Court concluded that the "value of the confession cannot be considered more than a piece of paper."[49] The Lahore High Court went on to note that, other than the confession, there was no evidence on the record to show that the murder was an honour killing and that all private witnesses, including Qandeel Baloch's parents, had resiled their statements. The trial court's basis for using its discretion to reject the compromise, i.e., that the murder was an honour killing, was therefore erroneous. On this basis, the Lahore High Court declared that Muhammad Waseem was "acquitted on the basis of compromise."[50]

The acquittal of Baloch's brother shows how the failure of law-enforcement officials to build a strong case works with the Qisas and Diyat amendments to obstruct convictions. The Lahore High Court concluded that there was insufficient evidence presented before it to support the rejection of a compromise. The analysis of the evidence by the Lahore High Court indicates that, even in the absence of a compromise, there were no grounds to convict Muhammad Waseem since his confession was deemed unreliable and all other private witnesses resiled.

In this chapter I have discussed that advocacy by women's-rights activists against honour killings in Pakistan over the last few decades has focused to a large extent on changing the law and that these efforts have not been successful. There has been no substantive reversal of the Qisas and Diyat amendments. Even while activists continue to advocate against these amendments, they should be aware of the fact that impunity for honour crimes will not end, and may not even decline significantly, with the repeal of Qisas and Diyat amendments. This is because changes in the law will not address the weaknesses in the criminal-justice system that lead to acquittals.

Advocacy against the Qisas and Diyat amendments assumes that a formal justice system, unimpeded by compromises and privately mediated settlements better serves the cause of gender justice. For this reason, advocacy against honour killings is also linked to activism against "parallel" or "informal" justice mechanisms, such as jirgas, panchayats and *faislo*. For the remainder of this chapter, I will use the term jirga to refer to these processes collectively, since this is the term that is often used generically in Pakistan to refer to traditional, community-driven settlement forums. Activism by women's-rights activists over the years has been unable to curb the influence of jirgas. In the next section, I consider the activism and the lessons it teaches us about the resilience of informal justice processes.

ADVOCACY AGAINST JIRGAS

Informal or tribal justice mechanisms wield considerable influence across Pakistan. Jirgas are presided over by male elders of communities or tribes and arbitrate a wide range of disputes, from property matters to criminal violations, including murders and sexual assaults. They act as alternatives to the formal court system and continue to assert legitimacy in communities across Pakistan, based on cultural or tribal norms, even without having any formal legal status.

For decades women's-rights activists in Pakistan have condemned jirgas for their promotion of patriarchal violence. Jirgas promote impunity for honour killings by encouraging and mediating compromises between the families of the victims and perpetrators. The terms of settlements that they negotiate often involve sexual or other forms of violence against women and girls. Jirga-mediated settlements sometimes require that parties resolve their differences by swapping brides, who are often underage. The practice of swapping brides to resolve disputes is sometimes referred to as *swara* or *vanni* and is specifically outlawed in the Pakistan Penal Code.[51] Nonetheless, as shown in a report of the National Commission on the Status of Women (NCSW) published in June 2017, the practice persists. The NCSW study documents several instances in 2014 where jirgas rendered decisions that involved violence against women.[52]

In spite of their regressive practices that condone and promote gender-based violence, jirgas enjoy social legitimacy, primarily because of the absence of trust in the formal justice system. The NCSW report notes, "While jirgas are often criticized in the mainstream media and by human rights activists for their anti-women orientation, for many others, locally constituted jirgas are perceived as more 'just' than the national justice system, more so outside urban provincial capital cities."[53]

In 2016, the government in Pakistan attempted to assign legal status to jirgas in the Federally Administered Tribal Areas in the northwest of the country with a proposed "Riwaj Bill."[54] The bill was never enacted. International development aid organisations have also supported measures to institutionalize jirgas as alternative dispute-resolution mechanisms that would fill the gaps of the formal judicial system.[55] These moves were strongly condemned by women's-rights activists on the grounds that jirgas do not and would not include women and that assigning any legal status to them would legitimise their settlements promoting and condoning patriarchal violence.[56]

In 2004, the Sindh High Court passed a judgment declaring that jirgas have no legal standing in Pakistan and therefore their decisions and directions do not have the force of law.[57] This judgement was not implemented. In 2012, the NCSW filed a petition against jirgas before the Supreme Court of Pakistan, asking the top court to declare jirgas to be illegal. The petition claimed that the "existence of parallel bodies or kangaroo courts" deprives persons of their right to liberty, justice, and equal protection under the laws. The petitioners emphasised that jirgas are inherently opposed to "due process of law."[58] The petition stated that "[e]fforts should be made by the State . . . and its three pillars to eliminate the patriarchal and inhuman practices in jirgas, panchayat and other similar bodies."[59] The petition sought a direction from the Supreme Court that jirgas and panchayats should be "declared unconstitutional and ultra vires for assuming the powers of courts" and that proceedings and orders of jirgas should be declared "void" and "action be taken against those who have participated in such illegal activities."[60]

The Supreme Court passed a judgement on the petition in 2019, recognizing that the decisions of jirgas often lead to serious violations of human rights, especially the rights of women, and affirmed that jirgas cannot act as courts.[61] The Supreme Court referred to Pakistan's international human-rights treaty obligations in the International Covenant of Civil and Political Rights and Convention on Elimination of Discrimination Against Women and noted that the "modes of operation" of jirga violate the provisions of these treaties.[62] Its decision noted that jirgas "trespass the jurisdiction of the legislature and the judiciary" and that the form of justice they provide is fundamentally flawed because there is no "procedural or substantive law" that dictates their proceedings.[63] The Supreme Court found that their proceedings violate the fundamental right to a fair trial and due process.

The Supreme Court did not, however, ban jirgas altogether. The decision acknowledges that jirgas are "a gathering of village elders to resolve a dispute which can within the permissible limits of the law be settled outside of courts."[64] It goes on to say that it does not wish for stigma or ill-feeling to be "attached to the term jirga or panchayat which may operate within the permissible limits of the law . . . to the extent of acting as arbitration, mediation, negotiation or reconciliation bodies/councils." The top court stated that jirgas cannot "adjudicate" matters as a parallel court, but they may act as "arbitration, mediation or reconciliation forums" even as their decisions are not legally binding since these bodies are not sanctioned under any law. This important caveat made by the Supreme Court acknowledges that jirgas exercise social legitimacy in communities as alternatives to the formal court system, which does not provide efficacious and speedy resolutions to disputes. Jirgas, panchayats, and other forms of mediation are sometimes required to reach meaningful resolution of matters that courts are incapable of effectively addressing.

This Supreme Court judgement was widely celebrated, and many feminists perceived it to mean that jirgas would no longer be allowed to dispense "justice." The judgement did not, however, add anything substantive to existing law and jurisprudence. It stated the obvious when it declared that jirgas are not in and of themselves prohibited, as people cannot be disallowed from pursuing avenues other than the judiciary to resolve claims and disputes. To the extent that jirgas "decree" violations of the rights of women that run contrary to Pakistan's laws and Constitution, they are liable to be tried for aiding and abetting crimes under existing laws. That jirgas continue to aid and abet such violations reflects a failure of the formal justice system, including the police and the courts, to hold them accountable. The primary value of the Supreme Court judgment is symbolic, as it acknowledges the human-rights violations perpetrated by jirgas and reiterates the responsibility of law-enforcement officials to prevent these violations. The judgment will not lead to any practical change, however, unless law-enforcement officials act to hold jirgas accountable. In May 2023, the Sindh High Court expressed frustration that jirgas continued to operate across Sindh and continue to mediate settlements that lead to violence against women.[65]

Advocacy around the petition and the response to the judgment reflect feminists' approval of the formal justice system and their aversion to "parallel" justice mechanisms that diminish the legitimacy of courts. This advocacy exemplifies the faith among feminists in Pakistan of the "adjudicative ideal," even though this ideal has been so difficult to put into practice. The activism against jirgas also appears to sidestep a fundamental reason why jirgas continue to operate: the formal law-enforcement system in the form of police and courts does not deliver resolution of disputes or speedy justice. As the NCSW report noted,

> Pakistan has failed to extend state presence in remote villages, leaving jirgas as the only means of justice and reconciliation in these areas. The formal justice system is perceived to be inefficient, slow, and expensive, since courts have backlog running into hundreds of thousands of cases and lawyer fees run into the course of the dispute and are exorbitant. The courts do not always deliver justice because of high degree of corruption at all stages, including police investigation and court hearings.[66]

It is not surprising that jirgas continue to operate and promote violence against women in their decisions even after the Supreme Court judgment. Jirgas can only be regulated by law enforcement—the police and the courts—and they do not do so consistently. It is also not simply the case that jirgas replace the formal justice system, because the latter often works with the former to extract benefits from settlement arrangements. As noted in the NCSW report, the police has an incentive to protect such mediation processes as it is often actively involved in extracting money from the settlements.[67] Courts order acquittals on the basis of settlements, thereby ensuring that the jirga-facilitated compromises are executed. It is therefore somewhat paradoxical to rely on the formal justice system to curb a practice that is very much enabled, perpetuated, and legitimized by the deliberate actions and inactions of formal state actors.

THE ADJUDICATIVE IDEAL

Advocacy against jirgas is based on a dichotomy—formal justice systems are "good," and informal, community-based processes are "bad." Women's-rights activists should be aware of the extent to which advocacy premised on this dichotomy lets the state off the hook. While jirgas in Pakistan have a terrible track record for condoning and promoting violence against women, the formal justice system has also consistently failed women. When women activists ask the Supreme Court to ban jirgas because they act as "kangaroo" courts that violate the rights of liberty and due process, they should also be aware that formal courts are often indistinguishable from kangaroo courts in their operation and also consistently violate human rights. This is not to say that women activists should not approach courts for relief or demand that the judiciary uphold fundamental rights. Rather, all such engagement should adopt a critical approach, one that eschews false dichotomies.

This advocacy also risks obscuring the responsibility of the formal judicial system towards perpetuating the legitimacy of jirgas. For most people, especially those belonging to poor and marginalised communities, police and courts are primarily forces for oppression and exploitation and not a better alternative to jirgas. Women's-rights activists must acknowledge that even women who stand to suffer from jirga decisions are embedded in communities that view jirgas as being more legitimate and effective than state authorities.

Women's-rights activists also should not turn a blind eye to the diverse ways in which crimes are perceived by communities in Pakistan, ways that do not conform to the feminist conceptualization of gender-based violence. Communities or tribes in Pakistan often interpret a crime against an individual as a violation against the entire community or tribe that must be avenged to restore the status quo. As Shah shows in her study of honour-based violence, individual accusations of *karo kari* are often magnified to involve entire communities and tribes and often develop into feuds that last many years.[68] Criminal proceedings against individuals in such cases are insufficient to restore a community's sense of honour or safety, and so jirga-based settlements are sometimes more effective in bringing closure and ending cycles of retribution. Settlements of such feuds that promote violence against women can of course never be acceptable to advocates for gender equality. At the same time, however, experience indicates that, when advocacy ignores the wide gap between social perceptions of justice on the one hand and feminist understandings of accountability for gender-based crimes on the other, it will not achieve more than limited success.

Advocacy against honour killings is based on optimistic faith in the ability of the carceral system to reduce patriarchal violence. For women's-rights activists, acquittals for honour killings signal a failure for the cause of gender justice, while convictions and incarcerations represent success and prove that the criminal system can deliver. Such an approach has the tendency to pathologise individual cases of crime and obscures the structural forces that promote gender-based violence. There is little acknowledgment, let alone questioning, among women's-rights activists of the assumptions that underly the push toward an increased number of convictions and specifically of the assumption that convictions deter gender-based crimes. There is also little questioning of the assumption that tougher sentences will prevent gender-based violence. Condemnation by activists of pleas of "grave and sudden provocation" to mitigate sentences for honour killings also presupposes that leniency for murderers in the form of shorter sentences undermines the cause of gender justice. The push to impose stricter sentences and remove possibilities of mitigation runs the risk of targeting individual offenders and does not address the social stereotypes about sexuality and gender that motivate honour-based crimes. The danger of obscuring structural causes in the pursuit of individual accountability is also present in calls for stricter penalties for rape and child marriages and the criminalization of domestic violence, as discussed in previous chapters.

Calls for strict application of rules in the criminal-justice system and the elimination of privately mediated compromises reflect a faith in the adjudicative ideal. The adjudicative ideal says that the primary goal of a justice process is to determine the facts and prescribe penalties or punishments accordingly. It is widely believed that a formal justice system lives up to or at least tries to live up to this ideal. Students of criminal-justice systems, however, have questioned the extent to which this ideal is followed in practice anywhere and whether it is practically desirable.

Upholding the adjudicative ideals requires the imposition of rules and processes that impose transaction costs in the form of lengthy judicial proceedings and legal and other expenses for the parties. This means, as Malcolm Feeley framed it in his classic study of lower criminal courts in Connecticut, United States, the "process" becomes the punishment.[69] The avoidance of rules and procedures in flawed criminal-justice systems may sometimes be more desirable for parties involved in a crime or a dispute. Feely explains that this is why defendants in the lower criminal courts he studied overwhelmingly prefer to plead guilty at the pretrial stage or to accept plea bargains rather than face protracted criminal trials.[70] Feeley's study shows how rules and procedures are replaced or circumvented through the use of discretion by actors in the legal system, including judges, police officers, and prosecutors. He notes, "In the administration of the criminal law, there is a strong drive for discretion. Decisions made under a strict application of rules often lead to outcomes that few find palatable."[71]

Evidence discussed in this book on many areas of gender-based violence highlights the costs imposed on all parties, especially survivors of gender-based violence and families of victims, when they pursue criminal procedures through law enforcement and courts. It poses this dilemma for women's-rights activists: with their resistance to compromises, jirga-mediated settlements, and discretionary mitigation of offences through pleas such as "grave and sudden provocation," activists want strict adherence to legal rules that makes no room for discretion, as such discretion will reflect patriarchal beliefs and almost inevitably discriminate against women. At the same time, feminists are confronted with the fact that "decisions made under a strict application of rules often lead to outcomes that few find palatable." When the prosecution is required to prove its case beyond a reasonable doubt, a fundamental requirement of the principle of due process in criminal cases, convictions become very difficult to attain. The acquittal of Qandeel Baloch's brother is an example of how the strict adherence to legal rules can lead to an undesirable outcome: the court rejected her brother's confession because it was made under conditions that violated procedural rules laid down by the Supreme Court. The dilemma faced by women's-rights activists is heightened by the fact that the adherence to rules and processes increases the burdens faced by survivors and family victims who approach the legal system by adding to delays and costs.

This dilemma is real and serious. Given the reality of informal justice processes led by nonstate actors, it is entirely understandable why women's-rights activists reject them and rely on the only alternative available, that of the formal justice system. At the same time, it is important for women's-rights activists to be aware of the limitations of the adjudicative ideal and of the paradoxes that arise from it. This awareness could be a first step toward imagining how gender justice and equality are possible outside the perceived binaries of the formal and informal processes.

NOTES

1. Kathy Gannon, "A Woman Sacrificed for Honor of Her Family," *Los Angeles Times*, Lahore, July 9, 2000, <https://www.latimes.com/archives/la-xpm-2000-jul-09-mn-50070-story.html>, accessed August 15, 2024.
2. BBC, "Qandeel Baloch: Court Acquits Brother of Pakistan's Star Murder," BBC, February 15, 2022, https://www.bbc.com/news/world-asia-60388111, accessed August 15, 2024.
3. Ibid.
4. Nafisa Shah, *Honour Unmasked: Gender Violence, Law and Power in Pakistan* (Oxford University Press, 2017), 1.
5. Ibid., 2.
6. Ibid., 196.
7. Sohail Akbar Warraich, "'Honour Killings' and the Law in Pakistan," in *'Honour' Crimes, Paradigms and Violence Against Women*, eds. Lynn Welchman and Sara Hossain (Zed Books, 2005).
8. Maliha Zia Lari, "A Pilot Study on: 'Honour Killings' in Pakistan and Compliance of Law," (study report, Aurat Publication and Information Service Foundation,

2011), 84. The report is critical of the practice of courts to mitigate honour killings on the basis of "grave and sudden provocation."

9. *Gul Hassan Khan v. Government of Pakistan and Another* (1980) PLD Peshawar 1.

10. Ibid.

11. *Muhammad Riaz v. The Federal Government* (1980) PLD Federal Shariat Court 1.

12. Tahir Wasti, *The Application of Islamic Criminal Law in Pakistan: Sharia in Practice*, Brill's Arab and Islamic Law series, vol. 2 (Koninklijke Brill NV, 2009), 107–9.

13. *Federation of Pakistan and Another v. Gul Hasan Khan* (1989) PLD Supreme Court 633.

14. Wasti, n 12, 100.

15. Ibid., 235–38.

16. Ibid., 287–88.

17. Ibid., 193.

18. *Yara v. The State* (1992) SCMR 1283.

19. Criminal Law (Amendment) Act 2004 (CLA 2004), Section 6.

20. Wasti, n 12, 196–97.

21. Pakistan Penal Code 1860, s 299(ee) (PPC).

22. Criminal Law (Amendment) Act 1997, Section 7.

23. *Ijaz Ahmad v. The State* (2000) PCRLJ 1116 Lahore High Court.

24. Lari, n 8, 37.

25. Shah, n 4, 123.

26. CLA 2004, s 2.Honour killing is defined as follows: "offence committed in the name or on the pretext of honour means an offence committed in the name or on the pretext of *karo kari sivah kari* or similar other customs or practices."

27. Ibid., s (8)(iv).

28. Criminal Law (Amendment) Act 2004 (CLA 2004), Section 6.

29. Lari, n 8, 33.

30. Ibid., 2.

31. "Resolution No. 249," Senate of Pakistan, March 2, 2016, https://senate.gov.pk/uploads/documents/resolutions/1457691647_547.pdf, accessed August 16, 2024.

32. "End 'Honor' Killings," Equality Now, February 29, 2016, https://equalitynow.org/news_and_insights/end_honor_killings/, accessed August 16, 2024.

33. Ibid.

34. Criminal Law (Amendment) (Offences in the name or pretext of Honour) Act 2016, s 2.

35. Ibid., s 6. The amended Section 311 of the Pakistan Penal Code provides as follows:

Where all the wali do not waive or compound the right of qisas, or if the principle of fisad fil arz is attracted, the court may, having regard to the facts and circumstances of the case, punish the offender against whom the right of qisas has been waived or compounded with death or imprisonment for life or imprisonment for either description of term which may extend to fourteen yearsProvided that if the offence has been committed in the name or on the pretext of honour the punishment shall be imprisonment for life.

36. Code of Criminal Procedure 1898, s 345; read with Schedule II.

37. BBC, "'Honour Killings': Pakistan Closes Loophole Allowing Killers to Go Free," BBC, October 6, 2016, https://www.bbc.com/news/world-asia-37578111, accessed August 16, 2024; National Public Radio, "Pakistan Toughens Penalties for Honor Killings," National Public Radio, October 6, 2016, https://www.npr.org/sections/thetwo-way/2016/10/06/496905205/pakistan-toughens-penalties-for-honor-killings.

38. Katie Dallas, "How Public Pressure Led to a Great Leap to #LeveltheLaw," Global Citizen, October 25, 2016, https://www.globalcitizen.org/en/content/level-law-honor-killing-pakistan/, accessed August 16, 2024.

39. Yousuf Katpar, "Man Who Killed Daughter in City Courts for 'Honour' Set Free," *The News*, May 30, 2023, https://www.thenews.com.pk/print/1075184-man-who-killed-daughter-in-city-courts-for-honour-set-free, accessed August 16, 2024.

40. Asad Jamal, "How Not to Legislate," *The News*, October 26, 2016, https://www.thenews.com.pk/print/159850-How-not-to-legislate, accessed August 16, 2024.

41. Ben Johnson, "Do Criminal Laws Deter Crime? Deterrence Theory in Criminal Justice Policy: A Primer," (research report, Minnesota House Research Department, 2019), 17, <https://www.house.mn.gov/hrd/pubs/deterrence.pdf>, accessed August 16, 2024.

Deterrence theory is difficult to test. Some studies have shown that the degree of certainty of detection and punishment is a stronger deterrent than the severity of punishment.

"Legislators seeking to discourage people from taking particular actions can use deterrence theory to inform policy choices. For example, if the goal is to reduce an action that is currently legal, studies suggest that the most effective policies would include criminalizing the behavior, establishing a reasonable consequence, developing an awareness campaign, creating periods of targeted enforcement, and publicizing the results of the enforcement campaign."

42. Shah, n 4, 142–43.

43. Ibid., 131–43.

44. Ibid., 123.

45. *Muhammad Wasim v. The State & Another* (2023) PCRLJ Note 81 Lahore High Court.

46. Ibid., para 4.

47. Ibid., para 20.

48. Ibid., para 22.

49. Ibid., para 23.

50. Ibid., para 26.

51. PPC, s 310A.

52. Nazish Brohi, "Women, Violence and Jirgas: Consensus and Impunity in Pakistan," 2nd ed. (review study, National Commission on Status of Women, 2017), 7–10.

53. Ibid., 14.

54. Iftikhar Malik, "Riwaj Act," *Dawn*, D.I. Khan, September 7, 2016, https://www.dawn.com/news/1282468, accessed August 16, 2024.

55. See Ayesha Khan, "Pakistan's Jirgas: Buying Peace at the Expense of Women's Rights?," Open Democracy, June 30, 2017, https://www.opendemocracy.net/en/5050/pakistan-jirgas-womens-rights/, accessed August 16, 2024.

56. Ibid.

57. *Mst Shazia v. Station House Officer and Another* (2004) PCRLJ Karachi 1523 Sindh High Court.

58. *National Commission of Pakistan and Others v. Government of Pakistan and Others* (2019) PLD Supreme Court 218 para 2.

59. Ibid.

60. Ibid.

61. Ibid., para 13.

62. Ibid., para 6–7.

63. Ibid., para 12.

64. Ibid., para 5.

65. Maryam Missal, "SHC Stands against Jirgas," Voicepk.net, Lahore, May 15, 2023, https://voicepk.net/2023/05/shc-stands-against-jirgas/, accessed August 16, 2024.

66. Brohi, n 51, 14.

67. Ibid., 34.

68. Shah, n 4, 153–81.

69. Malcolm M. Feeley, *The Process Is the Punishment: Handling Cases in a Lower Criminal Court* (first published 1979, Russell Sage Foundation, 1992).

70. Ibid., 28–33.

71. Ibid., 23.

Chapter 6

Assessing the Past and Looking Ahead

In Chapter One I suggested that some feminists in Pakistan now walk the halls of power. Governance feminism has been an important strand of the women's-rights movement in Pakistan. Since the 1980s, feminists in Pakistan have been very effective in their challenge to discriminatory laws and gaps in legal frameworks that deny women equal rights. They were able to build and grow NGOs that led legal and policy advocacy and developed partnerships with sympathetic members of political parties. The sustained efforts of women's-rights activists, the inclusion of women in legislatures, along with the support of an international women's-rights movement have meant that feminist ideas and goals have made their way into legislative enactments, rules, and procedures followed by bureaucracies and decisions of courts. These gains are fragile and subject to sustained backlash.

As feminists attempt to defend the gains made so far, the questions raised in the Introduction have crucial relevance:

> Exactly what forms of "feminism" make sense to power elites as they gradually let women in? What happens when feminists and feminist ideas find their way into legal institutions and change legal thought and operations? Whose nongovernmental organisations get funding from international aid and development agencies and from ideologically driven private donors? Once feminists gain a foothold in governance, what do they do there, and what particular legal forms are they most invested in? What are the distributive consequences of the partial inclusion of some feminist projects? Who benefits and who loses? Can feminism foster a critique of its own successes?[1]

This chapter assesses the gains of governance feminism and also considers the priorities and strategies of younger generations of feminists in Pakistan who are more skeptical of the effectiveness of laws and state institutions in addressing patriarchal violence.

EVALUATING FEMINIST GAINS

Exactly what forms of "feminism" make sense to power elites as they gradually let women in?

Gradually, over the decades from the 1990s to the 2010s, power elites in Pakistan recognised the role of the criminal-justice system in protecting women and girls from sexual violence. As the discussion on rape and honour killings shows, it became increasingly difficult for elites to deny that such violence can take place by Muslim men in a Muslim society. Instead, they decided that, to play the role of protectors of the honour of women and girls—and by extension that of society—they must be seen to take strict action against gender-based violence. In this context, it was the feminist push to increase criminalisation that eventually "made sense" to those in power. Criminal sanction creates the strongest perception that those in power are doing something about a problem. This is why the conservative PML-N (Pakistan Muslim League-N) introduced the 2016 Pakistan Penal Code amendments with the goal to increase convictions for honour killings and why the Imran Khan–led PTI government made sweeping changes to the definitions of rape in the Pakistan Penal Code in 2021 to broaden the scope of the crime.

What happens when feminists and feminist ideas find their way into legal institutions and change legal thought and operations?

The book's discussion on law reform around rape, domestic violence, child marriage, and honour killings shows that the legislative changes themselves are by no means sufficient evidence that a feminist idea has "made it." The poor implementation or nonimplementation of laws tells us the extent to which feminist ideas *actually* make their way into legal institutions and the degree to which these institutions *pretend* to incorporate feminist ideas. Common commentary around these laws is that they are either not implemented or are poorly implemented. This book attempts to complicate the generally accepted analysis by showing that each form of legislation has a different set of consequences, depending on the nature of the problem it is trying to address and the institutions that have the primary legal responsibility to enforce the law.

When feminists and feminist ideas find their way into law and legal institutions, they encounter both overt and subtle backlash. Overt backlash comes in the form of constitutional challenges to law reform or dismissive and even hostile attitudes of law-enforcement officials and courts toward survivors, victims' families lawyers, and activists trying to pursue the law. Subtle backlash is in the form of deprioritisation of projects and activities required to enforce these laws. Sometimes, as in the case of domestic-violence legislation in Sindh, there are slow, incremental shifts toward the feminist goals behind the law reform that became possible when activists, lawyers, and key players in the judiciary simultaneously worked toward the enforcement of the law. On other occasions, however, implementation of laws intended to protect women and girls from violence and coercion has counterproductive consequences. For example, child-marriage legislation in Pakistan has produced regressive outcomes because the interaction of legislation with the criminal-justice system and patriarchal norms reinforces restrictions on adolescents.

Whose nongovernmental organizations get funding from international-aid and development agencies and from ideologically driven private donors?

The agenda of the movement against violence against women received considerable support from NGOs funded by foreign donors. This book does not include a detailed study or mapping of donor-funded women's-rights–related NGO activity, but it has emphasized that violence against women has been a central agenda item for the international women's-rights movement from 1990s onward. NGOs and collectives in Pakistan have simultaneously made this issue a priority. Donors stepped in to fund the legal advocacy initiatives of NGOs, such as the Aurat Foundation, that made law reform in the areas of political participation and criminal law an important priority of their work. The Aurat Foundation and other NGOs also receive funding to train local government councilors, judges, and law-enforcement officials. For the last several decades, work that "centers" the state by making it the target of advocacy as well as a recipient of feminist expertise has received funding from international donors. NGOs led by women with strong professional skills and qualifications were and are able to absorb the international funding and grow the institutional capacities of their NGOs while making a space for themselves inside some state institutions.

Once feminists gain a foothold in governance, what do they do there, and what particular legal forms are they most invested in? Feminists in prominent NGOs and influential collectives with footholds in governance and women in parliaments advocate for a liberal state that removes obstacles to gender equality and increases opportunities for women's political participation. These advocacy projects are based on a faith in the state, through formal law and legal institutions, to address discrimination faced by women and girls in their families and to regulate violence sanctioned by communities on the basis of cultural norms or religious beliefs. Not all feminists behave the same way when they make inroads into power. Women legislators may have complete sympathy for and personal agreement with proposals brought to them by women's-rights activists through their NGOs, but they may fail to convince their political allies and fellow party members and therefore may be forced to compromise on their positions. Some feminists choose not to devote most or any of their energies to NGOs and remain active in unfunded, unregistered collectives. Some women's-rights activists in Pakistan choose to join political parties and contest elections, while others consistently remain outside state institutions. The diversity of roles that governance feminists adopt in many other domestic and international settings around the world is mirrored in Pakistan.

Discussion in the preceding chapters shows that, while some successes are attained through the formal court system, they are inconsistent and rare. The women's-rights movement has invested in the "adjudicative ideal," turning to criminal courts to punish cases of violence against women. The movement has strongly opposed informal justice mechanisms—jirgas, panchayats, and *faislo*—and has called on courts to take up the space that these mechanisms occupy for resolving disputes and settling harms. Women's-rights activists call for strict application of rules and procedures to exclude privately negotiated settlements and compromises, even though strict application of rules often means the acquittal of perpetrators of rape or murder due to insufficiency of evidence. Uncertainty of outcomes in the formal judicial system as well as the costs it imposes on survivors and victims' families make out-of-court compromises a more practical alternative for many, but women's-rights activists in Pakistan have by and large chosen to reject any such practical benefit and prefer to act as if the state can meet the adjudicative ideal.

Investment in formal systems is motivated by the very harmful patriarchal violence that jirgas condone and promote, but this reliance has also encouraged denial of the deep flaws in the formal justice system. Over the decades, there is little that the women's-rights movement has accomplished by way of reforming the formal criminal-justice system as a whole to make it more capable, efficient, and fair. Meaningful improvements to the judicial system require many political, cultural, and social reforms that call for broad-based movements, and the women's-rights movement alone cannot and should not be expected to usher in all systemic reforms.

Feminists invest a great deal of energy in legislative enactments and progressive judicial precedent. When it comes to measures that require sustained monetary investment over an extended period of time, they are limited in what they can do. They are constrained in their ability to develop protection mechanisms, as these require sustained investments in resources and personnel. Activists through their NGOs and collectives have set up shelters, helplines, and counseling services, but they have limited reach given the resource constraints of these organizations. Women legislators play leading roles in taking progressive legislation forward, but they have not been as effective toward motivating their political parties to engage in sustained implementation.

What are the distributive consequences of the partial inclusion of some feminist projects? Who benefits and who loses?

The inclusion of feminist demands for criminal punishment of gender-based violence represents a win for women's-rights activists and their NGOs and collectives that demand that the state accept responsibility for violence against women in the private sphere. When the state says that it will punish domestic violence or honour killings, it undermines the control of family members and community members over women and girls. It opens up the space for women and girls to approach the state for redress against violence. But this potential opening does not answer the question of who in fact benefits and who loses. In order to answer this question we have to consider not what the law says but what it actually does.

I show in the preceding chapters that significant burdens are imposed on survivors when they approach law-enforcement officials and courts. The burden for enforcing these laws falls largely on survivors, victims' families, and lawyers or activists who assist them with these cases. The psychological and financial burden on women and girls when they engage with these laws should be counted as a cost of implementation. The state absolves itself of the responsibility to undertake most of the protection mechanisms required by the laws. Even a "successful" outcome in the form of a conviction or imprisonment cannot be seen as a net benefit until the costs on the survivor of attaining the conviction are calculated.

Sometimes the distributive consequences of criminal laws are counterintuitive. With the domestic-violence legislation in Sindh, we see that women often file domestic-violence cases without seeking criminal convictions. Rather, they use court cases as bargaining chips to attain some freedom from abusive or controlling family members and withdraw cases after they attain some kind of compromise. Seeing how coercive control of sexuality is an important value for patriarchal societies, we must be sensitive to how laws regulating violence are deployed to preserve control over sexuality. Criminal-law legislation on child marriage, for example, is used by family members to control adolescents and is seldom used proactively by the state to stop a marriage forced on a child by parents. Assessing the distributive consequences of criminal-law legislation means that we must also consider the costs of arrests and incarcerations imposed on those accused of being perpetrators. There is always a possibility of wrongful imprisonment as well as a risk of excessive, disproportionate punishment; these costs must be considered when a demand for criminalization or enhancement of criminal penalties is made.

Some advocacy projects yield few distributional benefits other than a victory for feminist NGOs, collectives, legislators, and political parties.

Legislative amendments to curb honour killings in Pakistan have brought no substantive and effective change to the Pakistan Penal Code and the Code of Criminal Procedure. They have, however, been projected publicly as significant legal changes by actors campaigning against honour killings. This enhances the credibility of some NGOs and politicians that enacted the amendments but does not appear to have any significant impact on accountability for honour killings.

Some women's-rights activists consider legal changes to mark "symbolic" gains. A symbolic victory could signal an achievement for legislators, NGOs, collectives, and activists that pushed for the legal change, but this victory on its own is not enough. A symbolic gain should not be considered a win in and of itself unless it leads to material changes in the lives of women and girls. What can women and feminists do with the symbolic value of criminal legislation? A symbolic victory can perhaps open up space for rights-based claims by individual actors within a legal framework. The chapter on domestic violence shows how the enactment of a domestic-violence law creates space for activists, lawyers, and judges to begin to enforce remedies for survivors by invoking the letter and spirit of the law. Other victories that have important symbolic value, such as the raising of the minimum age of marriage for girls to eighteen from sixteen through legislative enactment in Sindh and judicial pronouncement, tend to promote harsh, punitive measures against young people—the very constituencies such laws are meant to protect.

There may be some unwelcome symbolic effects of criminal-law legislation that aims to remove the control of a woman by her family and community and brings her within the protection of the state. Such laws potentially enhance the scope of the punitive state, giving more power to law-enforcement bodies that do not have a record of using their power fairly and equitably. When feminists assert their faith in these institutions to attain gender justice, they should be aware of the risk that they are helping unjust institutions whitewash their own records. Co-optation of feminist goals by the state to improve its own image and gloss over injustices is a possible distributional consequence of criminal-law legislation.

Can feminism foster a critique of its own success?

There is considerable disillusionment among feminists and women's-rights activists in Pakistan regarding legal-advocacy successes. While some political parties, legislators, and NGOs are quick to claim credit for legislative enactments, there are many women's-rights activists and collectives who question the impact of these changes and are also skeptical about their potential.

In the first chapter, I introduced women's-right's activism of the 1980s as the foundation on which the wave of legal changes to address violence against women was built. Some women's-rights activists from that era continue to lead chapters of the WAF, and the NGOs that they founded play leading roles in legal advocacy to this day. Within this group, there is considerable reflection on and critique of the impact of "NGO-ization" and the extent to which this has depoliticized women activists.[2] This segment of women's-rights activism in Pakistan is critical of the nonimplementation of progressive laws but maintains its faith in the project of law reform itself. There is an acknowledgement that criminal laws are not a silver bullet, and social transformations are required to make legal reforms effective. However, while interacting with this strand of women's-rights activism, I observe at best fleeting or sporadic reflection on the role of criminal-law–reform advocacy within feminist movement building, the extent to which it should continue to be prioritised, and some of its unintended, paradoxical, and negative consequences.

A more rigorous assessment of criminal-law–reform advocacy projects is required; this can be accomplished by looking at the impact of each major legal change separately. The exercise of answering the questions about the distributive consequences of law reform—i.e., who wins and who loses?—should be done for each law and legal amendment that is purportedly made to advance gender justice. The motivation behind writing this book is to engage in such assessments from the standpoint of feminist advocacy in Pakistan and to foster more reflection and criticism.

LAW REFORM AND THE NEXT GENERATION

Much of this assessment and self-reflection will be led by a younger generation of feminists as they are the ones who will shape the upcoming goals of women's-rights activism. This brings me to the Aurat March collectives, which are the homes of many young feminists in Pakistan since the first Aurat March was held in Karachi in 2018. The success of the first march led to the creation of collectives in Karachi, Lahore, Hyderabad, Islamabad, and Peshawar. These collectives have organized annual marches since 2018 and also lead advocacy on feminist issues in between marches. Most of the membership of these collective comprises women born at least one or two generations after the activists of the 1980s. I was one of the organizers of the first Aurat March and have since then interacted regularly with members of the Karachi-based collective that sprang from it.

This younger generation of leaders is far more skeptical of the potential of law-reform advocacy. Their skepticism is based on a general disappointment in and cynicism about state institutions and political parties rather than on a systematic assessment of law reform that has already taken place. Among this generation there is a sense of futility about the role of law reform and legal institutions in the fight against patriarchy. Aurat March activists believe that patriarchal mindsets can be challenged more directly by raising feminist voices, primarily through marches, public protests, and activism on social media.

According to Moneeza Ahmed, one of the lead organizers of the Aurat March collective in Karachi since 2018, members of the current generation of Aurat March activists are largely motivated toward activism in response to patriarchal restrictions they face at home from family members and communities.[3] They are impatient with restrictions placed on them due to their gender and reject the cultural justifications put forward for these restrictions. The direct object of their activism is not the state but social and cultural attitudes that limit their freedoms, and they believe that it is crucial to express their opposition to these regressive attitudes on wide platforms to get their voices across. Their goal is to keep expanding the Aurat March platform so that it projects their objections to patriarchal norms and culture more often to more people. They believe this approach is more effective than reform of legal frameworks toward changing patriarchal mindsets. In other words, there is a shift in this generation of activists away from governance feminism, in sharp contrast to the approach of activists of the earlier generation.

In their approach to gender-based violence, Aurat March activists believe that changing mindsets through protest and interventions in social discourse is more effective than advocacy in enacting and implementing better laws.[4] This is partly due to their skepticism about whether such laws will be properly implemented; they therefore doubt whether devoting time and energy to engaging with these laws will yield sufficient gains. Aurat March activists do not believe that progressive laws will change the lives of women in meaningful ways. Nor do they believe that institutions such as the police and courts can be made to respond effectively to cases of gender-based violence. It is not the case, however, that Aurat March activists turn away from state actors and institutions entirely. Moneeza Ahmed says that Aurat March activists are regularly contacted by women facing domestic and sexual violence for support.[5] Aurat March activists try to guide women through the process by referring them to lawyers or connecting them to other NGOs and activists that work with police. If survivors choose to pursue cases in courts, Aurat March activists support them by attending court hearings. The engagement with the law and legal institutions, however, is limited to the extent desired by the survivors themselves. The activists do not push for women to approach courts or utilize criminal legislation.

I am not under the impression that skepticism about the role of law and legal institutions reflects a desire to deprioritize the problem of violence.

Activists from a younger generation are very conscious of pervasive violence, and much of their protest in public and online spaces relates to incidents of violence. For example, Aurat March chapters mobilized very swiftly after the rape on the Lahore motorway in 2020, organizing multiple protests across the country. Using social media, young activists ensured that the government and the media kept their focus on the incident several days after it occurred. The fact that a new generation of women's-rights activists in Pakistan continues to mobilize against incidents of violence shows that such violence is still perceived as a serious obstacle to equality and recognized as a tool wielded by the patriarchy. The continued prioritization of the anti–violence-against-women agenda refutes the view, discussed in Chapter 1, that this agenda was imported in domestic contexts as a result of international advocacy led by first-world feminists in the 1990s. The persistence of violence against women as an important issue for women's-rights activists across generations shows that this issue is an organic concern, based on real issues faced by women and girls on a daily basis in Pakistan.

Nor does the turning away from law and legal institutions reflect a rejection of punitive and carceral approaches among younger activists. When the accused rapists in the Lahore motorway rape case were sentenced to death, activists did not object to the imposition of the death penalty. Nor did they oppose the imposition of the death sentence on the murderer of a young woman, Noor Mukaddam, whose brutal killing in 2020 was widely covered by the media. Feminists across generations were outraged when Qandeel Baloch's brother was acquitted of her murder. When incidents of violence against women take place, a younger generation of activists calls for accountability and justice. Are these demands directed specifically to state institutions? Perhaps, but then there is little engagement by activists with the state institutions to follow up on these demands. The younger generation of activists does not specify the lapses in state institutions that lead to sexual violence; nor do they demand specific procedures and programmes that would increase the chances of conviction. If it is true that members of the younger generation of activists, particularly those within Aurat March collectives, believe that engaging with legal institutions is not worth the time or the effort, then it is understandable that their demands from them would not be specific either. But, in the absence of any forum for accountability other than the state-run institutions, their demands cannot be directed anywhere else. Beyond the state, there is a vacuum.

The "theory of change" on gender-based violence followed by the earlier generation of activists may be contrasted with approaches of the more recently formed feminist collectives as follows:

Earlier Activism

Take a violence case to court → attain conviction → establish a positive precedent → motivate state institutions to mirror response → deter gender-based violence → move closer to gender justice

New Wave of Activism

Condemn violence incident in media → organize protests against the incident → raise societal awareness and condemnation of gender-based violence → deter gender-based violence → move closer to gender justice

Whereas the mode of activism that stresses legal advocacy is based on a faith that gender-based violence is deterred when legal institutions act effectively, the newer mode of activism is driven by the belief that greater societal awareness about gender-based violence and vocal condemnation of it will reduce the number of incidents of gender-based violence.

Of course, both approaches mapped above are not mutually exclusive in theory or in practice. Activists who take cases to court often simultaneously raise media awareness about incidents of violence and organize public protests. Similarly, younger activists who lead media campaigns on incidents of violence also sometimes pursue these cases in court. The difference lies in emphasis and distribution of energies among the activities. For the older activists, the legal case and its outcome hold a crucial key for gender justice, while the younger activists believe that the consciousness-raising that comes through media and public discourse is the means to their end.

The preceding chapters discuss the limitations of the first approach. The "new wave" approach, however, is also subject to some constraints. It is not at all self-evident that increased social discourse on violence will itself deter violence in the absence of protection and accountability frameworks. While discourse may change the attitudes of many over the long term, it will not eliminate the problem in the short or medium term. During this interim, women and girls will remain very vulnerable in the absence of protection mechanisms.

Awareness raising and condemnation of gender-based violence is and will be countered by patriarchal and misogynist discourse, which is widespread in Pakistan in all forums, including on social media. Feminist discourse in the public sphere—like feminist law-reform advocacy—is subject to backlash. Feminists will have to consistently counter the impact of regressive discourse. They also have to contend with the fact that social media discussion tends to be very polarized and lends itself far more to aggressive disagreement than to dialogue and reasoned persuasion. Often feminists online are "preaching to the choir," with little opportunity to change the most rigid of mindsets. Social media tends to be a space where already-held views are further hardened rather than transformed.

Transforming attitudes through social discourse is also challenging when the religious right takes up so much space and asserts the power to inflict violence with impunity in Pakistan. In this context, it is particularly difficult for feminists to challenge patriarchal values that purportedly are based on religious injunctions. In the preceding chapters, I discussed how appeals to Shariah impede progressive reforms of legal frameworks and prevent implementation of gender-related progressive laws. Just as campaigns for law-reform advocacy are challenged by the religious right, public protests and media campaigns are also subject to challenges from religious groups and political parties. Aurat March protestors over the years have been repeatedly accused of espousing principles that are against Islam. Their calls for gender equality are labelled obscene and vulgar. Petitions have been filed in high courts to prevent Aurat marches from taking place, on the ground that they violate public order and the morals of society. Criminal complaints of blasphemy have also been filed against some Aurat March organizers. These criminal complaints, which so far thankfully have not led to criminal prosecution, are very frightening, not only because a conviction carries a death penalty but also because a mere accusation of blasphemy is sometimes sufficient to incite fatal mob violence and lynchings. Developing a response or counternarrative to claims that Aurat March demands are against Islam is therefore important to gain credibility in public discourse in Pakistan.

The earlier generation of activists—the ones who organised against Zia ul Haq's drive to Islamize laws—believed in and advocated for secular legal frameworks. There was internal discussion among women's-rights activists in the 1980s about whether they should challenge Zia's impositions by appealing to Islam and demonstrating how his law reform is not in fact compliant with the religion. Another option before them was to challenge him from a secular, rights-based standpoint, by showing how his law and policy reforms violated the rights of women to equal protection under the law.[6] The WAF chose the latter option after much deliberation.[7] As activist Tahira Abdullah says, "You cannot win against the mullah on his wicket."[8] Over the years, the WAF has remained true to its belief in the value of secular laws. The Karachi chapter of the WAF released a manifesto prior to the 2018 national elections that called for a "secular and pluralistic state" as well as a reform of religion-based family laws.[9]

Even after Zia ul Haq's rule, mainstream political parties continued to implement conservative agendas and caved to the religious rights repeatedly, especially on issues involving gender equality and rights of minorities. With state support—especially through the military establishment—violent religious hardliners developed strongholds throughout the decades of the

1990s, 2000s, and 2010s. Lynchings of persons accused of blasphemy and mob violence against religious minorities increased.[10] In this environment, women's-rights activists and the civil-society organizations that they lead—such as the Human Rights Commission of Pakistan (HRCP) and the Aurat Foundation—represent an increasingly isolated and marginalized voice for secular discourse.

Members of the more recent generation of feminists are not as emphatic about their belief in secular frameworks and institutions. This is in large part because growing threats of violence from reactionary forces have stifled discourse that challenges claims about religious injunctions made under the garb of religious authority. While members of Aurat March collectives believe in the separation of religion and public institutions,[11] they do not explicitly call for secular constitutional or legal frameworks. Instead, Aurat March activists make their demands without directly challenging claims about the role of women and gender equality in Islam. Nor do they have positions on how regressive laws that are justified by appealing to Islamic law—such as the Qisas and Diyat amendments or the blasphemy prohibition in the Pakistan Code—should be reformed or repealed. While the earlier generation of feminists grappled with the question of whether to call for reform by appealing to correct interpretations of Shariah or by asserting that religion-based justifications can never trump fundamental human rights, the younger generation is trying to sidestep these questions. A clear position on secularism is not articulated even within the collectives.

Given the inclination of the religious right in Pakistan to resort to violence and the state's tendency to tolerate and even actively promote the religious right's unlawful tactics, it is understandable why the newer generation of feminist activists considers it both futile and dangerous to demand secularization of state and society. The persistent opposition of the religious right to Aurat March and to the demands of the young feminists, however, undermines the strategy of bringing about change through public discourse. A reasoned response to the religious right's conception of state and society is required if feminists want to advance gender equality by transforming public discourse.

EXPLORING ALTERNATIVES

Some conception of accountability frameworks and protection mechanisms is therefore crucial even as feminists focus on consciousness-raising around violence. The strategy of highlighting individual cases of violence is used commonly by the younger generation of activists as it is perhaps the most effective way to evoke condemnation of patriarchal violence. It is difficult to focus on an individual case, however, without calling for some form of justice or accountability for that particular incident of violence. Raising awareness through an incident of violence, therefore, requires some appeal to a forum for justice and redress, and feminists should identify this forum.

I do not believe that laws prohibiting violence and guaranteeing protection to vulnerable persons can be dispensed with while women and girls are exposed to such grave risks of violence. Nor do I believe, as I mentioned in the first chapter, that carceral and punitive approaches should be rejected entirely, as such approaches are sometimes necessary, particularly in the absence of other alternatives to accountability and protection. While these approaches remain necessary, feminists resisting gender-based violence should explore how they may be utilized and improved, while seriously assessing their limitations and, as emphasized above, their distributive consequences. It would be worrying if a new wave of women's-rights activists rejected governance feminism by simply sidestepping the questions raised in the beginning of this chapter. Skepticism of governance feminism should not entail a nihilism about legal and policy frameworks. Feminists should develop conceptions of justice that do not always centre carceral and punitive institutions and that focus on the needs of survivors and communities instead.

The overreliance on criminal justice has led to frustrations. This also explains why a younger generation of feminists is not as invested in criminal justice and struggles to imagine an alternative form of accountability. An impassioned statement released by the Aurat March collective in Lahore in August 2021 conveyed frustration with the state's obsession with penal approaches. The collective condemned statements by legislators, including women representatives, calling for perpetrators of rape and child sexual abuse to be hanged publicly. Its statement says that the "idea that violent punishments or spectacles of brutality will act as a deterrent to crimes such as rape and murder is ill-informed" and notes that "[p]atriarchal violence happens because of a culture of silence, lack of accountability and structural complicity."[12] The acknowledgement of the limitations of penal approaches to gender-based violence is an important step toward imagining alternatives.

In recent years, there have been some discussions around using restorative-justice approaches as alternatives. Restorative-justice approaches allow the survivor to seek some form of accountability other than prison for the perpetrator.[13] They generally involve dialogues between the survivor and the perpetrator, sometimes involving family and community members. Such approaches can be successful when the survivor prefers an acknowledgment of the harm done to her, an apology, or a commitment from the perpetrator to take rehabilitative measures. Through restorative-justice approaches, the survivor also avoids the harrowing experience of interacting with the police and the courts.

In the very preliminary discussions around restorative justice in Pakistan, feminists expressed concern that restorative-justice approaches let the state off the hook by taking sexual crimes to the private sphere.[14] This is a valid concern when feminists have struggled for so long for the state recognize its responsibility to end sexual crimes. Restorative-justice approaches, however, do not remove the role of the state to promote accountability. State support, provided through offering resources and developing legal and policy frameworks, is essential for such approaches to work. Such approaches will deemphasize the punitive role of the state and encourage both state and society to employ forms of accountability that may actually lead to rehabilitation and even prevention.

ENRICHING THE ANTI–VIOLENCE-AGAINST-WOMEN AGENDA

In some ways Aurat March activists are very well positioned to enrich existing frames through which violence against women is viewed. In the first chapter, I discussed the criticism that the global anti–violence-against-women agenda essentializes women by portraying them as generic "victims," while obscuring differences among them, differences in their class, nationality, race, and other factors. In doing so it foregrounds the role of culture, depicting violence as the product of timeless cultural phenomena, while ignoring the modern economic, political, and social forces that promote patriarchal violence. The typical subject of the anti–violence-against-women agenda is the cisgender woman or girl who is abused by her family or community members, and the violence is justified by appeal to religious or cultural values. This interpretation of victims' identities glosses over many facts about the subjects that shape their identity and the complex role that religion and culture play as these factors interact with a range of other contemporary forces. This simplistic portrayal lends itself to state-centric approaches that tend to laud the punitive powers of the state to regulate and punish nonstate actors that use religious or cultural values to justify patriarchal violence.

To challenge these assumptions embedded in the anti–violence-against-women agenda, Ratna Kapur urges feminists to shift from a simplistic victim-centric approach and to focus on the complicated positionalities and experiences of women who face and resist violence.[15] She suggests that feminists focus on "peripheral" and "resistive" subjects. The peripheral subject experiences multiple layers of discrimination on grounds in addition to her sex. A focus on the peripheral subject will bring to light the multiple, overlapping forms of oppression that, in addition to patriarchal dominance, shape the experiences of women and make many of them vulnerable to violence.

The resistive subject is one who challenges the status quo in the face of her vulnerability to patriarchal violence.[16] She is consistently resisting constraints and trying to carve more freedoms and opportunities for herself. She does not passively wait for a saviour—in the form of upper-class, professional, or white women from the developed world—to protect her from violence. The resistive subject challenges the convention of a "good woman" and so cannot be typecast as a one-dimensional victim of patriarchy. Foregrounding the resistive subject disrupts essentialist views about a culture and casts light on how women are constantly shaping gender norms in societies that are in flux. Focusing on the resistive subject helps us to understand how violence is the result of a range of complex forces, including contemporary political and economic conditions, rather than the result of only timeless, traditional cultural values.

Aurat March activists are very well placed to foreground peripheral and resistive subjects because of the alliances they have forged and the causes they have taken up in recent years. The Aurat March collective in Karachi for example has developed close ties to the transgender community and works closely with its members to advocate for their recognition as equal citizens. The movement for transgender rights in Pakistan is spearheaded by the *khwaja sira* community, whose members are transgender persons who have existed as a distinct community in the Indian subcontinent for centuries.[17] The gender expression of *khwaja siras* is effeminate, and therefore they can be most accurately described as transgender women if we are to adopt globally recognized terms, but we should keep in mind that their self-identity is distinctly shaped by their historical place in South Asia. *Khwaja siras* are economically vulnerable as they are denied employment opportunities in the mainstream. They also face violence regularly and are denied protection from law-enforcement agencies.

Over the last two decades, the *khwaja sira* community in Pakistan has organized to demand political rights. This community achieved a landmark victory in 2009, when the Supreme Court of Pakistan ordered that *khwaja siras* have the right to national identification cards denoting their gender identity.[18] A national identification card in Pakistan is crucial for admission to educational institutions, to gain formal employment, to vote, and to have access to many other basic services. *Khwaja siras* were routinely denied identification cards due to incongruence between their gender identity and the sex assigned to them at birth. The Supreme Court ruling acknowledged their fundamental right to state recognition to enable their access to crucial services. In 2018, the Transgender (Protection and Promotion) Rights Act was passed, guaranteeing the right of all persons to recognition of their "self-perceived gender identity."[19] The law also guaranteed the right of transgender persons to access health-care services, education, and employment without discrimination. The religious right and conservatives mounted a campaign against this law almost two years after it was passed. The law was challenged before the Federal Shariat Court. The campaign spearheaded by Jamaat-i-Islami claimed that the law was exploited by gays and lesbians to legitimize their sexual relations and that many persons falsely claimed to be *khwaja siras* so that they could engage in "deviant" sexual behaviour. The campaign made ample use of social media to discredit *khwaja siras* and maligned leading *khwaja sira* activists.

Khwaja siras are both peripheral and resistive subjects who face systemic discrimination due to their gender identity and their marginalized socio-economic status. Their successful advocacy for political recognition and economic rights triggered a backlash against them, which led to increased victimization and risks of violence. Aurat March activists have actively supported *khwaja siras* by defending their rights on social media and organizing protests. By foregrounding *khwaja siras* as the subjects of advocacy against patriarchal violence, feminist activists can combine resistance to the multiple forces—cultural, political, and economic—that perpetuate patriarchal violence, while exposing the regressive agendas of the religious right.

Another example of a resistive subject who became an icon for feminist activists in Pakistan is Qandeel Baloch. With her titillating videos, provocations to mullahs, and huge public following, Qandeel Baloch challenged traditional norms about gender and sexuality. Her popularity was an indication of society's appetite for fresh, original, and funny ripostes to conventional morality. In her life and work, she was the very opposite of the passive victim of a conservative, Muslim society. Rather, she offered an example of how contemporary women, from economically deprived backgrounds in conservative states, use social media to gain an income and a place in popular culture. After her murder, her example became a cautionary tale. With a focus on Qandeel's resistance, feminist activism against violence can expose tensions between women's economic aspirations and opportunities and dangers generated through modern media and the resilience of patriarchal mindsets. This will enable movements to develop strategies that challenge the diverse range of factors that promote violence against women.

Increasingly, resistance movements in Pakistan are led by women activists. The movement to end injustices against the people of Balochistan is spearheaded by Balouch women, such as Mahrang Balouch and Sammi Deen Balouch. Like many Balouch women, Mahrang and Sammi Deen Balouch have lived through the abduction and torture of immediate male relatives.[20] Their experiences have pushed them to mobilize peacefully against human-rights violations, in particular extrajudicial killings and enforced disappearances. These women activists are resistive subjects who show how violence by state actors impacts women and families; thus, they encourage us to broaden the frames through which we view gender-based violence.

Resistive and peripheral subjects invite more complex analyses and solutions. They make space for activism that is more likely to eschew dichotomies, such as carceral/anti-carceral and formal/informal justice. Instead, activism should draw on many different forces, including the redistributive power of the welfare state, the legitimating power of community-driven justice processes, and the awareness-raising potential of mass media. These engagements must always be critical, with a recognition that the sheer power of such forces can be easily deployed to crush rather than enhance freedoms.

These strategies also create room for bringing economic hierarchies into the discourse on violence against women. Peripheral subjects, such as *khwaja sira* activists or working-class women such as Qandeel Baloch, are economically marginalized, making them more vulnerable to violence. They represent the so-called precariat of modern capitalist societies, and their gender compounds the many layers of discrimination they face. Their resistance is against patriarchal norms intertwined with socioeconomic structures that control labor and sexuality. As discussed in the first chapter and illustrated in subsequent discussion on the different types of law reform, the anti–violence-against-women discourse tends to privilege gender identity over other factors driving oppression. There is real scope for new generations of women's-rights activists to expand the frames of activism against patriarchal violence, connecting it to transformative visions of societies as a whole.

NOTES

1. Janet Halley, "Preface: Introducing Governance Feminism," in *Governance Feminism: An Introduction*, eds. Janet Halley and others (University of Minnesota Press, 2018), ix.
2. See Ayesha Khan, *The Women's Movement in Pakistan: Activism, Islam and Democracy* (I. B. Tauris, 2018), 284–86.
3. Moneeza Ahmed, interview by Sara Malkani and Farieha Aziz, Karachi, April 13, 2024.
4. Ibid.
5. Ibid.
6. Khan, n 2, 105–10.
7. Khan, n 2, 110.
8. Khan, n 2, 109.
9. "Women Action Forum—Karachi: A Women's Manifesto for General Election 2018," https://electionpakistan.com/womens-action-forum-karachi-a-womens-manifesto-for-general-election-2018/, accessed August 16, 2024. The manifesto

states, "WAF holds that an independent civil divorce law should be legislated with a focus on safeguarding the rights of women and children."

10. Engage Pakistan, "The Untold Truth of Pakistan's Blasphemy Law (2018)," https://engagepakistan.com/assets/resources/Pak_blasphemy_report2018.pdf, accessed on August 15, 2024.

11. Moneeza Ahmed, interview by Sara Malkani and Farieha Aziz, Karachi, April 13, 2024.

12. Aurat March Lahore, Facebook, August 21, 2020, https://www.facebook.com/photo?fbid=1194613911014068&set=pcb.1194617707680355.

13. Sara Malkani, "Restorative Justice," *Dawn*, November 14, 2020.

14. Online consultation on restorative justice, organized by Farieha Aziz, with women's-rights activists, on May 7, 2021.

15. Ratna Kapur, "The Tragedy of Victimisation Rhetoric: Resurrecting the 'Native' Subject in International/Post-Colonial Feminist Legal Politics," *Harvard Human Rights Journal* 15 (2002): 1, 29–36.

16. Ibid.

17. Alizeh Kohari, "The Guru Who Said No," Pipe *Wrench*, 2022 <https://pipewrenchmag.com/pakistans-khwaja-sira-fight-for-the-right-to-be/>, accessed August 16, 2024.

18. Amna Rashid and Umar Rashid, "Constitutional and Legal Guarantees for Transgender in Pakistan: Reforms and Failures in Law," in *Towards Gender Equality in Law*, eds. Gizem Guney, David Davies, and Po-Han Lee (Palgrave MacMillan, 2022).

19. Transgender Persons (Protection of Rights) Act 2018, Section 3.

20. Zofeen Ebrahim, "'She Has Won Our Hearts and Minds': Can One Woman Unite the Baloch People in Peaceful Resistance?" *The Guardian*, August 31, 2024, < https://www.theguardian.com/global-development/article/2024/aug/31/can-one-woman-unite-the-baloch-people-in-peaceful-resistance-balochistan-pakistan-mahrang>, accessed on November 18, 2024.

References

Aaj News. "Arzoo Case: Medical Board Declares Girl Underage." *Aaj News*, November 9, 2020. https://english.aaj.tv/news/30247528/.

Aaj News. "Timeline of the Dua Zahra Case." *Aaj News*, July 22, 2024. https://english.aaj.tv/news/30293228/timeline-of-the-dua-zahra-case.

Afiya Shehrbano Zia. "Contesting the Class Question: Moving Beyond Piety and Patriarchy." In *Womansplaining: Navigating Activism, Politics and Modernity in Pakistan*, edited by Sherry Rehman. Folio Books, 2021.

Ahmad Tariq. "Pakistan: Sindh Province Rejects Bill Against Forced Conversions." Library of Congress, November 15, 2019. https://www.loc.gov/item/global-legal-monitor/2019-11-15/pakistan-sindh-province-rejects-bill-against-forced-conversions/.

Ahmed Saeed. "Conviction Rate in Sexual Crimes Cases Stands at 3.6% in 2022." Voicepk.net, Lahore, March 27, 2023. <https://voicepk.net/2023/03/conviction-rate-in-sexual-crimes-cases-stands-at-3-6-in-2022/>.

Ali Azhar v. Arzoo Fatima and 5 Others (2022) PLD Sindh 1.

Alizeh Kohari. "The Guru Who Said No, Pipe Wrench." 2022. <https://pipewrenchmag.com/pakistans-khwaja-sira-fight-for-the-right-to-be/.

Al Jazeera. "Pakistani Court Upholds Gang-Rape Acquittals." *Al Jazeera*, April 21, 2011. <https://www.aljazeera.com/news/2011/4/21/pakistani-court-upholds-gang-rape-acquittals>.

Amir Wasim. "Child Marriage Restraint Bill Sails through Senate." *Dawn*, Islamabad, April 30, 2019. <https://www.dawn.com/news/1479317>.

Amir Wasim. "Bill against Child Marriages Divides Parties in NA." *Dawn*, Islamabad, May 1, 2019. <https://www.dawn.com/news/1479444>.

Amna Rashid and Umar Rashid. "Constitutional and Legal Guarantees for Transgender in Pakistan: Reforms and Failures in Law." In *Towards Gender Equality in Law*, edited by Gizem Guney, David Davies, and Po-Han Lee. Palgrave MacMillan, 2022.

Arzoo Fatima v. Province of Sindh and Others, C.P. No. D-5364 of 2020 (High Court of Sindh).

Asad Jamal, "How Not to Legislate." *The News*, October 26, 2016. https://www.thenews.com.pk/print/159850-How-not-to-legislate.

Asha Bedar and Farieha Aziz. "Domestic Violence in the Time of COVID-19 and Beyond." *Bayan Bi-Annual Socio-Legal Journal* VII (2021).

Associated Press of Pakistan. "CII Rules Out DNA as Primary Evidence in Rape Cases." *Dawn*, Islamabad, September 23, 2013. <https://www.dawn.com/news/1044879>.

Asma Jahangir and Hina Jillani. *Hudood Ordinances, A Divine Sanction?* Rhotas Books, 1990.

Atif Zareef and Others v. The State (2021) PLD Supreme Court 550.

Atika Rehman. "UK Sanctions Controversial Sindh Cleric." *Dawn*, London, December 10, 2022. https://www.dawn.com/news/1725577.

Ayaz Gul. "Pakistan Drops 'Un-Islamic' Chemical Castration as Penalty for Rapists." *Voice of America*, Islamabad, November 19, 2021. <https://www.voanews.com/a/pakistan-drops-un-islamic-chemical-castration-as-penalty-for-rapists-/6320005.html>.

Ayesha Khan. "Pakistan's Jirgas: Buying Peace at the Expense of Women's Rights?" Open Democracy, June 30, 2017. <https://www.opendemocracy.net/en/5050/pakistan-jirgas-womens-rights/>.

Ayesha Khan. *The Women's Movement in Pakistan: Activism, Islam and Democracy*, I. B. Tauris, 2018.

Azka Wahid v. Province of Punjab, W.P. 32798 of 2023 in Lahore High Court, decision dated April 9, 2024.

Bakhshi v. Bashir Ahmed (1970) PLD Supreme Court 323.

BBC. "'Honour Killings': Pakistan Closes Loophole Allowing Killers to Go Free." BBC, October 6, 2016. <https://www.bbc.com/news/world-asia-37578111>.

BBC. "Qandeel Baloch: Court Acquits Brother of Pakistan's Star Murder." BBC, February 15, 2022. <https://www.bbc.com/news/world-asia-60388111>.

Ben Johnson. "Do Criminal Laws Deter Crime? Deterrence Theory in Criminal Justice Policy: A Primer." Minnesota House Research Department, 2019, 17. <https://www.house.mn.gov/hrd/pubs/deterrence.pdf>.

Catharine MacKinnon. "Feminism, Marxism, Method and the State: Toward Feminist Jurisprudence." *Signs: Journal of Women, Culture and Society* 8, no. 4 (1983): 635.

Constitutional Petition No. S-728 of 2016 before Sindh High Court, order dated September 19, 2023.

Dawn. "Domestic Violence Bill to Push Up Divorce Rate: CII." *Dawn*, Islamabad, August 25, 2009. https://www.dawn.com/news/855084/domestic-violence-bill-to-push-up-divorce-rate-cii.

Dawn. "DNA Evidence for Rape." *Dawn*, October 13, 2021. <https://www.dawn.com/news/1651746>.

Dawn. "F-9 Rape Case: Victim's Lawyer Demands Inquiry into Suspects' 'Extrajudicial Killing.'" *Dawn*, February 17, 2023. <https://www.dawn.com/news/1737649>.

Dawn. "Girls Can Marry of Their Own Will: SC." *Dawn*, Islamabad, December 20, 2003. <https://www.dawn.com/news/130393/girls-can-marry-of-their-own-will-sc>.

Dawn. "SHC Orders Social Welfare Official to Look after Arzoo at Shelter Home." *Dawn*, November 24, 2020. https://www.dawn.com/news/1592050.

Dawn. "SHC Wants Darul Aman Employee Booked for Rape of Inmates." *Dawn*, Karachi, May 4, 2021. <https://www.dawn.com/news/1621937>.

Dawn. "SHC Wants Probe Report in Darul Aman Rape Case Submitted in Time, Offenders Tried." *Dawn*, Karachi, May 16, 2021. <https://www.dawn.com/news /1623789>.

Dawn. "Two Killed in 'Encounter' Were Involved in F-9 Park Rape Case: Police." *Dawn*, Islamabad, February 17, 2023. <https://www.dawn.com/news/1737527/two -killed-in-encounter-were-involved-in-f-9-park-rape-case-police>.

Elizabeth Bernstein. "The Sexual Politics of the 'New Abolitionism.'" *Differences—A Journal of Feminist Cultural Studies* 18, no. 3 (2007): 143.

Engage Pakistan. "The Untold Truth of Pakistan's Blasphemy Law." 2018. https:// engagepakistan.com/assets/resources/Pak_blasphemy_report2018.pdf.

Farida Shaheed and Sohail Akbar Warraich. "The Context of Women's Activism." In *Shaping Women's Lives: Laws, Practices and Strategies in Pakistan*, edited by Farida Shaheed, Sohail Akbar Warraich, Cassandra Balchin, and Aisha Gazdar. Shirkat Gah, 1998.

Farieha Aziz. "Dealing with VAW." *The News*, June 27, 2020. <https://www.thenews .com.pk/print/678241-dealing-with-vaw>.

Fatima Razzaq. "Victim of Neglect: Multan's Center for Helping Women in Distress Fails to Achieve Its Objective." *Lok Sujag*, March 24, 2022. <https://loksujag.com /story/violence-against-women-centre-multan>.

Fatima Yasmin Bokhari. "Accountability for Rape: A Case Study of Lodhran." Centre for Human Rights, University College Lahore, 2018, 45.

Federation of Pakistan and Another v. Gul Hasan Khan (1989) PLD Supreme Court 633.

Geo News. "Lahore CCPO Blames Motorway Rape Victim for Choice of Route, Travelling Late at Night." Geo News, September 10, 2020. <https://www.geo.tv/ latest/307200-ccpo-lahore-blames-motorway-rape-victim-for>.

Girls Not Brides. "Child Marriage Atlas: Pakistan." 2020. <https://www.girlsnot-brides.org/learning-resources/child-marriage-atlas/atlas/pakistan/>.

Glen Kessler. "Musharraf Denies Rape Comments." *The Washington Post*, September 18, 2005. <https://www.washingtonpost.com/archive/politics/2005/09/19/ musharraf-denies-rape-comments/5f2e0d4c-5ff2-4273-81e5-878cd59a1744/>.

Gul Hassan Khan v. Government of Pakistan and Another (1980) PLD Peshawar.

Habibullah v. The State (2011) SCMR 1665.

Hafiz Abdul Waheed v. Mrs. Asma Jehangir and Another (2004) PLD Supreme Court 219.

Haroon Janjua. "Protests and Fury at Pakistan's 'Rape Epidemic' after Woman Attacked in City Park." *The Guardian*, Islamabad, February 9, 2023. <https:// www.theguardian.com/global-development/2023/feb/09/pakistan-rape-epidemic -woman-attacked-park-islamabad>.

Hassan Shehzad. "The Female Warriors." *The News*, January 25, 2022. <https://www.thenews.com.pk/magazine/you/926944-the-female-warriors>.

Hina Jilani. "In Her Own Voice." In *Womansplaining*, edited by Sherry Rehman. Folio Books, 2021.

Iftikhar Malik. "Riwaj Act." *Dawn*, D.I. Khan, September 7, 2016. <https://www.dawn.com/news/1282468>.

Ijaz Ahmad v. The State (2000) PCRLJ 1116 (Lahore High Court).

Imtiaz Ali. "Pakistan's First Anti-Rape Crisis Cell Set Up at Civil Hospital Karachi." *Dawn*, August 4, 2023. <https://www.dawn.com/news/1768385>.

Indira Jaising. "Unscrambling the Images: Conflict in the Shared Household." In *Conflict in the Shared Household: Domestic Violence and the Law in India*, edited by Indira Jaising and Pinki Mathur Anurag. Oxford University Press, 2019, 4.

Ishaq Tanoli. "Aarzoo Refuses to Go Home after SHC Finds Her Marriage 'Not Legally Valid.'" *Dawn*, November 10, 2020. < https://www.dawn.com/news/1589502>.

Ishaq Tanoli. "Dua 'Free to Decide' Where She Wants to Go." *Dawn*, Karachi, June 9, 2022. <https://www.dawn.com/news/1693895>.

Ishaq Tanoli. "FIA Chief Told to Cooperate with Sindh Police to Recover Dua Zehra." *Dawn*, Karachi, June 4, 2022. <https://www.dawn.com/news/1692944>.

Ishaq Tanoli. "SHC Rules Dua Zehra Can't Be on Her Own in Lahore, Police Empowered to Move Her to Karachi." *Dawn*, July 21, 2022. <https://www.dawn.com/news/1700838/shc-rules-dua-zehra-cant-be-on-her-own-in-lahore-police-empowered-to-move-her-to-karachi>.

Ishaq Tanoli. "Underage Marriage: SHC Allows Arzoo to Leave Shelter Home, Return to Her Parents." *Dawn*, December 22, 2021. <https://www.dawn.com/news/1665223>.

Janet Halley. "Preface: Introducing Governance Feminism." In *Governance Feminism: An Introduction*, edited by Janet Halley, Prabha Kotiswaran, Rachel Rebouché, and Hila Shamir. University of Minnesota Press, 2018.

Janet Halley. "The Move to Affirmative Consent." *Signs: Journal of Women in Culture and Society* 42, no. 1 (2016): 257.

Jurgen Schaflechner. "'Forced' Conversion and (Hindu) Women's Agency in Sindh." *South Asia Chronicle* (2017). https://edoc.hu-berlin.de/server/api/core/bistreams/194bc6db-594c-4178-a9e9-b187f34f5d6a/content.

Kathy Gannon. "A Woman Sacrificed for Honor of Her Family." *Los Angeles Times*, Lahore, July 9, 2000. <https://www.latimes.com/archives/la-xpm-2000-jul-09-mn-50070-story.html>.

Katie Dallas. "How Public Pressure Led to a Great Leap to #LeveltheLaw." Global Citizen, October 25, 2016. <https://www.globalcitizen.org/en/content/level-law-honor-killing-pakistan/>.

Maddie Brockbank and Saara Greene. "Beyond the Carceral/Anti-carceral Binary: Considerations for Addressing Gender-Based and Sexual Violence." *The British Journal of Social Work* 52, no. 8 (2022): 5027.

Madeeha Syed. "The Case of Missing Arzoo." *Dawn*, December 27, 2020. <https://www.dawn.com/news/1598113>.

Madhu Mehra and Amrita Nandy. *Why Girls Run Away to Marry: Adolescent Realities and Socio-Legal Responses in India*. Partners for Law in Development, 2019.

Maheen Sultan and Pragyna Mahpara. "Backlash in Action? Or Inaction? Stalled Implementation of the Domestic Violence (Prevention and Protection) Act 2010 in Bangladesh." Working paper, vol. 2023, no. 590. Institute of Development Studies, 2023.

Mahmood Farooqui v. State (Govt of NCT of Delhi) (2017) (Delhi High Court).

Mariyam Suleman Anees. "'Honor Killings' Continue Unabated in Pakistan." *The Diplomat*, July 28, 2022. <https://thediplomat.com/2022/07/honor-killings-continue-unabated-in-pakistan/>.

Martin Lau. "Twenty-Five Years of the Hudood Ordinance—A Review." *Washington and Lee Law Review* 64, no. 4 (2007): 1291.

Maryam Missal. "SHC Stands against Jirgas." Voicepk.net, Lahore, May 15, 2023. <https://voicepk.net/2023/05/shc-stands-against-jirgas/>.

Mst. Hina v. Province of Sindh and 4 Others (2019) PLD Sindh 363.

Mst. Shazia v. Station House Officer and Others (2004) PCRLJ Karachi 1523 (Sindh High Court).

Muhammad Imran v. The State and Another (2024) Criminal Petition No. 725 of 2023 Supreme Court of Pakistan.

Muhammad Riaz v. The Federal Government (1980) PLD Federal Shariat Court 1.

Muhammad Wasim v. The State and Another (2023) PCRLJ Note 81 (Lahore High Court).

Mumtaz Bibi v. Qasim and 4 Others (2022) PLD Islamabad 228.

Mushtaq Ahmed v. The State (2007) SCMR 473.

Nafisa Shah. *Honour Unmasked: Gender Violence, Law and Power in Pakistan*. Oxford University Press, 2016.

Nadeem Shah. "Pakistan's First 'Violence Against Women Center' Inaugurated in Multan." *The News*, Multan, March 29, 2017. <https://www.thenews.com.pk/latest/195270-Pakistans-first-Violence-Against-Women-Center-inaugurated-in-Multan>.

Naeem Sahoutara and Ali Ousat. "The Strange Case of the Silent Women." *Dawn*, November 10, 2019. <https://www.dawn.com/news/1515863>.

Nancy Fraser. *Fortunes of Feminism: From State Managed Capitalism to Neo-Liberal Crisis*. Verso, 2013.

National Commission of Pakistan and Others v. Government of Pakistan and Others (2019) PLD Supreme Court 218.

National Institute of Population Studies (NIPS) and ICF. "Pakistan Demographic and Health Survey 2017–18." Survey report. NIPS and ICF, 2019.

National Institute of Population Studies (NIPS) and ICF. "2019 Pakistan Maternal Mortality Survey Summary Report." Survey report. NIPS and ICF, 2020. <https://dhsprogram.com/pubs/pdf/SR267/SR267.pdf>.

National Public Radio. "Pakistan Toughens Penalties for Honor Killings. National Public Radio, October 6, 2016. <https://www.npr.org/sections/thetwo-way/2016/10/06/496905205/pakistan-toughens-penalties-for-honor-killings>.

Nazish Brohi. "Gap Analysis of Service Providers for Gender-Based Violence in Punjab and Sindh." Report. Oxfam and Legal Aid Society, 2020.

Nazish Brohi. "Women, Violence and Jirgas: Consensus and Impunity in Pakistan." 2nd ed. National Commission on Status of Women, 2017.

Nida Usman Chaudhry. "The State of Women's Representation in the Judiciary 2023: Supplementary Report." Report. Women in Law Initiative Pakistan, 2024.

Population Council and United Nations Fund for Population. "Child Marriage in Sindh: A Political Economy Analysis." November 2021.

Prabha Kotiswaran. "Governance Feminism in the Postcolony: Reforming India's Rape Laws." In *Governance Feminism: An Introduction*, edited by Janet Halley, Prabha Kotiswaran, Rachel Rebouché, and Hila Shamir. University of Minnesota Press, 2018.

Pratiksha Baxi. *Public Secrets of Law: Rape Trials in India*. Oxford University Press, 2014.

Professor Muhammad Ibrahim Khan and Others v. Province of Punjab and Others (2023) PLD Federal Shariat Court 1.

Punjab Commission on the Status of Women. "Sheltering Women From Harm: Dar-ul-Amans of Punjab." 2016. <https://pcsw.punjab.gov.pk/system/files/ShelteringWomenfromHarmDarulAmansofPunjabAchievementsandChallenges2016.pdf>.

Punjab Commission on Violence Against Women. "Special Mechanisms to Address Violence Against Women in Punjab: A Study of Model Gender-Based Violence Court in Lahore & Violence Against Women Centre in Multan."

Rana Yasif. "LHC to Initiate Contempt for 'Two-Finger Test.'" *Dawn*, Lahore, October 13, 2023. <https://tribune.com.pk/story/2440899/lhc-to-initiate-contempt-for-two-finger-test>.

Rashid Javed and Mazhar Mughal. "Girls Not Brides: Evolution of Child Marriage in Pakistan." 2020. Global Labor Organization (GLO), Essen discussion paper, no. 731. <https://www.econstor.eu/bitstream/10419/226830/1/GLO-DP-0731.pdf>.

Ratna Kapur. "The Tragedy of Victimization Rhetoric: Resurrecting the Native Subject in International/Postcolonial Feminism Legal Politics." *Harvard Human Rights Law Journal* 15 (2002): 1.

Rehan Abeyratne and Dipika Jain. "Domestic Violence Legislation in India: The Pitfalls of a Human Rights Approach to Gender Equality." *American University Journal of Gender, Social Policy & the Law* 21, no. 2 (2013).

Report of the Commission of Inquiry for Women, Pakistan (1997).

Sadaf Aziz & Others v. Federation of Pakistan & Others (2021) PCrLJ 205 Lahore High Court.

Sadaf Chaudry. "'The Pain Was Unbearable': Thousands of Women Subjected to Banned 'Virginity Tests.'" *Vice*, Karachi, September 17, 2021. <https://www.vice.com/en/article/93y4v3/pakistan-virginity-tests-the-pain-was-unbearable-thousands-of-women-subjected-to-banned-virginity-tests>.

Salman Akram Raja v. Government of Punjab (2013) SCMR 203.

Sara Malkani. "Restorative Justice." *Dawn*, November 14, 2020. <https://www.dawn.com/news/1590293>.

Sessions Case No. 179 of 2008 (April 6, 2013) Judgement of Court of II Additional District and Sessions Judge Karachi.

Sessions Case No. 179 of 2008 (October 5, 2021) Court of II Additional District and Sessions Judge Karachi.

Shafi Baloch. "SHC Sends Dua Zehra to Shelter Home, Orders Medical Test to Determine Age." *Dawn*, June 6, 2022. <https://www.dawn.com/news/1693439>.

Shafi Baloch. "'She Is Completely Free': SHC Allows Dua Zehra to Decide Who She Wants to Stay With." *Dawn*, June 8, 2022. <https://www.dawn.com/news/1693769>.

Sheh-e-Azam and Haider Kaleem. "Massive Protests in Karachi & Lahore in the Aftermath of Motorway Rape Incident." Voicepk.net, Lahore and Karachi, September 13, 2020. <https://voicepk.net/2020/09/womenprotests/>.

Sherry Rehman. "The Parliament Percentage." In *Womansplaining: Navigating Activism, Politics and Modernity in Pakistan*, edited by Sherry Rehman. Folio Books, 2021.

Sohail Akbar Warraich. "'Honour Killings' and the Law in Pakistan." In *'Honour' Crimes, Paradigms and Violence Against Women*, edited by Lynn Welchman and Sara Hossain. Zed Books, 2005.

Sushil Kumar Sharma v. Union of India and Others (2005) 6 SCC 281 Supreme Court of India.

Tahir Wasti. *The Application of Islamic Criminal Law in Pakistan: Sharia in Practice*. Brill's Arab and Islamic Law series, vol. 2. Koninklijke Brill NV, 2009.

Terence McKenna. "Land, Gold and Women Part 2: The Case of Shazia Khalid." CBC News, February 28, 2006. <https://www.cbc.ca/news2/background/pakistan/mckenna_pakistan-pt2.html>.

The Express Tribune. "DNA Testing Lab in Sindh." *The Express Tribune*, August 4, 2019. <https://tribune.com.pk/story/2027474/dna-testing-lab-sindh>.

The Express Tribune. "Senate Panel 'Turns Down' Bill on Minorities Rights." *The Express Tribune*, Islamabad, February 2, 2021. <https://tribune.com.pk/story/2282277/senate-panel-turns-down-bill-on-minorities-rights%3Famp=1>.

The Friday Times. "'A Minor Cannot Consent To Marriage': Sensational Reporting Of Dua Zehra Case Condemned." *The Friday Times*, April 25, 2022. <https://thefridaytimes.com/25-Apr-2022/a-minor-cannot-consent-to-marriage-sensational-reporting-of-dua-zehra-case-condemned>.

The Friday Times. "Punjab Protection of Women against Violence Act 2016 Notified Across Punjab." *The Friday Times*, December 12, 2022. <https://thefridaytimes.com/12-Dec-2022/punjab-protection-of-women-against-violence-act-2016-notified-across-punjab>.

The Guardian. "A Question of Honour." *The Guardian*, May 27, 1999. <https://www.theguardian.com/world/1999/may/27/gender.uk1>.

The News. "18 Major Flaws Identified in Anti-Rape Criminal Law Ordinances." *The News*, May 6, 2021. <https://www.thenews.com.pk/print/830972-18-major-flaws-identified-in-anti-rape-criminal-law-ordinances>.

New York Times. "Rape Victim Can Travel, Musharraf Says." *New York Times*, Islamabad, June 30, 2005. <https://www.nytimes.com/2005/06/30/world/asia/rape-victim-can-travel-musharraf-says.html>.

The State v. Abdul Khalique (2011) PLD Supreme Court 554.

World Bank. “Female Labor Force Participation in Pakistan: What Do We Know?” World Bank Group, February 2018. <https://documents1.worldbank.org/curated/en/444061529681884900/pdf/Female-labor-force-participation-in-Pakistan-what-do-we-know.pdf>.

UN Committee on the Rights of the Child (UNCRC). “General Comment No. 20 (2016) on the Implementation of the Rights of the Child during Adolescence.” December 6, 2016. UN Doc CRC/C/GC/20.

UN Committee on the Rights of the Child (UNCRC). “General Comment No. 24 (2019) on Children’s Rights in the Child Justice System.” September 18, 2019. UN Doc CRC/C/GC/24.

Xari Jalil. “Punjab Domestic Violence Act: Black and Blue But Nowhere To Go.” Voicepk.net, Lahore, August 22, 2022. <https://voicepk.net/2022/08/punjab-domestic-violence-act-black-and-blue-but-nowhere-to-go/>.

Xari Jalil. “Women Recount 1983 Protest against Discriminatory Laws.” *Dawn*, Lahore, February 13, 2020. <https://www.dawn.com/news/1534095>.

Yara v. The State (1992) SCMR 1283.

Yousuf Katpar. “Man Who Killed Daughter in City Courts for ‘honour’ set free.” *The News*, May 30, 2023. <https://www.thenews.com.pk/print/1075184-man-who-killed-daughter-in-city-courts-for-honour-set-free>.

Yudhvir Rana. “Two Pakistani Hindu girls Being Falsely Proved Adult.” *Times of India*, April 2, 2019. < https://timesofindia.indiatimes.com/world/pakistan/two-pakistani-hindu-girls-being-falsely-proved-adult-pakistan-hindu-body/articleshow/68691659.cms>.

Zaffar Abbas. “Pakistan’s New-Look Parliament.” BBC, November 21, 2002. <http://news.bbc.co.uk/1/hi/world/south_asia/2498425.stm>.

Zahid Gishkori. “Domestic Violence Bill a Copy of Indian Law: Fazl.” *The Express Tribune*, Islamabad, April 7, 2012. <https://tribune.com.pk/story/360999/domestic-violence-bill-a-copy-of-indian-law-fazl>.

Zainab Z. Malik. “Call for Reform: Pakistan Must Ban Two-Finger Test for Rape—and Now.” Scroll.in, December 25, 2017. <https://scroll.in/article/862310/call-for-reform-pakistan-must-ban-two-finger-test-for-rape-and-now>.

Zofeen Ebrahim. “‘She Has Won Our Hearts and Minds’: Can One Woman Unite the Baloch People in Peaceful Resistance?” *The Guardian*, August 31, 2024. < https://www.theguardian.com/global-development/article/2024/aug/31/can-one-woman-unite-the-baloch-people-in-peaceful-resistance-balochistan-pakistan-mahrang>.

Zubair Ashraf. “Main Suspect to Be Tried for Rape in Arzoo Underage Marriage Case.” *The News*, December 10, 2020. https://www.thenews.com.pk/print/756222-main-suspect-to-be-tried-for-rape-in-arzoo-underage-marriage-case.

Index

About the Author

Sara Malkani is a lawyer with over thirteen years of experience in practicing law. She represented a domestic-violence survivor in a trial that led to the first conviction under domestic-violence laws in Pakistan. Along with reproductive-rights activists she initiated a public-interest litigation that led to the establishment of obstetric fistula-repair facilities and the recruitment of gynecologists in public hospitals in Sindh. As a legal adviser to the international organization, Center for Reproductive Rights, she has engaged in advocacy before United Nations treaty bodies and special procedures. Prior to her work in Pakistan, Sara practiced labor and employment law in Los Angeles, California, where she represented teacher and port worker unions in litigation and arbitration proceedings. Sara has a juris doctor from the University of Michigan Law School at Ann Arbor and a BA with high honors from Princeton University, where her thesis was awarded the Class of 1869 Prize in Ethics.

www.ingramcontent.com/pod-product-compliance
Ingram Content Group UK Ltd.
Pitfield, Milton Keynes, MK11 3LW, UK
UKHW020209290926
15470UKWH00001B/87